Economics of Indo-Soviet Trade

ECONOMICS OF INDO-SOVIET TRADE (1953-1990)

(A cost-benefit analysis)

DILIP KUMAR GHOSH
M.A., Ph.D.

GIAN PUBLISHING HOUSE
New Delhi-110002

GIAN PUBLISHING HOUSE
5, Ansari Road, Daryaganj
New Delhi 110 002

Consultant: Prof. V. R. Panchamukhi

This publication is financially supported by the ICSSR. The responsibility for the facts stated, opinions expressed or conclusions reached, is entirely that of the author and that the ICSSR accepts no responsibility for them.

ISBN-81-212-0394-5

PRINTED IN INDIA

Published by Mrs. Gayatri Garg for Gian Publishing House, New Delhi-110 002.
Laser typeset by Professional Laser Graphics, New Delhi-110019.
Printed at Goyal Offset Works, Delhi.

PREFACE

The book is primarily an outgrowth of my thesis entitled contribution of Soviet trade to Indian economy (1953-74") which has been awarded Ph.D. Degree in Economics from the University of Calcutta. Although the period covered under the study was 1953 - 74, it has been updated till 1990 with a postscript reviewing the historical changes that are taking place in Soviet Domestic and Foreign economic relations under "Perestroika" and the major changes that are taking place in India's internal and external economy.

At a more personal level, I like to put on record my deep gratitude to Professor Dhires Bhattacharya, formerly head of the department of Economics, Calcutta University for his unfailing inspiration and invaluable guidance while writing the book. Needless to say, I alone remain responsible for errors and views expressed.

I remain grateful to the authorities of ICSSR, New Delhi for the publication grant of the book. I also offer special thanks to Gian Publishing House, New Delhi, for publishing the book within a reasonable time frame. Finally, I would be failing in my duty if I do not mention the contribution of my wife, Mrs. Suchitra Ghosh who throughout the gestation period of the book gladly put up with my failure to attend to the family needs.

Dilip K. Ghosh

St. Xavier's College
Calcutta

CONTENTS

INTRODUCTION

The main purpose of this study is to evaluate the impact of Indo-Soviet trade on Indian economic development during the time-frame 1953-90. For this purpose we divide the entire period into two important sub-periods : (a) 1953-74 and (b) 1975-90. The former period occupies an important place in India's current economic history, since this period covers the first four five-year plans of the country. During this period, India had to pass through a period of stagnant export-earnings but rapidly increasing import requirements due to emphasis on the development of heavy industries. From the Soviet point of view also, this period is important because Soviet Bloc trade with the developing countries received a tremendous boost with its small and tentative post Stalinist beginning in 1955.

Prior to the Second World War, the Soviet Union considered herself the only citadel of Communism surrounded by a hostile capitalist world. Logically, her foreign policy was, therefore, primarily one of self-sufficiency and isolationism. The main role of Soviet foreign trade during the period was only to remedy the internal deficiencies in the country. After World War II, however, the situation became different. The Soviet Union, assuming the leadership role in the socialist camp embarked on competition with the Western capitalist world. Since the end of World War II, the volume of Soviet foreign trade has been growing at a rapid rate. It can be seen from Soviet trade statistics that from the 1950s Soviet trade has increased by about 50 per cent every five years. There has been a further acceleration in the more recent period, 1971-74. Table 1.1 shows the details of Soviet foreign trade during the entire period 1946-74. The share of the centrally planned economies in Soviet foreign trade started declining gradually from the late 1950s and correspondingly the shares of the advanced capitalist countries and the Third World increased significantly. Between 1960 and 1970, the share of the less developed capitalist countries in Soviet and East European exports increased from 8.1 to 14.8 per cent, while in imports it increased from 8.8 to 11.1 per cent.[1]

India has been the foremost among the developing countries

1. Statistical Review of Trade between countries having different social and economic systems, UNCTAD Secretariat, TD/B/410, Geneva, August 23, 1972, p. 6.

Table 1.1

Foreign Trade of the USSR, 1946-74

(in million roubles and current prices)

Year				Trade with centrally Planned Economies			Trade with Advanced Capitalist Countries			Trade with developing Countries		
	Export	Import	Trade balance	Export	Import	Trade balance	Export	Import	Trade balance	Export	Import	Trade balance
	1	2	3	4	5	6	7	8	9	10	11	12
1946	588	692	-104	340	357	-17	209	282	-73	39	53	-14
7	694	670	24	434	395	39	240	219	21	19	56	-37
8	1177	1102	75	691	679	12	420	259	161	66	163	-97
9	1303	1340	-37	988	916	72	251	315	-64	64	109	-45
1950	1615	1310	305	1350	1023	327	236	204	32	29	83	-54
1	2062	1792	270	1690	1435	255	306	271	35	66	86	-20
2	2511	2256	255	2097	1765	332	347	388	-41	67	103	-36
3	2653	2492	161	2260	2020	240	348	400	-52	45	72	-27
4	2901	2864	37	2386	2195	191	426	528	-102	88	141	-53
1955	3084	2755	329	2454	2177	277	503	402	101	128	176	-48
6	3254	3251	3	2460	2462	-2	553	540	13	241	249	-8
7	3943	3544	399	2974	2543	431	643	628	15	327	373	-46
8	3869	3915	-46	2823	2918	-95	632	591	41	415	406	9

9	4905	4566	339	3719	3417	302	799	791	8	388	439	-51
1960	5007	5066	-59	3790	3581	209	913	1004	-91	304	481	-177
1	5399	5245	154	3889	3732	157	984	1006	-22	526	507	19
2	6328	5810	518	4415	4109	306	1023	1175	-152	890	526	364
3	6545	6353	192	4590	4484	106	1135	1281	-146	821	584	237
4	6915	6963	-48	4866	4812	54	1181	1587	-406	868	564	304
1965	7357	7253	104	5001	5049	-48	1346	1470	-124	1010	734	276
6	7957	7122	835	5286	4738	548	1581	1601	-20	1091	784	307
7	8687	7683	1004	5739	5351	388	1741	1634	107	1207	698	509
8	9571	8469	1102	6421	5730	691	1887	1965	-78	1264	774	490
9	10490	9294	1196	6914	6026	888	2056	2275	-219	1520	992	528
1970	11520	10559	961	7530	6873	657	2154	2540	-386	1836	1146	690
1	12425	11232	1193	8116	7360	756	2482	2601	-119	1827	1271	556
2	12734	13310	-576	8286	8519	-233	2441	3441	-1000	2008	1350	658
3	16060	15802	258	9115	9217	-102	3750	4589	-839	2937	1738	1199
4	20738	18834	1904	11092	10304	788	6258	6146	112	3388	2384	1004

Sources : 1946-66 : Vneshniaia torgovlia SSSR : Statisticheskii sbornik, 1918-66, Moscow, 1967.
1967-74 : Vneshniaia torgovlia SSSR, Moscow, various issues.

in having growing trade and economic relations with the Socialist countries. In 1947, when India became independent and established diplomatic and commercial relations with the Soviet Union, few could have visualised that the trade between these two countries with different economic and political systems would grow so rapidly and at such a phenomenal pace. Total Indo-Soviet trade in 1950-51 was barely Rs. 0.22 crores, while in 1975-76, it crossed Rs. 700 crores. This spectacular growth in trade in a span of less than three decades is an excellent example of fruitful trade and economic co-operation between the two countries with different social systems. The growth in Indo-soviet trade becomes all the more significant when viewed in a historical perspective. After independence in 1947, all the foreign trade of India was directed to Britain or to countries where Britain had strong political and business influence, mainly Western Europe and the U.S.A. The soviet Union was an unexplored and totally new territory so far as India's foreign trade was concerned. Yet within a short span of time the Soviet Union began to occupy a place of distinction in India's foreign trade which demonstrated the vitality of the newly developing Indo-Soviet relations. In the early half of the 1950's when Indo-Soviet trade was quite small in absolute terms and as a proportion of India's total trade, it was keenly felt that trade between these countries could get a boost if trade relations were based on bilateral agreements concluded by India with the USSR and Eastern Europe were almost like convertible currency agreements, since the outstanding balance at the end of any trade agreement period were eligible to be converted into sterling for settlement purposes. But with the foreign exchange crisis faced by India during her Second Five Year Plan (1956-61), the USSR and Eastern Europe were agreeable to a change in terms by accepting settlement in non-convertible rupees. All outstanding trade balances at the end of any agreement period were to be settled by the export of mutually agreed commodities. Thus, aided by the self-balancing "rupee payments" mechanism, trade between the two countries (India and USSR) grew rapidly in the 1960's and early 1970's and has now reached a qualitative, though not a quantitative, plateau. Added to this was the appreciable amount of economic assistance extended to India especially by the USSR, that gave further stimulus to growth in trade between India and the Soviet Union.

Since 1953, there has been five trade agreements between India and the Soviet Union. These trade agreements have set out to achieve several objectives, viz. (1) to establish direct trade contacts with USSR and other centrally planned East European countries, (2) to obtain capital goods and raw materials without straining India's convertible foreign exchange reserve, (3) to stabilise prices of India's traditional exports, (4) to reduce dependence on India's traditional export markets, (5) to create markets for India's non-traditional products, (6) to maintain a balance between export and import values a bilateral balancing of trade.

In the subsequent chapters we intend to study the extent to which Indo-Soviet bilateral trade agreements have been successful in achieving these objectives. The study has some contemporary interest because many doubts have been raised recently regarding the overall benefits of Indo-Soviet trade to India. The doubts raised relate to (1) Whether by engaging in greater trade with the East European bloc of countries India is diverting its trade away from the convertible currency areas and thus losing valuable free foreign exchange; (2)Whether India is trading at a loss in terms of prices and (3) Whether India is getting products of comparable quality by way of imports from the USSR and Eastern Europe.

In Chapter 1, we take up the study of the analytical and historical background of Indo-Soviet trade in the post-independence period. We start with the role of foreign trade in the economic development of a developing economy like India with special reference to the significance of bilateral trade agreements. We shall see that there has been a good deal of controversy in the course of the last century or so regarding the interrelationships between foreign trade and economic development in the less developed countries of the world. There are two important lines of argument regarding this interrelationship. One line of argument upholds the positive effects of commodity exchange and capital flows upon the growth of the poor economies. This analysis runs in terms of static comparative cost theory. Another important variant of the above line of analysis runs in terms of a "vent for surplus" theory which provides scope for increased use of hitherto unemployed/underemployed resources through participation in world trade and commerce. The other main variant emphasising the beneficial role of trade in the historical context runs in terms of international trade serving as an engine of economic growth.

The second important line of argument has emphasized the detrimental effect of foreign trade in less developed economies pointing out the "enclave character" of export development and its backwash effects on the rest of the economy. It has been observed that the primary producing countries have not been as successful as developed countries in international trade. These primary producing countries are also experiencing shrinking exportable supplies faced with a declining demand for their products in industrially advanced countries. As a logical consequence of this, there has been a wide gap between the import needs for accelerated economic development in less developed countries and their import capacity measured by the trend in their export earnings. In addition to these, export earnings of primary producing countries are subject to wide fluctuations. Plans for export development should be considered as an inherent part of any country's overall development strategy. It is in this context that the role of bilateral trade and payments agreements should be considered for the expansion of export-trade in the developing countries. Although bilateral trade is inferior to multilateral trade from the "specialisation effect" point of view, when we take into consideration the composite effect of "specialisation and payments", it becomes difficult to deny the importance of bilateral trade from the purely national point of view.

Taking India as a case study, we find that India's export earnings remained virtually stagnant during the first decade of India's planning (1951-61). This was due to the fact the world demand for commodities like tea, jute manufactures, coffee, cotton textiles, vegetable oils, cashew kernels, leather and leather manufactures and coir products which accounted for 70 per cent of India's total export earnings showed no strong upward trend. India's traditional trading partners such as the U.K., U.S.A. and Japan dominated the markets for these commodities. Increasing competition in the world markets for tea, jute, coffee and cashew kernel led to a reduction in India's importance in the world export market for these products. The above analysis of the stagnation in world demand for India's primary products is only a part of the whole story. One should also take into account factors like the internal demand and supply position within India as well as the policies of the Govt. of India and the Planning Commission. Whatever may have been the reasons for India's stagnant export earnings, there would be no differences of opinion regarding the need for reorientation of India's export policy in the context of her growing need for export earnings for development purposes. We know that during the First Five year Plan (1951-55) India's export earnings financed 83.4 per cent of India's total imports; but during the Second Five Year Plan (1956-61) the proportion of imports financed by current export earnings fell to 56.2 per cent. India discovered a great opportunity, in the Soviet offer of bilateral trading agreements, for the expansion of her exports.

From the Soviet point of view the adherence to bilateralism originated from a very pragmatic decision. The USSR and other East European countries clearly realised that the scarcity of free foreign exchange on both sides was the most important stumbling block in trade expansion with the less developed countries. Bilateralism with emphasis on bilateral balancing provided a way out. Moreover, in such an approach, there was an element of certainty about the commodities and quantities to be exchanged. For centrally planned economies like that of Soviet Russia, there is much advantage in knowing in advance what precisely would be available from other countries and what must be provided for despatch abroad. The Soviet Union would receive much needed tropical goods (consumers' goods) in exchange for its industrial products. In other words, bilateralism enabled the primary producing countries like India to exchange their surplus primary commodities for capital goods of the USSR and other centrally planned economies. The coining of the slogan "Trade is aid" by the USSR and other East European countries is the outcome of the realisation of these beneficial effects.

It is interesting to note that aid and trade are used interchangeably in the Soviet Bloc literature on foreign economic relations. There is an obvious link between the credit granted trade with the countries of the Third World. Soviet economic aid to India started flowing with the signing of an agreement to build a steel plant at Bhilai in 1955. The Soviet Union is now responsible for building up of over 60 per cent of India's heavy and basic industries in the public sector from a level of "Zero-investment" in 1955. The Soviet Bloc aid to developing countries like India has, on the whole, been useful in more ways than one. It has helped to change the aid-climate in favour of more concessional and long-term loans for development purposes, helped the development of industries which the Western countries were not prepared to finance and opened new markets for the products of the developing countries like India. The economic relationship between the Soviet Bloc and some of the developing countries such as India will certainly continue to be important.

In Chapter 2, we undertake an analysis of Indo-Soviet trade agreements in the context of Indian planning. Since 1955-56, the strategy of India's planning has been to lay particular emphasis on "heavy" or "capital-goods" industries. It is generally agreed that the core of development lies in rapid industrialisation and diversification of the economy. Rapid industrialisation, in its turn, depends upon the development of basic industries like iron and steel, non-ferrous metals, coal, cement, heavy chemicals as well as industries which make machines for making machines. In other words, the development of basic and key industries was a necessary condition for achieving economic self-sufficiency in developing countries like India. On the other hand, since the USSR had concentrated on the development of heavy industry during her plan period, the internal cost structure in that country had become advantageous for her to increase exports of machinery and import raw materials specially primary products.

An analysis of Indo-Soviet trade agreements shows that the trading pattern between the two countries is determined broadly by five year trade agreements. This five year period does not exactly correspond with India's Five-year development plans; yet these agreements do take into account the likely requirements of each country in the next five years. The First Trade Agreement which was signed for the period 1953-58 covered the last three years of India's First Plan and the first two years of the Second Plan. The Rupee was accepted as the unit of account by both the countries and trade surpluses on either side were to be settled in sterling during the currency of the agreement as well as on the expiry of the agreement. Hence the payment arrangement was in effect multilateral.

In all the trade agreements between the two countries, the main objective was to provide for "every possible development and strengthening of trade relations between the two countries on principles of equality and mutual benefit". It has been observed that during the First Trade Agreement period (1953-58), while India's total exports and imports increased by 1.2 and nearly 2 times respectively, India's exports to and imports from the USSR increased by about 14 and 39 times respectively. Against this background of a growing trend of Soviet trade with the developing countries, we find that Soviet exports to developing countries as a whole increased by about 7 times, whereas Soviet exports to India increased by about 39 times during 1953-58. During the same period, Soviet imports from developing countries increased by about 14 times. India's imports from the USSR consisted mainly of machinery and equipment and industrial raw materials. The USSR Ministry of Foreign Trade reported that during 1954-58, the yearly average of India's imports from the Soviet Union was as follows in percentage terms : machinery and equipment 59.2 p.c., rolled ferrous and non-ferrous metals 33.1 p.c., fertilizers 0.4 p.c, pulp and paper 1.4 p.c. India's exports to the USSR were mostly made up of consumer goods, the supply of which came to be regarded as constraints for the successful implementation of economic development plans in the USSR.

One of the distinctive features of the first and subsequent trade agreements has been that India for the first time was able to organise her foreign trade with the USSR on a planned basis. A close scrutiny of Soviet exports items to India in the First Agreement shows that out of a total of 39 export items from the items from the Soviet Union to India, 38 items were in the nature of capital goods and industrial raw materials necessary for the industrialisation of Indian economy. Regarding India's exports to USSR, we find that all the 20 items were in the nature of India's traditional export goods which are mostly agriculture based.

The First Trade Agreement was only a stepping stone fo bigger co-operation in the economic field between India and th USSR. The first long-term credit of Rs. 647.4 mn was offered by the Soviet Union in 1955 in order to cover the cost of importing machinery and technical know-how from the USSR for setting up the first public sector steel plant at Bhilai in the Indian state of Madhya Pradesh.

The Second Trade Agreement signed for the period 1958-63 between India and USSR marked a clear departure from the payment provisions of the earlier agreement. Rupee balance was no longer allowed to be converted into sterling on demand, but could be utilized for the purchase of Indian or Soviet goods as the case might be. In the first agreement, India's exports to the USSR consisted of 5 or 6 commodity groups but in the second agreement the figure rose to 40 groups of commodities. On the other hand, Soviet exports to India were limited to items of machinery, raw materials and some goods of industrial use like ferrous and non-ferrous metals, agricultural machinery etc. In the list of Soviet exports to India, the contribution of the single item-machines and equipments constituted 56.5 p.c. of India's total imports from the USSR. The Third Trade Agreement which was signed for the period 1963-68 and further extended to 1970 gave an additional impetus to Indian imports of Soviet capital goods for her industrialisation programme. During this period, machinery and other capital equipments accounted for as much as 72 per cent of the total Indian imports from the USSR. Among other imports oil products and fertilisers were important. On the other hand, the role of ferrous metals was sharply declining due to the growth of capacity output of steel where Bhilai Steel Plant with Soviet assistance provide to be an important contributing factor. Machinery equipment, ferrous and non-ferrous metals, fertilisers, oil and oil products constituted nearly 90 p.c. of all imports from the Soviet Union. The remaining 10 p.c. of imports from the Soviet Union consisted of textile fibres, chemicals, medicinal and pharmaceutical products.

So far as India's exports to the USSR are concerned, we find that although the emphasis was still on traditional export commodities like, tea, jute manufactures, hides and skins, cashew kernels etc., there occurred a gradual change in favour of manufactures specially those of engineering industries. These manufactures are as follows : footwear, clothing, chemicals, iron and steel and a number of engineering goods. This diversification in the commodity composition of Indian exports can be taken as a sign of healthy trade relations between the two countries.

In the export list of India, agricultural products, were gradually yielding place to engineering products like metal-cutting precision tools/pumps, compressors, components and ancillary for chemicals and oil industries/textile machinery including hosiery machinery and needles/fans, air conditioners and other electro-technical appliances/zip fasteners/razor blades. This movement is somewhat inevitable in the sense that the establishment of industrial base in India by capital goods import from USSR and other countries will generate capacities for production and exports of engineering goods and other manufactured products. On the other hand, India's exports to USSR being primarily consumer goods in previous trade agreements, it was quite likely that the demand for these goods would not continue to grow at an equally high rate in the subsequent trade agreement periods. From the Third Agreement, Russia's exports to India were more in the nature of industrial raw materials, spares and components of Soviet assisted projects. Imports of conventional types of plant and machinery have been on the decline as a result of indigenous production in India.

The Fourth Trade Agreement which was signed for the period 1971-76 revealed an extension of the degree of diversification of Indian exports to and imports from the USSR aimed at during the Third Trade Agreement period (1963-68-70). In the list of India's exports to USSR, the change in the Fourth Agreement was more in favour of industrial machinery and equipments which were products of Soviet assistance, engineering goods and simple manufactures like readymade garments, woollen textiles and knitwear, jute bags and cloth etc. India's imports from the USSR turned more in favour of equipments, spare parts and industrial raw materials. The importance of turn-key projects was gradually on the decline. Besides the significant increase in total trade between the two countries during the Fourth Trade Agreement period, the Soviet Union agreed to supply asbestos, copper, newsprint, zinc, kerosene and fertilisers of which supply was stopped by the U.S.A during the 1971 war. Another significant development of this trade agreement was the conversion deal which provided the supply of 15,000 to 20,000 tones of raw cotton to be processed and converted into textiles for export to the Soviet Union. The agreement likewise provided opportunities for Soviet supply of steel of conversion into steel screws for re-export to the Soviet Union; supply of stainless steel for conversion into cutlery for purchase by the USSR, supply of automobile ancillaries by India and the offer of credit by the USSR for setting up export-oriented industries in India.

Prof. Kidron's* general observation regarding Soviet Bloc trade with the developing countries is not applicable to India's trade with the USSR. His observation was that Soviet Bloc exports to developing countries consisted mainly of manufactures and armaments in particular, while raw materials, food and beverages from the developing countries still accounted for 85 p.c. of their exports to the Block countries. In the early years of Indo-Soviet trade agreement, India's exports indeed consisted mostly of primary tropical products and her imports also consisted of manufactured products from the USSR. But when we consider the evolution of the trade pattern between the two countries, we find that products manufactured in India had almost edged out primary products form the list of exports since the mid 1060's. In order to substantiate the point, we can simply point out that till 1970 the Soviet Union bought about 600,000 tons of steel structural from the Bhilai Steel Plant and till 1973, the Soviet Union had agreed to buy 250,000 tons of steel products from the Bokaro and Bhilai Steel Plants.

The joint Indo-Soviet effort in shipping also formed an important part of trade relations between the two countries. It is well known that India loses a huge amount of foreign exchange on freight charges for its imports. India, therefore, strove to have her own fleet of cargo vessels to meet the increasing demands of foreign trade. Indo-Soviet shipping service which started in 1955 has registered an increase of 8 p.c. in gross registered tonnage since then and there are now 15 Soviet ships carrying goods to as many as 20 Indian ports.

In Chapter-3, we make an attempt to assess the costs and benefits of Indo-Soviet trade. In this connection, we have examined the following important points (1) whether India could have established links with the socialist bloc (particularly the USSR)

* M. Kidron : Pakistan's Trade with Eastern Bloc countries, New York, 1972.

to get an increasing share of its trade without the help of rupee payments agreements; (2) whether rupee trade led to any diversion of India's trade from the traditional markets; (3) how far India, under rupee trade agreement was able to get prices for her exports and imports comparable to what were obtainable in the world market; and (4) how far rupee restricted the flexibility of commercial policy in the trading countries.

Regarding point (1) our conclusion has been that it would have been difficult for India to establish trade links with the Socialist Bloc without rupee trade agreement. In absolute terms India's exports to USSR, which stood at Rs. 28.8 crores in 1960-61, increased to Rs. 418.2 crores in 1974-75. It would not have been possible for India to increase her trade with the Socialist Bloc to this extent without rupee trade agreements.

Regarding the point (2) above, we think we have been able to establish through commodity-wise analysis that there was some amount of diversion of trade towards the Soviet Blocr during the period of our study. In tea exports, such diversion took place because India committed herself to export good quality tea to the USSR under the terms of the trade agreements. This quality tea could have been sold easily in the convertible currency markets of Western Europe and so India was losing its convertible currency earnings from high-grade variety tea. In the international market for common-quality tea, India was facing severe competition from the East African countries. Soviet market for this quality of tea was helpful in stabilising the prices of tea in the international/domestic markets. India's exports of tea to the traditional markets declined from 174.8 mn kg in 1960-61 to 145.5 mn kg in 1973. By contrast, India's exports of tea to USSR and other East European countries increased from 11.1 mn kg in 1960-61 to 47.6 mn kg in 1973. The larger off-take of tea by the Soviet Bloc countries was helpful in stabilising the prices of Indian tea. Another important factor which needs careful consideration is that had there been no Soviet bloc market for Indian tea and India tried to maintain her share in the traditional western market there would have been a further fall in tea prices which would have reduced India's export earnings from tea.

In the same way, coffee exports to the Soviet Bloc countries reduced India's capacity to satisfy the demand for coffee in western markets. In coffee, export quota was fixed by the International Coffee Agreement and India failed to fulfill its quota due to her exports of coffee to USSR and other East European Countries under her bilateral trade agreements with the East European Countries in 1963-64. Next year, the quota was reduced by 4000 tons. On the other hand some of the East European Countries which were signatories to the International Coffee Agreement were in a position to exceed their share of exports to quota countries by about 50 p.c. in the late 1960's.

Exports of jute manufactures generally consist of exports of hessian cloth and sacking bags. Good quality raw jute is needed for the manufacture of hessian cloth and India's capacity to produce good quality jute being limited, exports of hessian cloth to the USSR and Eastern Europe may have resulted in some diversion of trade. By contrast, exports of sacking bags in which Pakisatan was a powerful competitor may be regarded as largely an addition to existing exports.

Other commodities which we have taken care of in our analysis are : cashew kernels, raw wool, hides and skins (raw), tobacco (unmanufactured). The commodities noted above constituted the bulk of India's exports to USSR and Eastern Europe upto India's Fourth Plan.

Our broad conclusion is that trade with the USSR and Eastern Europe did not involve any large scale diversion of India's export trade from the Western markets. If we consider this diversion in the context of capturing and finding new markets in the Soviet Bloc, the total diversion effect is negligible. But if we find that some of the commodities imported from India by USSR and Eastern Europe were being re-exported to Western Europe, there is an additional cost involved in the sense that India was losing free foreign exchange earnings, the demand for which is persistent in India's developing economy. Actually the question of re-exports cannot be answered properly without a full knowledge about domestic production and consumption over and above figures relating to trade. In this regard the real difficulties that we face are (1) unless the country is a big exporter of commodity its name is not mentioned in the foreign trade statistics of Western

Europe, (2) many commodities are often exported through third countries. So what we need is a comprehensive survey regarding trade, production and consumption of all Eastern and West European markets. Another difficulty is that Soviet official trade statistics do not make any distinction between exports and re-exports. Again, goods purchased from the one country and resold to another by a foreign-based but Soviet owned commercial enterprise are included in Soviet exports as well as imports. All these problems make it difficult to throw light on question of Soviet re-exports.

Considering all these difficulties, we can adopt the following wider and more realistic interpretation of re-exports : when a country exports some goods from other countries, re-exports can be said to take place. So when USSR imports tea from India not for meeting increased domestic demand for tea but for increasing its capacity for tea exports, it may be regarded as a case of re-export of Indian tea. We know that the USSR is a regular buyer of Indian and Ceylonese tea on a large scale but is generally not an exporter of tea to the West. But in 1971 and 1972 it exported 1367 and 81 tons respectively to the U.K. market at prices of 536 and 546 rouble per ton[2]. Soviet Union's own production of Georgian tea plus imports from India provided an opportunity for tea re-exports. The increasing amount of off-take of coffee by the USSR from India may also be an indication of re-exports. However, though many developing countries including India have registered their protests against re-exports at the Algiers meeting of the "Group of 77" and in Lima Conference, USSR remains the single exception against whom no similar protests were voiced.

The most important issue centres round point (3), where we have raised the question of comparative price advantage which India obtained on her exports to and imports from the USSR and other East European countries *vis-a-vis* other countries. An important argument often raised against Indo-Soviet trade is that Soviet Union practises price discrimination in her trade with the developing countries. J. R. Carter** has charged that the Soviet

2. Soviet Official Publication : Vneshniaia Torgovlia SSR, Moscow.

** J. R. Carter : The net cost of Soviet Foreign Aid, New York, 1971. F. Pralger Publishers, p.35, 124-25.

Union sells its commodities at 15 to 20 per cent higher than the world prices and purchases primary commodities form the developing countries at a rate of 15 to 20 p.c. lower than the world prices. He has drawn up a table of 80 common commodities entering into Soviet trade with the industrial West and developing countries. He has selected two years, 1959 and 1965 for comparison. To take a few examples, the less developed countries paid the Soviet Union in 1958 11,182,000 roubles for 1,843 tractors, while the same number of tractors cost the industrial West only 7,019,000 roubles. Thus the less developed countries paid about 2,500 roubles more for every tractor bought in the Soviet Union.

The important causes of price discrimination may be enumerated as follows : world market prices for machinery and equipment are more remunerative than for primary commodities. Hence the developing countries selling primary commodities are likely to lose against the machinery selling Soviet Union.

The Soviet Union as well as the East European countries generally experience an acute shortage of free foreign exchange. Lower prices charged for commodities sold to the industrial West can be explained by distress selling of goods by the Soviet Union and Eastern Europe. The main purpose of this sale is to acquire convertible currency.

So far as India is concerned, one way of verifying the fact is to study both and import unit values involved in Indo-Soviet trade with those for trade with other countries. It is true that unit values may not be equal to actual prices, but they are very close to these prices and we take them for approximate prices of commodities.

We have taken into our calculation almost all the important goods that enter into Indo-Soviet trade. We have found that unit values paid by the Soviet Union were low and sometimes very low in jute manufactures, hides, skins and tobacco. In all other export commodities, the unit values for Soviet Union were generally higher then those for Western markets like UK and U.S.A.

We have also demonstrated that the unit value fluctuations of India's export to USSR were confined within a narrow limit of

2 points, whereas the unit value index numbers of India's export to the rest of the world declined continuously. At the same time India obtained slightly higher prices for her exports to USSR and other East European countries for some commodities, but it is not possible to say that these prices were significantly higher than those received elsewhere because of differences in the quality of commodities.

Unit value comparison regarding India's imports from the Soviet Union and other countries is even more difficult to undertake. It has been observed that for import of industrial raw materials, unit values from the Soviet Union were not generally higher than those in those in western markets. Therefore for merchandise trade alone, India's net barter terms of trade were comparable with those from the rest of the world. But industrial raw materials constituted only 30 p.c. of India's total imports form the USSR and machinery-import constituted at least 50-60 p.c. of India's total imports from the Soviet Union. Machinery imported from the Soviet Union was of a special kind and therefore the assessment of reasonable price for them was not possible. Available evidence showed that prices of machinery and equipment from the Soviet Union were higher than prices offered by other countries. No taking into account all imports and exports, India's net barter terms of trade *vis-a-vis* the Soviet Union were probably inferior to those with the rest of the world.

Regarding our last point centering round the question of flexibility of commercial policy of trading countries, we may point out that Indo-Soviet bilateral trade agreements have provided for the diversification of export-import trade of the Indian economy to quite a significant extent. In the early years of the trade agreements, India received capital goods-turnkey projects for her industrial development in exchange for her traditional primary commodities like tea, jute, coffee, cashew kernel, spices, tobacco etc. But this commodity composition of India's exports and imports underwent a change in later agreements. This shows the flexibility of the trade policy implicit in Indo-Soviet bilateral trade. In later trade agreements (particularly from the Third Agreement) India's imports moved more in favour of industrial raw materials, spares and components of Soviet assisted projects. Imports of conventional types of plant and machinery were on the decline.

In the commodity composition of India's export-goods agricultural products like metal-cutting precision tools/pumps, compressors, components and ancillaries for chemicals and oil industries/textile machinery etc. India has also been able to secure high-priority goods through bilateral trade.

Our broad judgement after considering all these factors, has been that Indo-Soviet bilateral trade has, on the whole, benefited India during the period under study (1953-73). But it is difficult to say whether a solid foundation for future development of this trade has been laid or not. There are two important sources of uncertainty regarding the future development of this trade : (1) India is not an indispensable supplier of any commodity to the Soviet Union and therefore India's bargaining power is relatively weak. This position has to be changed. (2) If Sino-Soviet relations improve India may not be so much needed as supplier because at one stage Indian supplies had replaced those from China.

The other important issue centres round the question of repayment in kind. On the basis of our study, we have reached the conclusion that since by and large India's exports to the Soviet Union are additional in nature and terms of trade are not significantly inferior to those elsewhere, the burden of repayment in kind is not possibly higher than that in covertible currency. The basis for this conclusion will be explained in the relevant chapter.

In Chapter-4, we discuss the contribution of Soviet trade and aid to the growth of Indian industries. The Eastern Bloc countries consider trade as a special kind of aid. Soviet trade and credit arrangement with India have their bearing on the creation of an industrial infra structure in India.

The First Five Year Plan of India (1951-56) had relatively few industrial targets. The Second Five Year Plan (1956-61) called for a marked shift in favour of capital goods industries, the theoretical framework of which was provided by the two sector growth model developed by P. C. Mahalanobis. The same type of model was developed by Feldman in the 1920's in the Soviet Union. Although there are some similarities between Mahalanobis and Feldman types of model, it would be a case of extreme over simplification to conclude that Indian planners adopted the strategy of development of heavy industries due to USSR's willingness to offer credits. In the Indian Plans the adoption of overall objectives and strategy was influenced more by domestic factors than by Soviet inspiration. But the relative priorities of sectors and industries might have been influenced by the availability of Soviet credit because of the foreign exchange constraint prevailing at the time. We have seen that the proportion of Soviet Bloc aid to India grew steadily from practically zero level during the first Plan to under 6 p.c. of total aid during the Second Plan under 12 p.c. during the Third Plan. The major portion of this aid came from the Soviet Union alone.

Indo-Soviet collaboration for development began the signing of the first credit agreement on Feb. 2, 1955 for the construction of the Bhilai Steel Plant. This agreement was significant in the sense that it was the first major agreement of its kind signed by the Soviet Union with any non-communist country. Soviet assistance accounted for 8.8 per cent of total foreign aid authorised to India upto 1969-70. Among all the aid-giving countries, the Soviet assistance to India was utilized for the development of heavy industries in the public sector. The proportion of grants in the total aid has been rather small since Soviet preference has always been for loans. The Soviet Union offered credits at 2.5 p.c. interest to be repaid in 12 annual instalments with the export of Indian goods. Such terms for credit assistance were at that time unknown to the western world.

Soviet credit assistance was quite significant in the development of Steel Plants in India. During the 1950's, Indian demand for steel was continuously rising at the rate of 12 p.c. per year. But India's production of steel stood at barely 1 million ton. Soviet assistance for building up the steel industry in India was of crucial importance. Bhilai Steel Plant (1955) and Bokaro Steel Plant (1964) are two significant milestones in the field of steel production in the country. The Soviet Union provided credit of Rs. 647.4 million for setting up the Bhilai Steel Plant. Between commissioning of the plant in 1959 and 1973, the plant produced 22.7 million tons of steel and 16 million tones of rolled stock. A substantial amount of Bhilai's steel output is now exported to Argentina, Bangladesh, Burma, Dubai, Hongkong, Iran, Iraq,

Indonesia, Kuwait, both North and South Korea, Thailand, Malaysia, Sudan, Egypt, U.S.A., USSR etc. In 1973-74 steel exports fell on account of a fall in international demand and India could earn only Rs. 46 million. In the period between 1959-60 and 1971-72 Bhilai has provided India in excise duty, interest on loan and amortisation Rs. 3,770 million as against the total investment of Rs. 4,300 million. In 1974-75, out of total production of steel of 4.90 million tons in the country, 35 p.c. was from Bhilai. Profit-wise, Bhilai tops the list among the public sector Steel Plants.

The production cost of Bhilai Steel Plant is the lowest. The following table gives a picture of production cost of steel in different plants.

Table - *1.2*

Comparative Cost of Production in different Steel Plants in India

Name of Plant	*Cost per ton (1970-71)*
Bhilai	Rs. 363
Durgapur	Rs. 450
Rourkela	Rs. 429 (Open hearth steel)
	Rs. 374 (Convertor steel)
IISCO	Rs. 446
TISCO	Rs. 413

Source : CPU-Report, Hindusthan Steel Ltd, Fifth Lok Sabha, 1971-72.

Bokaro Steel Plant which is also a product of Indo-Soviet co-operation came at a time when India's steel requirements were growing fast. The Soviet Union offered to provide a credit of 200 million roubles for meeting the cost of supply of some basic equipments and materials for setting up the steel plant. The prestigious Indian firm M. N. Dastur and Co. was actively associated with the early planning of the Bokaro Steel project and had the competence to assess critically the proposed Soviet designs. It was the first time that, on being confronted by a competent assessment of their project by an Indian team of experts, the Russians failed to satisfy Indian public opinion and had to have recourse to political manoeuvering. Dastur and Co.'s cost reduction study of the Soviet proposals questioned the desirability of installing 100 ton converters in the steel melting shop on grounds of technical economies of scale as well as capital costs.

Equally damaging was the criticism of the slabbing mill which, in view of the Dastur study was likely to be obsolete quite soon. This was being built in spite of the fact that new technique had already been developed in the USSR and adopted at several plants. The implication is that Russia was deliberately providing India with an inferior technology. Dasturt Co's report also indicated that the Soviet Project did not take due consideration of coke and iron ore availability in India and it most extensively questioned the Soviet project report's excessive provision for importing consulting and specialist services, specially during the construction of the project. However, a distinguishing feature of the Bokaro Steel Plant was that 63.5 p.c. of its equipments, 92.5 p.c. of its steel structure, 77 p.c. of refractories and other materials were supplied from indigenous sources like Heavy Machinery Plant at Ranchi, Mining Equipment Plant at Durgapur, Heavy Electrical Equipment Plant at Hardwar and Precision Equipment at Kota which were also set up with Soviet economic and technical assistance, while hardly 10 p.c. of equipment and structures were supplied from indigenous sources from Bhilai. This shows how Soviet economic assistance has been directed for promoting self-reliance in Indian economy and has saved considerable amount of foreign exchange which would have been otherwise required for setting up the fourth steel plant in the public sector.

Industrialisation and modernization of a country depend largely on the growth of oil consumption. The international oil industry is dominated by seven major international oil companies. It is against this background that India wanted to develop her oil industry. Regarding the question of co-operation between these Oil Cos., and the Govt. of India important differences arose on the question of equity shares in refineries, the setting up of refineries and reduction in the price of crude. Being unable to get the co-operation of these Oil Cos., the Govt. of India decided to acquire the know-how of oil production from whatever source was available and in the shortest possible time. The Soviet Union came forward with the objective of breaking private sector monopolies in oil. Another indirect benefit of Soviet entry was that the Western private firms made counter offers with more favourable terms for India. Refineries of Cochin, Madras and Haldia are examples to the point. India's total investment in oil exploration upto 1970 was Rs. 4,000 million. This amount of investment yielded better results than the same amount of investment (Rs. 4,000 mn) in Rourkela and Durgapur Steel Plants which resulted in substantial cumulative losses.

Another important field in which Soviet contribution has been of great help is Drugs and Pharmaceuticals industry. About 95 p.c. of total production of drugs was controlled by private foreign companies. The people of low income countries like India were forced to pay high prices for the drugs. The Pharmaceutical Inquiry Committee in 1961 had found that patent rights were mostly responsible for exorbitant drug prices in India. The Govt. of India was therefore looking for help in order to establish a dependable drug industry. No western country was willing to help without heavy royalty payments. The Soviet Union showed its willingness to assist India in the field of drugs. The Soviet Union made an offer of Rs. 9.52 crores for establishing plants for the manufacture of synthetic drugs, antibiotics, surgical instruments, glandular products etc. in the public sector. This credit offer involved an interest payment at the rate of 2.5 p.c. only per annum with no provision for royalty payments. Soviet-aided IDPL projects could not make their expected impact on the drug market by bringing down the prices of drugs since they could not make any profit upto 1970.

The Heavy Machine Building Plant at Hathia aided by the USSR along with the Czechoslovakia-aided Foundry Forge Plant and Heavy Machine Tool Plant was constituted into a corporation known as the Heavy Engineering Corporation Ltd. This plant supplied all structural and metallurgical equipment that was required for Bhilai's sixth blast furnace. Over and above this it also manufactured over 19,520 tons of structural and 7,056 tons of equipment towards its total share of 84,511 tons required for the first stage$_2$ of the Bokaro Plant. The Central Electrical and Mechanical Workshop at Korba, M. P. was established with Soviet assistance to meet the demand for major repairs and spare parts manufacturing facilities required for the operation of both open cast and underground mining machinery and equipment in and around M. P.

The Heavy Electrical Equipment Plant at Hardwar, U.P., built with Soviet economic and technical aid was expected to contribute towards the development of power engineering in India. The Mining and Allied Machinery Corporation at Durgapur, W.B. has become a base for mechanising Indian Coal Industry.

Regarding Soviet aid to other sectors of the Indian economy, we may point out the establishment of the Precision Instrument Plant at Kota producing automatic control instruments which are nerves, eyes and ears of large enterprises. Korba Aluminium Plant, M.P. set up with Russian and Hungarian economic assistance is trying to meet India's need for aluminium. In the field of power generation also the Soviet Union has helped in setting up 16 power stations in the country (11 thermal and 5 hydropower stations).

Soviet aid also flowed to Indian agriculture. The Soviet help to set up large scale agricultural farms in the public sector at Suratgarh, Rajasthan and Jetsar, Rajasthan, to build a tractor factory at Loni in U.P. in the private sector and the gift of a small amount of improved seeds did help to some extent in improving agricultural production in the Indian economy.

The Soviet Union has also helped India in the development of coal and copper industries. The National Coal Development Corporation (NCDC), Ranchi, Bihar which is the largest single coal producing unit in India executed projects with Soviet collaboration. They are : The Kathwara Washery in the Bokaro-Kargil area in Bihar, two underground mines of Banki and Surakachar; the Manikpur open-cast mine. In the field of copper, the Soviet Union under its 15-year agreement with India will help in developing India's largest copper deposit in Malanjkhand (M.P.) which was discovered in 1968.

The Soviet Union is now the major supplier of sophisticated military equipment to India. After the Indo-China War of 1962, the Govt. of India asked the U.S. Govt. for $ 500 mn. in military assistance, to be spread over a period of 5 years, for the modernisation of India's armed forces. But the U. S. Govt. responded half-heartedly with only $ 70 mn. worth of military equipment and refused to grant any more, presumably for fear of offending Pakistan. The Govt. of India then turned towards the Soviet Union who gave the required help and more. From that time onwards, the Soviet Union emerged as the biggest supplier of arms to India. The sophisticated military equipments supplied by the USSR include : AN-12 heavy transport planes, IL-14 and TU 124 transport planes, MI-4 and MI-8 helicopters, Mig-21 fighter intercepters, Mig-21 UTI trainers and SU-7B fighter bombers, K-13 "Atoll" air to air missiles, SA-2 surface to surface missiles, PT-26 amphibious tanks and T-54 and T-55 main battle-tanks, OT-62 and OT-64 armoured personnel carriers, landing craft, patrol boats frigates, submarines, motor torpedo boats. Besides, India also manufactures Mig-21 fighter interceptors under licence from the Soviet Union. Indian engineers have introduced certain new features to suit the country's need and have come out with a new model Mig-21 M.

The structure of Industrial production in India has gradually shifted away from consumer goods industries to a growing role for capital goods and intermediates. Soviet aided projects made an important contribution in this transformation.

To sum up : Indo-Soviet trade and economic relations have come a long way since the small and tentative post-Stalin beginning in 1955. Aided by the useful self-balancing "rupee payments mechanism", trade between the two countries grew rapidly in the 1960s and early 1970s. Defence supplies and their accounting are an obscure area but trade figures which include repayment in the form of exports of rouble credits for development and other purposes show that in 1973 the two-way trade amounted to Rs. 412 crores and went upto Rs. 645 crores in 1974. The latter figure is not entirely a happy augury for India since it represents the cost exaltation of imports-particular petroleum products and fertilizers which India has to pay for by increasing its rather stately priced exports. By 1980, it is expected that the trade turnover between the two countries would increase by 100 per cent. The value target is not over ambitious but it would call for better matching of needs and capabilities rather than more of the same thing.

India's import needs and export capabilities have altered significantly over the years. This would be true, perhaps to a lesser extent, of the Soviet Union as well. Machinery imports used to account for a substantial part of the supplies from the Soviet Union in the early years but with a much wider and deeper industrial bases built up in India, they are no longer needed. For the same reason, Indian exports to the Soviet Union have become more diversified to include manufactures and non-traditional consumer-oriented Soviet economy. Further re-adjustments are called for. Although India's exports of non-traditional goods to Soviet Union and other East European countries have increased, such increase has not been substantial. Traditional items like tea, cashew kernels, tobacco, textiles, species, mica and oilseed cakes continue to dominate India's exports. India's share in USSR imports fell from 2.31 p.c. in 1970 to 1.88 p.c. in 1974 and 1.38 p.c. in 1975. The following suggestions have been made for the increase and diversification of India's exports to the Soviet Union : regular contact with the importing organisation, intensive publicity, provision of after-sales service facilities, periodic visit by experts, effective participation in trade fairs and introduction of air cargo services. These suggestions need to be pursued with vigour and imagination in view of the increasing opportunities that are available for trade and industrial collaboration between these two countries.

The S.T.C. and its subsidiaries as well as other State Trading Agencies have to play a major role in developing India's trade with East Europe. S.T.C's exports to East Europe increased from Rs. 27 crores in 1971-72 to Rs. 92 crores in 1975-76. S.T.C's exports have consisted mainly of canalised items like semi-processed leather, leather shoes, lemongrass, oil, castor oil, shellac and shellac products. But it has not achieved much success in exporting non-canalised items like cotton textiles, jute goods, coir products etc. It has been noted that the socialist countries preferred to buy direct from private manufactures instead of routing their purchases through the S.T.C. It is quite likely if there is an assurance of good quality, fair prices, timely supply and prompt delivery that the role of S.T.C. in Indo-Soviet trade will improve in future.

Efforts have also to be made to diversify India's exports to the Soviet Union through conversion deals, joint ventures in third countries and production co-operation. For example, the scope for conversion deals has been identified in industrial fasteners, wire ropes, hand tools, forged items and automobile components. Production co-operation may be envisaged in respect of electronics, aluminium and cotton. The view is sometimes expressed that because of the difficulty in balancing trade with some of the East European countries, it would be desirable to switch over to the convertible currency system. It is suggested that this change would help eliminate or reduce switch trade and such practices as over-and-under-pricing and encourage India and the countries concerned to trade on the most favourable terms. Any set back to India's exports arising from the change to the new system could be safeguarded by the accumulation of large foreign exchange reserves. An appropriate decision in this respect will have to taken in respect of each trading partner after mutual consultation. Recently India terminated her rupee trade with Yugoslavia. It will be useful to study to what extent this has helped the two countries to strengthen their trade and economic relations for mutual benefit. Since the volume of trade with the U.S.S.R. is quite sizeable and since the economic relations with the U.S.S.R. are of more basic importance, a switch over to free currency trading arrangement with the U.S.S.R. needs perhaps to be postponed until a later stage. Meanwhile the experiment in respect of trade with other East European countries would provide a valuable guidance for deciding whether the country can safely go ahead with convertible currency payments arrangements by terminating the currently useful system of bilateral agreements.

CHAPTER 1

INDO - SOVIET TRADE IN THE POST - INDEPENDENCE PERIOD

Indo-Soviet trade has witnessed spectacular expansion in the recent decades. The Soviet Union has emerged as one of India's major trade-partners not only in East Europe but in the entire world. This growth in Indo-Soviet trade took place under the stimulus provided by the framework of bilateral trade and payments agreements which were initiated from 1953. The First Trade Agreement with the Soviet Union was signed in December 1953 and was valid for a period of five years ending 1958. This agreement opened a new avenue for India for obtaining capital goods like machinery, industrial raw materials like rolled ferrous and non-ferrous metals for her industrialization programme which was accepted as one of the basic objectives of India's Second Five Year Trade Agreement (1 st April, 1956 to 31 st March, 1961). But the First Trade Agreement (1953-58) could not provide full mutual convertibility and lacked the flexibility of the later agreements. In Article 8 of the Agreement it was pointed out that "any balance in the rupee accounts maintained by the State Bank of the U.S.S.R with the Reserve Bank of India or with a commercial bank (banks) authorised to deal in foreign exchange will be convertible on demand into sterling at the usual bank's selling rate for sterling as fixed from time to time by the Indian Exchange Banks Association. The above-mentioned balance will also be convertible into sterling after the expiry of the present Agreement".[1]

The Agreement provided for every possible development and strengthening of trade relations between both countries on "Principles of equality and mutual benefit". Basically there was little difference between this type of payment agreement and multilateralism. The rupee was to serve only as a unit of account for payment purposes and final settlement of balance at the end of the agreement period was to be effected in sterling. This mecha-

1. Indo-Soviet Trade Agreement, 1953.

nism of payment and settlement of balances is usually referred to as an exchange settlement scheme whereby convertible currency or gold is generally accepted as means for settling the balances. At the end of each agreement, these countries were entitled to get their outstanding rupee balances converted into sterling.[2]

If we analyse the progress of Indo-Soviet trade during the First Trade Agreement period (1953-58), we find that the total value of Indo-Soviet trade, taking export and import together, was Rs. 2.8 cr. in 1953-54 and it increased to Rs. 65.7 cr.[3] in 1957-58. Although trade between two countries had started growing during this exchange settlement period, its growth was not sufficiently rapid until the exchange settlement scheme was replaced by an off-set settlement mechanism which introduced an element of genuine bilateralism in India's trade with the U.S.S.R. In the off-set settlement scheme, all payments, commercial and non-commercial would be made in inconvertible rupees and outstanding balances at the expiry of the agreement, would be settled by the export of mutually agreed items. This off-set settlement system which was introduced from the Second Trade Agreement (1958-63) gave a further stimulus to India's trade with the U.S.S.R. after 1960.[4] India has had four trade agreements with the U.S.S.R upto 1975-76. India's exports to U.S.S.R were Rs. 28.8 cr. in 1960-61 which increased to Rs. 418.2 cr. in 1975. Imports from the U.S.S.R also increased from Rs. 15.8 cr. to Rs. 402.5 cr. during the same period.

This tremendous increase in the quantum of Indo-Soviet trade stands in sharp contrast with the small amount of trade between the two countries in the early years after independence. Starting as a trickle of barter deals in 1951, trade between the two countries has now assumed a vast dimension of economic co-operation in the from of trade and aid enabling the economy of India to achieve self-reliance in a number of crucial sectors. The Soviet economic and technical assistance is now available for

2. Arya, P. N. : A study of India's bilateral trade and payments agreements, USAID, New Delhi, 1968, p. 35.
3. Value at post-devaluation rates (1966).
4. Dharma Narain : Aid Through Trade, T.O/B./C3/57, UNCTAD Secretariat 1968, p.22

nearly 100 projects in the fields of metallurgical industry, heavy engineering, power generation, heavy electrical, precision instruments, mining, oil industry, pharmaceuticals, agriculture, defence and shipping.

Before we review the present state of Indo-Soviet trade relations, it would be useful if we pay some attention to the theories of trade and their influence on economic development as propounded by Western economists with special reference to Soviet-type of bilateral trade and payments agreements.

Role of Foreign Trade in the Economic Development of a Developing Country like India

In the historical development of Asia, Africa and Latin-America, foreign trade has played a very important role. In these countries, production for exports accounts for 10 to 25 p.c. of the total gross domestic product and a still higher proportion of monetary GDP. Similarly, imports also constitute an equally large share of aggregate national expenditures of these economies. Commodity exports provide the single most important source of foreign exchange earnings in the less developed countries, accounting for more than three times the value of gross capital flows into these countries. Table 1.1. brings out the salient features of the situation.

Regarding the importance of foreign trade in underdeveloped countries, a U.N. study figures for the ratio of trade to income for several underdeveloped countries, compared these with corresponding data from some of the richer countries , and brings out the quantitatively greater dependance on trade for the underdeveloped countries.[5] Hans Singer has also pointed out that "foreign Grade tends to be proportionately most important when incomes are lowest".[6] B. Higgins has also suggested that "underdeveloped countries outside the arid zone are unstable mainly because of their orientation towards exports".[7]

5. U.N. (1953) Commodity Trade & Econ. Development, U.N., p.10.
6. H. Singer (1950) : The distribution of gains between investing and borrowing countries, A.E.R. Vol.10, No.2, p.473.
7. B. Higgins (1959) : Economic Development Norton, p.155.

Table 1.1

Selected components of the balance of payments of the less developed countries as a whole, 1960-69 (in $ U.S. billions)

Receipts :	*1960-62*	*1965*	*1969*
Commodity exports	26.9	37.2	49.8
Official flows (gross)	5.6	7.9	8.3
Private investment	3.3	4.9	5.9
Net services and private transfer payments	0.3	0.4	0.6
Total	36.1	50.4	64.6
Uses :			
Commodity imports	30.1	39.5	49.0
Debt service	2.2	3.2	
Other investment payments	3.2	4.9	14.2
Miscellaneous	1.0	1.5	
Changes in reserves	-0.4	+1.3	+1.4
Total	36.1	50.4	64.6

Sources : UNCTAD (1969) U.N. Monthly Bulletin of Statistics OECD (1970), Development Assistance Review , I.M.F., International Financial Statistics.

Macbean has cast doubt on the above idea that underdeveloped countries usually suffer from excessive export instability. He has observed that the unweighted average for the ratio of trade to income for a large group of underdeveloped countries is smaller than for a large sample of rich countries. The actual ratios are 46.6 per cent for fifty-two underdeveloped countries and 52.7 per cent for 17 developed countries. The calculations were made from date in Coppock 1962, Table A-2, omitting communist bloc countries.[8] A correlation analysis of the association between per capita income, a rough indicator of the stage of economic development and the ratio of exports and imports to national income yields a coefficient of 0.28, which seems to in-

8. A.I. Macbean (1966) : Export Instability and Econ. Development Allen & Unwin, Chap.3.

dicate a slight tendency for trade to be proportionately larger for rich than for poor countries, though the correlation is barely significant at the 0.05 level.

These results are independently corroborated by the findings published by Kuznets[9] using both historical and cross-sectional analysis and Michaely,[10] classifying thirty-three countries into large and small, developed and underdeveloped. Michaely's figures show that within each class on average it is the developed countries which have the higher ratio of exports to gross national products (GNP).

In the 19th and 20th centuries, there has been a somewhat unprecedented burst in the volume of world trade. Part of this growth was due to even more rapid rate of growth of production for exports in the underdeveloped countries of Asia, Africa and Latin America. This expansion was concentrated almost exclusively on the export of primary produce which occurred through development in mining, plantation and peasant agricultural production.

There is a good deal of controversy over the interrelationship between international trade and economic growth during the last century or so in the less developed countries. In order to understand the interrelationship, it would be helpful for our purpose to undertake a brief survey of modern trade theories.

SURVEY OF TRADE THEORIES

(a) The Classical Theory of International Trade

According to the classical theory, a country should produce and export the commodity in which its comparative advantage is greater and the country should import the commodity in which its comparative advantage is lower than in the other country. Trade, thus provides a dynamic force which helps the trading partners to enjoy increasing returns and economic development. It widens the extent of the market and the scope of the division of labour which permits a greater use of machinery, stimulates innovations and raises the productivity of labour. Adam Smith wrote in the "Wealth of Nations" : "Between whatever places

9. Kuznets, S. (1959), Six Lectures on Economic Growth, Free Press (pp.89-107).
10. Michaely, M. (1962), Concentration in International Trade Amsterdam, Trade 17.

foreign trade is carried on, they all of them derive two distinct benefits form it. It carries out that surplus part of the produce of their land and labour for which there is no demand among them, and brings back in return for it something else for which there is a demand. It gives a value to their superfluities, by exchanging them for something else, which may satisfy a part of their wants, and increase their enjoyments. By means of it, the narrowness of the home market does not hinder the division of labour in any particular branch of art or manufacture from being carried to the highest perfection. By opening a more extensive market for whatever part of the produce of their labour may exceed the home consumption, it encourages them to improve its productive powers, and to augment its annual produce to the utmost, and thereby to increase the real revenue and wealth of society."[11]

There are two leading ideas in this passage. Firstly, international trade provides an outlet for the surplus product above domestic requirements. This leads to the development of what has come to called "'event-for-surplus" [12] theory of international trade. Secondly, international trade also improves the division of labour and raises the general level of productivity within the country by widening the extent of the market. This develops into what may be called the "productivity" theory.

Specialisation in comparative cost doctrine means a movement along a static "production possibility curve" which assumes given resources and the given techniques of the trading country. Thus specialisation in comparative cost theory is a reversible process, since it represents a reallocation of resources. But specialisation in the Adam Smithian productivity doctrine involves adopting and reshaping the production structure of the country to meet the export demand and is therefore not easily reversible. This signifies that a country specializing for the export market is "more vulnerable" to change in terms of trade than is allowed for in the

11. Adam Smith : *The Wealth of Nations,* Vol.1, p.413.

12. This term is borrowed from Prof. J.H. Williams, who in turn quoted it from a passage in J.S. Mill's principles, in which Mill was criticizing this particular aspect of Smith's theory of international trade, William, J.H. (1929), "The theory of international trade reconsidered", Econ. Journal, Vol.39, June.

comparative costs theory.[13]

In the 19th century world trade climate the productivity aspects of international specialisation dominated completely the vulnerability aspect and it developed beyond a free-trade argument into an export drive argument. That explains, how international trade came to be thought of as highly beneficial in raising productivity and stimulating economic development both in developed and underdeveloped countries.

(b) The Staple Export Theory

For the underdeveloped world aiming at economic growth the arguments underlying the "staple export" theory are probably more appropriate. According to this theory, staple exports would provide the necessary incentive for economic growth, these being a leading sector in the economy. The process of diversification in the economy would concentrate around this export sector and it would distribute the growth activity both inside and outside the economy via its spread effect through backward, forward and demand linkages. It has been observed that many countries have achieved economic growth by export of primary staple products - Australia and Canada by export of wheat, Japan by the export of silk and Denmark by that of dairy products.[14]

As an extension of the theory, it is suggested that underdeveloped countries can also achieve the same goals by following these examples and so these countries should concentrate on export demand for their products instead of concentrating on a protective type of trade policy.

(c) "Vent-for-Surplus" Theory

As has already been noted Adam Smith pointed out that international trade helps to overcome the narrowness of the home market and provides an outlet for the surplus product over and above domestic requirements. This develops into "Vent-for surplus" theory of international trade. For the application of this

13. H. Myint : The "classial theory" of international trade and underdeveloped countries, Econ. Journal, Vol. 68, June, 1958, pp. 318-20.

14. G. Meier, International Economics of Development : Theory and Policy, New York, 1968, p.222.

theory in the context of his developing countries, Hla Myint uses a slightly different argument from Adam Smith's. According to Myint, the main function of international trade is to provide outlet in the form of markets for the surplus productive capacity of the subsistences sector in underdeveloped countries, rather than to reallocate given and fully employed economic resources. It is generally true that most of the underdeveloped countries have underutilized resources, particularly in land and labour in their subsistence sector. International trade provides a mechanism through which these under-employed resources can find better scope for use. This export expansions can take place without a reduction of output in the domestic sector and without noticeable change in the techniques of peasant production. The aim of the developing countries should be to facilitate the spread of exchange economy to the export sector and exchange economy can take place in the following ways : First, the exchange economy may grow extensively with important in transport and communications and the law and order situation. Secondly, free imports of cheap manufactured consumer goods should be permitted since they would provide incentive to increase peasant production of export crops. Thirdly, protection should be discouraged since it retards the growth of an exchange economy. The 19th and 20th centuries witnessed an enormous and probably unprecedented burst in world trade; part of this phenomenon was no doubt due to rapid growth of production for export in the developing countries of Asia, Africa and Latin America. This latter expansion was almost exclusively in the export of primary produce and it occurred in one of there ways through mining development, estate or plantation development, and growth in peasant agricultural production for export. Substantial amounts of foreign capital and manpower were invested in mining and development. In peasant agriculture, foreign investment was of less significance; such investment tended to be concentrated in the commercial sector rather than in production itself.[15] The economic gain from this expansion of exports was enjoyed by the European powers and the colonial economies. But there is no difference of opinion regarding the inequitable of gains between the metropolitan centres and the periphery.

15. G. K. Helleiner (1972) : *International trade and economic development*, Penguin (P.16).

(d) Foreign Trade as an "Engine of Growth"

Some theories of the Western economists consider foreign trade as an engine of economic growth in the trading countries. In other words, these theories put more emphasis on the beneficial effects trade in the form of increased knowledge of production and organisational techniques, altered demand pattern and other specialisation-effects, all of which increase production and alter the production function itself.

The economic development of Britain in the 19th century contributed to shape the international division of labour. This division of labour ensured expansion of foreign trade for a number of underdeveloped countries. The British "industrial workshop" became the workshop for the whole world, while overseas countries served as British "granary" and provided her with raw materials and food stuff. The British population increased by about 3 times and real national income increased tenfold between 1815 and 1914, but imports expanded as much as 20 times.[16] British overseas trade accounted for one-fourth of world trade in 1860. The British demand for raw materials and food-stuffs set up and international division of labour based on comparative advantage "natural" possibilities transmitted itself to the developing countries which were very often attached to them as colonies.

From this the conclusion was drawn that the establishment of free trade between the developed and underdeveloped countries was a *sine qua non* for the smooth working of the international division of labour. So high tariffs used in underdeveloped countries to protect their industries would not be any real benefit to them.

Critics of the above theory pointed out that the so called "natural endowment" could not be regarded as an unchangeable factor determining the international division of labour for all time. It is indeed difficult to believe that the 19th century division of labour made the most rational use of the endowments of each particular country. The Sahara desert is an example to the point.

16. R. Nurkse : "Pattern of Trade and Development" in his "Equilibrium and Growth in the World Economy", Cambridge, Mass., 1961, p.284.

Some fifteen to twenty years ago it was a barren desert which has now become one of the leading oil-producing areas in the world. To take another example cotton plantations in Egypt would never have been possible on such a scale had there been no American Civil War.[17] These instances show that any particular pattern of specialisation among countries was neither final nor sacrosanct.

Regarding the transmission effect of international trade, it has been observed that the process of "transmission" of capitalism form Europe to the colonies was slow and on a very limited scale. The trade relations between colonies and colonial was powers could not normally dismantle the existing social and economic structure in the colonial countries. The specialisation of colonies was determined by the colonial powers either according to their own needs or because of profits going to the intermediaries between the colony and other countries. Thus almost the whole of export income was absorbed by the profits of foreign capitalists and made to finance luxury imports.

Again the path of economic development under this system was not smooth, since any recession at the centre tended to have an immediate impact in the peripheral regions in the form of reduced demand for primary products, deterioration in the terms of trade and reduction in the flow of investment funds.

In spite of these criticisms, one may accept a limited role for trade as an engine of growth in the 19th century. But changed circumstances and the expansion of protectionism in the 20th century have greatly diminished this transforming role of international trade. Ranger Nurkse has rightly pointed out that though international trade could bring may benefits to the developing countries via an increase in the demand for the products of these countries, it is no longer an engine of growth for these developing countries. There are important factors emanating from developed countries which limit the growth of export from the underdeveloped countries of the world. Prof. Nurkse has pointed out some of these factors : a shift in the composition of industrial output (in the advanced countries) from industries with a high raw material content of finished output to those with a low

17. Ignacy Sachs (1965) : *Foreign Trade and Economic Development of Underdeveloped Countries*, Asia Publishing House, p.25.

content; low income elasticities of consumer demand for many agricultural commodities, once a high standard of living has been reached; growing technological advances leading to economies in the industrial uses of primary raw materials; and the displacement of natural raw materials by synthetic and other man-made substitutes made from a few basic elements mostly of local origin.[18] These factors have resulted in an increasing trade gap between the developed and underdeveloped countries. From 1948 to 1970, gross world exports increased by 413 per cent while exports form developing countries increased by 213 per cent. The share of developing countries' exports to total world exports fell from 29 per cent in 1948 to 17.2 per cent in 1970.[19]

It is true that the Nurksian thesis of deficiency of foreign demand is applicable only to primary products. But the production of manufactures for exports also encounters many difficulties in underdeveloped countries. As M. Singh has pointed out, there is at the very start, the problem of mastering the technical know how; then production has to be expanded in order to acquire a "reasonable utilization of economies of scale", and finally the developed countries with a permanent competitive advantage over the "late-starters" may have a high degree of reluctance to import manufactures from underdeveloped countries. All these do not imply however that development of "new manufactures" in underdeveloped countries is quite impossible.[20]

The Nurksian thesis of demand difficiency has been challenged by some economists. According to them, it is not the demand factor that is at fault, it is rather the supply factors in the developing countries that are weakening the economic growth stimulus. The domestic distortions are defective land tenure systems, poor irrigation, defective trade policies which act as disincentive to exports, lack of transport and communication facilities and of a capital market. It is emphasized by these economists that if these domestic distortions could be removed, then and then only international trade would function as an engine of eco-

18. R. Nurkse : *Patterns of Trade and Development Blackwell,* Oxford, 1961, p.26.
    M. Singh : *India's Export Trends,* Oxford Univ. Press, 1964, p.1.
19. GATT, International Trade; U/N. World Econ. Survey, new York, 1969, 1970.
20. M. Singh : *India's Export Trends,* Oxford Univ. Press, 1964, pp..1-2.

nomic growth.[21] These domestic distortions, it is true, are present more or less in every developing country and thus hamper the growth of exports in such countries. An impartial view regarding the role of international trade in primary producing countries should take into account not only these distortions but also the thesis of demand deficiency for the primary products, as developed by Prof. Ranger Nurkse.

To sum up : In the course of the last century or so, there has been a good deal of controversy regarding the interrelationship between international trade and economic development in the developing countries of the world. One line of argument runs in terms of the positive effects of international exchange and capital flows upon the growth of poor countries. The analysis in this case depends mainly on conventional static argument in terms of the comparative cost theory which emphasises that a country should produce and export the commodity in which its comparative advantage is greater and import the commodity in which the comparative disadvantage is higher. An important variant of this line of analysis follows in terms of the ''vent-for-surplus'' theory which emphasises the increased use of its available resources formerly unemployed through the participation in the world market economy. The other main line of argument which emphasises the beneficial effects of trade in the historical context runs in terms of international trade serving as an engine of economic growth.

The second important line of argument has put emphasis on the detrimental effect of international trade in the less developed countries. The supporters of this line of argument have emphasized the "enclave character" of export development and its "backwash" effects on the rest of the economy, the destruction of indigenous industries by imported substitutes, the demonstration effects lowering saving propensities and thus hampering the rate of growth of domestic capital formation and the tendency of secular deterioration in the commodity terms of trade.[22]

21. Robert E.Baldwin, *Economic Development and Growth,* John Wiley and Sons, New York, 1967, pp.54-55, H. Myint : *The Economics of Developing Countries,* F.A. Praeger, New York, 1965, p.147.

22. G.K. Helleiner : *International Trade and Econ. Development,* Penguin, 1972 p.18..

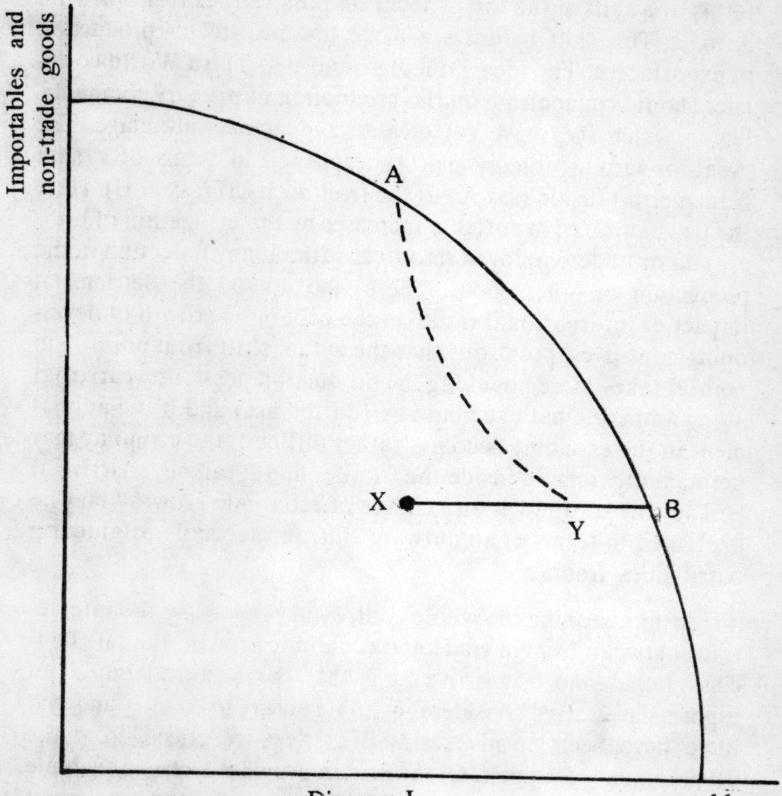

Diagram I.

One can conveniently explain the above controversy regarding the impact of international trade on the economic growth of a country in terms of diagram No.1 .[23] The "opening up" of developing countries to the world market can be explained in terms of a shift along the production possibilities frontier from A to B. This shift indicates a move towards greater production of exportables. The idea gained ground that Third World countries should concentrate on the production of primary commodities in which they have got greater comparative advantage. The "vent-for-surplus" theory may be explained in terms of a shift from a point inside (say X) to the frontier itself (say at B). Here the production of exportable increases by the utilization of hitherto un or underemployed resources without any reduction in the production of other goods. Those who uphold the detrimental impact of international trade on the economic growth of developing countries, point out that the actual shift from point A to point B takes place not along the production possibility curve but along an inside path such as AY (dotted arc) and if the adjustment in the economy becomes rather difficult, the economy may permanently remain inside the frontier and it can never arrive at B. The role of trade as an "engine of economic growth" may be explained in terms of an outward shift in the whole production possibilities frontier.

After analysing the whole controversy regarding the interactions between foreign trade and economic growth, the safe conclusion that one may arrive at is that the historical impact of exports have varied considerably from country to country and that there have been positive as well as negative effects from the development of exports. Great Britain provides a classic example where exports of wool, and later textiles, sparked off development in the 19th century. The country during 1870-1913 recorded an export level of roughly 1/5th of its national income and 1/3rd of its industrial output. After the First World War, however, the proportion of gross national product exported declined from around 18.8 p.c. in 1909-13 to 8.4 p.c. in 1944-48. It then picked up reaching a level of 16 p.c. during 1949-53, to drop again to 13.8 p.c. during 1957-63. The movements in trade demonstrated a parallel effect on the growth of Britain's industrial output and

23. *Ibid.*, p.19.

its national product. In case of Japanese economic growth, the export of silk has been the major propulsive factor in the early stages of development. Foreign trade played a vital role in that it not only widened the market for her goods, but also provided the crucial raw materials for her industrial development. During 1914-17, the proportion of exports to gross got established. Other examples of export-led growth could be found in the U.S.A. during 1790-1860, Canada and Switzerland during 1900-1913. Exports of grains have been a major factor in the early stages of development of both U.S.A. and Canada, although in later stages factors like the expansion of a domestic market consequent on the efficient development of transport and the stream of technological innovations that followed in succession have been the decisive factors in U.S.A's growth.[24] But it is widely accepted that the primary producing countries have not been as successful as developed countries in international trade. Apart from shrinking exportable supplies, the primary-producing countries are also faced with a declining demand for their products in the industrial countries.

Role of Bilateralism in Providing a Solution to the Problem of Lagging Export Trade in Developing Countries

Multilateral trade with multilateral convertibility of currencies is very regarded as the best method for enjoying the maximum advantage from international specialisation. It follows from this as a matter of logical corollary that any restriction on trade will reduce world welfare and thus ultimately the level of national welfare. Bilateral trade and payments agreements provide an example of trade restrictions. This method of trade-restriction may gain at the expense of some third country. This approach to trade was most dominant upto 1930 in the policy decisions of international trade and commerce. Economic theory now recognises explicitly that non-discrimination is not always good when a country is faced with severe balance-of-payments difficulties that call urgently for import restrictions. Bilateral trade and payments agreements have been tried in the 1930s in order to enlarge trade at a time when it was threatened by acute scarcity of gold and convertible currencies. Bilateral trade and payments agreements

24. National Council of Applied Econ. Research : Export Strategy for India, New Delhi, June, 1969 , pp.2-4.

provided an alternative to the traditional mechanism of gold and convertible currency when the volume of trade was declining due to acute scarcity of gold and convertible currency. One notices a high degree of similarity between the problems of developing countries of to day and European countries during the inter-war period. Income-elasticity of demand for a wide range of primary products being less than one, the rising income in the development countries does not lead to increased consumption of primary commodities. The spread of technological advance through greater efficiency in material use and the development of synthetics has also contributed to a slowing down in their rate of consumption of traditional commodities. The progress in the field of chemicals and petrochemicals has affected the demand for natural commodities such as shellac, jute, leather, natural rubber, wood etc. It is observed that since 1953 roughly a third of the increase in industrial raw material consumption consisted of aluminium and synthetic materials.[25] Restrictive trade policies followed by the developed countries. In addition to these, export earnings of primary producing countries thus being sluggish and small, the import-capacity of many of these countries is severely limited. Several devices are therefore, adopted by these countries to overcome this constraint, the most important of which is "foreign aid". But no country can depend on 'foreign aid' permanently for its economic growth. Moreover, the inadequate flow of foreign capital could become a severe constraint on economic growth itself. It is in this context, that the role of export-earnings needs reconsideration.

Plans for export development should be considered as an inherent part of any country's overall development strategy. It is in this context again that the role of bilateral trade and payments agreements should be considered for the expansion of export trade in the developing countries. It is true that bilateral trade is inferior to multilateral trade from the standpoint of "specialisation effect". But if we take the composite effect of "specialisation and payments", the importance of bilateral trade and payments agreements is difficult to ignore from a national point of view

25. National Council of Applied Econ. Research : Export Strategy for India, New Delhi, June, 1969 , pp.2-3.

since it has got some direct bearing on the dynamic aspect of trade.[26] From the national point of view trade intervention in the form of tariff and quota restrictions in the context of free and multilateral trade has been justified even in international trade theories. T. Scitovsky has also pointed out that "in appraising the social desirability of an economic action from the international point of view, all repercussions of that action must be fully taken into account whereas, from the national point of view, the welfare of domestic national alone is relevant and the losses suffered and benefits gained by foreigners are ignored".[27] Prof. G. Myrdal in a similar spirit has advocated double standards of morality supporting restrictive trade policies in the case of developing countries in order to maintain their trading position and removal of restrictions by advanced and developed countries which have no structural balance-of-payments difficulties.[28]

The exports of Third World countries (including petroleum-producing countries) have in general failed to keep peace with the growth of exports from the developed countries. This point has been upheld by the GATT report of 1958.[29] As a logical consequence of this, there has been a wide gap between the import needs for an accelerated economic growth in underdeveloped countries and their import-capacity generally measured by the trend in their export-earnings. It is also widely recognised that due to factors such as low income-elasticities of demand for primary products, advances in modern techniques of production utilising synthetic substitutes for natural raw materials etc. the chances open to underdeveloped countries to expand their exports to the traditional markets are extremely limited. It is now widely recognised that problems created by the export-lag accelerating stresses and strains on the balance of payments of these countries can be solved, to some considerable extent by mutual trade

26. Indian Institute of Foreign Trade : India's Trade with East Europe, 1973, New Delhi , p.25.

27. T. Scitovsky : "Two Concepts of External Economies", Journal of Political Economy, April, 1954 , p.150.

28. G. Myrdal : *International Economy,* Harper and Brothers, New York, 1956, pp.288-89.

29. GATT Report, Trends in International Trade, Geneva, 1958.

expansion, within the context of bilateral trade and payments agreements.

India's Export Development and Bilateral Trade and Payments Agreement

Since independence in 1947 India has entered into a large number of bilateral trade agreements. Such agreements unquestionably were meant for strengthening the foreign trade of the country, at least in the short-run. Some of these agreements involved exchange of concession for concession with other countries and these helped to liberalise India's trade. For example, India agreed to treat certain O.E.E.C countries as falling within soft currency areas for purposes of import and export control. The O.E.E.C. countries concerned, in turn, extended to India the liberalisation measures that they had adopted in importing from other members of the O.E.E.C. A large number of these agreement merely contained an "indicative" list of commodities in which it was thought that mutual trade was possible. The trade agreements served merely to bring to the notice of the other party that surpluses of certain goods were available for export. But the actual level of trade in them would still be determined by normal commercial considerations.

India's trade with the U.S.S.R and the other Centrally Planned East European Countries (CPEECs) was quite small both in absolute terms and as a proportion of India's total trade in the early years of the 1950s. It was then realised that bilateral trade relations between India and these countries could give a boost to India's exports. All the trade agreements prior to 1958 were almost like convertible currency agreements in the sense that the outstanding balances at the end of any agreement period were eligible to be converted into sterling for settlement purposes. But with the acute foreign exchange crisis faced by India during the Second Five Year Plan (1956-61), these socialist countries agreed to change the character of settlement in favour of the inconvertible rupee so that outstanding balances at the end of any agreement period were to be settled by the export of mutually agreed commodities.

This switchover from the exchange settlement mechanism to the off-set settlement mechanism introduced an element of genuine bilateralism in India's trade with USSR and other East European countries. The scheme constituted a self-liquidating system which incorporated within itself the mechanism of repayment on the basis of reciprocity.[30] Although trade had started growing during the exchanges settlement period, its growth was not rapid until the exchange settlement came to be supplemented by sizeable credits mainly from the USSR. In other words, after February 2, 1955 when the first credit agreement (Bhilai Steel Plant credit) was signed between India and the Soviet Union, annual average of India's exports and imports to and from the USSR which stood at Rs. 286 lakhs and Rs.105 lakhs respectively increased to Rs. 2,345 lakhs and Rs. 1,833 lakhs on an annual average basis during 1950-60. The off-set settlement system gave a further stimulus to India's trade with these countries after 1960. Part of the imports from the socialist countries came to be financed by loan assistance received from these countries and the rest by Indian exports. This bilateral trade enabled India to import plant and equipment, industrial raw materials and components which were vital to Indian economic development in exchange for its staple products such as tea, coffee and tobacco, crude materials such as iron-ore, leather-goods and traditional manufactures such as jute goods. The main advantage on an off-set settlement lay in the fact that it contributed to the balancing of trade at a higher level always stimulating the search for finding new exportable goods. The element of aid was demonstrated in terms of allowing India to pay for her imports in inconvertible rupee currency. Thus bilateralism in the strict sense of the term started after 1960. As brought out in Table 1.2 India's export earnings from the USSR financed 138 per cent of India's total imports form USSR during the First Five Year Plan period. During the Second and Third Five Year Plan the proportion of Imports financed by current export earnings fell to 131 per cent and 89 per cent respectively.

In order to understand the logic behind the trade expansion after 1960, one should take into consideration its background as well as look into the reasons for the preference of USSR and

30. Dharam Narain : Aid Through Trade, TO/B/C3/57, UNCTAD Secretariat, 1968, p.22.

other East European economies in favour of the bilateral trade and payments mechanism.

Table 1.2

Average annual value of India's exports and imports to and from USSR during the first three plan periods (In million rupees)

	First Plan	Second Plan	Third Plan
Exports	29	240	587
Imports	21	183	657
Export-Import ratio	138%	131%	89%

Source : DGCI and S : Monthly Statistics of Foreign Trade of India.

Bilateralism Form Soviet Point of View

Historically the basic feature of Soviet foreign trade in the post Second World War period is to be found in its adherence to bilateral trade and payments system. This adherence originated from a very pragmatic decision rather than ideological conviction. After the Second World War, the USSR and other East European countries realised clearly that one of the most important stumbling blocks in the matter of trade expansion with the less developed countries was the scarcity of convertible foreign exchange on both sides. Under the cirumstances bilateral trade with emphais on bilateral balancing was considered to be the only solution. Moreover, in such an approach to trade, there was an element of certainty about the commodities and quantities to be exchanged. In the framework of planning this certainty was expected to be of great help in the matter of integration of prospective imports and exports with the plan targets. Bilateralism was thus designed to overcome the element of uncertainly that was necessarily associated with multilateral arrangements.

In centrally planned economies like that of Soviet Russia, there is much advantage in knowing in advance what will be available from foreign import sources and what must be provided for despatch abroad. Bilateral arrangement provided greater opportunities to expand imports by payment through exports than would have been possible under a multilateral system. It was also pointed out that bilateralism would rule out competition in international trade and provide an easy way of disposing the accumulated surpluses in the economy.[31]

There is no denying the fact that on of the important problems that the USSR and other East European countries had faced and still now face is the shortage of free foreign exchange. In this context bilateralism was undecidedly of help in the import of much needed tropical goods (consumers' goods) in exchange for Soviet industrial products.[32]

In spite of these advantages, bilateralism was marked by some defects. Compared to multilateral exchange, bilateralism was somewhat primitive in nature. It narrowed down the choice of imports and markets too. The quality of goods was unlikely to be of the best standard.[33] With a full knowledge of all these shortcomings, the USSR still opted for a bilateralism in the interests of long term stability and predictability. Moreover, this system better suited the bureaucratic set up of the trade organisations in the USSR. The Less Developed Countries could dispose of their surplus commodities unwanted elsewhere in the East European markets and in return import the much-needed capital goods.[34]

The other features which marked Soviet foreign trade during this period were mutuality and reciprocity. According to the principles of mutuality and reciprocity, countries trading with the Soviet Union would be expected to accord it Most Favoured Nation (MFN) treatment in trade. MFN treatment signifies that one country extends to another country terms of trade no less favourable then those accorded in similar situations to nationals and companies of third countries. Reciprocity also implied that concession regarding tariff and other trade barriers could be awarded on a bilateral basis.

The UN World Economic Survey of 1958 was explicit regarding the significant increasing in the exports of primary commodi-

31. Samuel Pisar, *Coexistence and Commerce*, McGraw Hill, New York, 1970, Chap.9.
32. Raymond Mikesell and J. Behrmain, *Financing Free World Trade with Sino-Soviet bloc*, Princeton Univ. Press, New Jersy, 1968, pp.25-29.
33.. S. Pisar, op cit., p.173 ff.
34. Alec Nove, *The Soviety Economy*, 1968, pp.213-18. George Allen and Unition, London.

Table 1.3

Authorisation of Foreign Aid

(Rs. crores)

Source	Type of assistance	Upto the end of 3rd Plan	1966-67	1967-68	1968-69	1969-70	1970-71	1971-72	1972-73	1973-74	Total upto 1973-74
1	2	3	4	5	6	7	8	9	10	11	12
(1) Bulgaria	Loans	-	-	11.3		-	-	-	-	-	-
(2) Czechoslovakia	Loans	61.1	-	-	-	-	-	-		80.0	-
	Grants	0.4	-	-	-	-	-	-	-	-	-
	Total	61.5	-	-	--	-	-	-	-	80.0	-
(3) Hungary	Loans	-	25.0	-	-	-	-	-	-	-	-
(4) Poland	Loans	36.1	-	-	-	-	-	-	-	-	-
(5) Yugoslavia	Loans	18.1	31.2	-	-	-	-	-	-	-	-
(6) USSR	Loans	489.6	250.0	-	-	-	-	-	-	-	-
	Grants	5.0	2.5	0.8	0.7	-	-	-	-	-	-
	Total	494.6	252.5	0	0.7	-	-	-	-	-	-
(A) USSR and East European countries together	Loans	604.9	306.2	11.3	-	-	-	-	-	80.0	1002.4
	Grants	5.4	2.5	0.8	0.7	-	-	-	-	-	9.4
	Total	610.3	308.7	12.1	0.7	-	-	-	-	80.0	1011.8

(B) Total for all donor countries	Loans	3808.8	1034.1	398.5	753.1	421.8	705.4	774.5	639.6	1129.5	9665.3
	Grants	392.0	79.7	16.8	68.4	26.0	56.5	36.0	36.6	41.1	753.1
	PL 480/665 etc. assistance	1510.8	392.7	303.5	135.3	186.5	-	118.7	-	-	2637.5
	Grand Total	5711.6	1506.7	718.8	946.8	634.3	761.9	929.2	679.2	1170.6	13055.9
(C) A as percentage of B	Loans	15.88	29.61	2.83	-	-	-	-	-	7.08	10.37
	Grants (including special assistance)	0.28	0.52	0.24	0.34	-	-	-	-	-	0.27

Notes :
(1) All the above figures are taken from Annual Economic Survey published by the Government of India.
(2) Conversions in rupees are at the pre-devaluation rate of exchange ($1 = Rs. 4.7619) upto the end of the Third Plan, and at the post-devaluation rate of exchange ($ 1 = Rs. 7.50) for the subseqent years upto 1971-72. From 1972-73 the rupee figures have been derived on the basis of the central rates which prevailed following the currency realignment of December 1971. From 1973-74, the quarterly average of the exchange rate of the rupee with individual donor currencies has been applied to the corresponding quarterly data of aids authorised.
(3) A uthorisation figures for 1973-74 excludes wheat assistance from USSR.
(4) Constituent items may not add upto totals because of rounding.

Table 1.4

Utilisation of Foreign Aid

(Rs. crores)

Source	Type of assistance	Upto the end of 3rd Plan	1966-67	1967-68	1968-69	1969-70	1970-71	1971-72	1972-73	1973-74	Total upto 1973-74
1	2	3	4	5	6	7	8	9	10	11	12
(1) Bulgaria	Loans	-	-	-	0.2	0.2	-	-	-	-	-
(2) Czechoslovakia	Loans	12.6	13.4	7.4	16.1	8.2	1.3	1.4	6.7	6.6	-
	Grants	0.4	-	-	-	-		-	-	-	-
	Total	13.0	13.1	7.4	16.1	8.2	1.3	1.4	6.7	6.6	-
(3) Hungary	Loans	-	-	-	-	-	0.7	-	-	-	-
(4) Poland	Loans	11.3	1.0	1.8	1.4	4.2	2.8	2.4	0.6	2.4	-
(5) Yugoslavia	Loans	9.7	5.6	3.4	12.0	10.0	13.3	-	0.7	-	-
(6) USSR	Loans	282.1	36.1	46.4	56.6	49.4	36.8	14.0	9.5	14.7	-
	Grants	5.0	1.0	1.1	0.7	-	-	-	-	-	-
	Total	287.1	37.1	47.5	57.3	49.4	36.8	14.0	9.5	14.7	-
(A) USSR and East	Loans	315.7	55.8	59.1	86.3	72.0	54.9	17.8	17.5	82.0	711.1
European	Grants	5.4	1.0	1.1	0.7	-	-	-	-	-	8.2

countries together	Total	321.1	56.8	60.2	87.0	72.0	54.9	17.8	17.5	32.0	719.3
(B) Total for all donor countries	Loans	2768.7	674.7	793.2	679.8	660.7	658.9	671.7	649.9	828.6	8386.2
	Grants	336.9	97.1	60.7	6.2	26.1	43.5	50.5	12.0	20.7	712.7
	PL 480/665 etc. assistance	1403.2	359.6	341.7	157.6	169.5	89.0	111.9	4.3	-	2636.8
	Total	4508.8	1131.4	1195.6	902.6	856.3	791.4	834.1	666.2	849.3	11735.7
(C) A as percentage of B	Loans										
	Grants (inclu-	11.40	8.27	7.45	12.69	10.89	8.33	2.64	2.69	3.86	8.47
	ding special assistance)	0.31	0.21	0.27	0.31	-	-	-	-	-	0.24

Note : See footnotes to Table 1.3.

ties by the less developed countries as a result of their entry into bilateral trade and payments agreements with the USSR and other centrally planned economies. These trade agreements enabled the Less Developed Countries to exchange their surplus primary commodities for capital goods.[35] An elaboration of these beneficial effects of Soviet foreign trade led to the coining of the slogan "trade is aid" by the USSR and other East European countries.

Aid and Bilateral Trade

In Soviet Bloc literature, 'aid' and 'trade' are used interchangeably. It is true that all but a minute fraction of Soviet Bloc credits to the developing countries are serviced and repaid in goods. According to M. Kidron credit is considered by these countries to be the "Only correct method of expanding foreign trade with the countries of the Third World". He also mentions that Russian economists have gone so far as to develop a form of 'credit-ruble trade multiplier' to estimate the number of rubles of trade created are not granted exclusively to increase trade, yet their primary links are to trade creation and expansion. There is lot of validity in Kidron's remark that what seems to be purely political is so only in the short-run and ultimately becomes economic. He has rightly observed that by the early 1960s Soviet Bloc countries were "clearly beginning to count and reject, the cost of purely political trade".[36]

Soviet economic aid to India started to flow from 1955 with the signing of an agreement to build a steel plant at Bhilai. The Soviet Union is now responsible for the building up of over 60 per cent of India's heavy and basic industries in the public sector from a level of "zero-investment" in 1955. Before 1950, the economic relations between USSR and India was negligible. But in 1970s the USSR has been one of India's major trade partners and major contributors of economic aid. The tables 1.3 and 1.4 provide and idea regarding the authorisation and utilisation foreign aid in India economy. The share of East European countries' loans in total loans authorised and utilised upto the final year of

35. U.N. World Economic Survey : 1958, New York, 1959 p.165.
36. M.Kidron : Pakistan's Trade with Eastern Bloc Countries, Praeger Publishers, New York, 1972, p.6-7.

the 4th Plan (1973-74) was 10.37 per cent and 8.47 per cent respectively. In grants, their share was almost nil. As a bloc they were second only to consortium countries in importance, the latter accounting for over 90 per cent of aid utilised so far. A second feature which is evident from the tables is that there is a considerable time-lag between authorisation and utilization of East European credits. This time-lag is mainly due to two factors : the practice of allocation of aid long in advance of the implementation of the period projects and of tying aid to projects.

It should be observed that the quantum of Soviet Bloc aid is not a correct indicator of its importance to India. The USSR introduced a new style of aid-giving which was guided by three principles : to give loans rather than grants; to charge low rates of interest and to accept repayment in kind. Moreover, the USSR made available the first official credits for public sector industrial projects in drugs, oil refineries and heavy engineering products. Soviet aid also had a profound impact on the aid policies of the Western countries. After the Soviet entry into the aid-giving business, the emphasis in the US aid programme shifted from grants to loans. In the field of aid, the USSR was the first donor to accept the principle of giving development loans on concessional terms, by offering lower rates of interest. Gradually this idea was taken up by other donor countries. Since 1965, the UK has given a few interest-free loans.[37] By introducing competition in the aid giving business, the USSR forced others specially the USA, to review aid policies and programmes, and India was one of the main beneficiaries of the new policies.[38]

Another novel feature of Soviet Bloc aid to India has been that it is repayable in Indian currency. In other words, it becomes a "payment in kind". This arrangement certainly helped to ease India's foreign exchange shortage. But it would be misleading to suggest that no foreign exchange cost was involved. A. Datar on the basis of a commodity-wise study of India's exports to these countries in repayment of debts could be sold in hard currency

37. Asha L. Datar (1972) : *India's Economic Relations with the USSR and Eastern Europe 1953* to *1969*, Cambridge University Press, p. 43.

38. *Ibid*, p. 63.

areas [39] and was therefore a loss since the proceeds from exports to the East European countries could not be used for financing imports from other sources.

There is another important difference between the aid from the Soviet Bloc and that the Western countries. In the latter, most of the credits tied either to a project or to purchase in the country of origin, whereas in the former, credits are tied both ways. This may mean that cost of aid-tying is likely to be higher in the case of Soviet Bloc aid. This is so because in the case of Soviet countries, the creditors and the suppliers of the equipment are the same.

Another difference between the Soviet Bloc and Western economic assistance is the creditor countries' attitude towards "technical assistance". Except some small grants, Soviet Bloc aid is to be paid for and ties to specific projects. Western technical assistance is largely "grants" and often provides general opportunities for training in favoured fields (*e.g.* Fulbright or Commonwealth Scholarships). On the other hand, the Soviet Bloc has provided elaborate training programmes far superior to those put on private concerns in their overseas branches. Bhilai Steel Plant provides an instance in which the Soviet aid-givers provided for training up 686 engineers and skilled workers in the USSR and 450 workers and 501 engineers in India. As A. Datar has pointed out "In general the Soviet side not only trained Indian personnel for positions of responsibility but were willing to let them work in designing and drawing and for example accepted their blueprint for such an intricate plant as a coal washery".[40] However, this attitude has been hardening in recent years. This has been noticed in their negotiations on Bokaro when they refused to use the report prepared by the Indian consultants and did not utilize the skilled staff available in India. It is interesting to note how the Soviet negotiators gradually edged out the consulting firm of M.N. Dastur and Co. who were initially responsible for the overall design and engineering of the plant.[41]

39. Asha L. Datar (1972) : *India's Economic Relations with the U.S.S.R. and Eastern Europe 1953 to 1969*, Cambridge University Press, p. 182.

40. *Ibid.*, pp.64-65.

41. P. Desai : Bokaro Steel Plant : A Study of Economic Assistance, 1972, p.15.

To sum up : Soviet Bloc aid to developing countries like India has, on the whole, been useful in more ways than one. It has helped to change the aid-climate in favour of more concessional and long-term loans for development purposes, helped the development of industries which the Western countries were not prepared to finance and opened new markets for the products of the developing countries like India. The economic relationship between the Soviet Bloc and some developing countries such as India will certainly continue to be important. However, there is already an increasing tendency towards "hardened commercialism" among the Bloc countries. With increasing political understanding between the East and West, such commercial tendencies will be further strengthened and the Bloc countries will try to drive hard bargains with the developing countries including India which the latter may find difficult to resist without some kind of collective bargaining on their side.

Indian Foreign Trade Situation

Against the background so far considered, let us review the Indian foreign trade situation. Prior to the outbreak of the Second World War in 1938-39, undivided India had a foreign trade of Rs. 325 crores, comprising of Rs. 170 crores worth of exports and Rs. 155 cr. worth of imports. Prior to partition in 1946-47, the foreign trade of undivided India amounted to Rs. 656 crores, with exports at Rs. 321 crores and imports at Rs. 335 crores. Before the Second World War, India in a general way enjoyed a favourable balance of trade. The direction of Indian trade was mostly with the commonwealth countries, the USA and Japan. The share of finished products in India's export formed about 50 per cent in 1938 and about 80 per cent of India's imports were manufactured goods.[42] After the War from 1946-47 India began to experience an increasing amount of adverse balance of trade upto 1971-72. Only in 1972-73, the country experienced a very small surplus in her balance of trade. The country had to pass through a stage of stagnation in exports during the whole of 1950s. Exports varied between Rs. 946.7 cr. in 1950-51 and Rs. 1,008.1 cr. in 1960. Value of imports followed a strong upward trend over the period from Rs. 1,025.1 cr. in 1950-51 to Rs. 1,515.2 crores in 1959-60. The average annual growth

42. S.K. Srivastava, Trade of India, S.Chand & Co., Delhi 1956, pp.120-130.

Table 1.5

India's Export Earnings from Principal Commodities, 1951-60
(Million Rupees)

	1951-2	*1952-3*	*1953-4*	*1955-6*	*1956-6*	*1956-7*	*1957-8*	*1958-9*	*1959-60*	*1960-1*
1	*2*	*3*	*4*	*5*	*6*	*7*	*8*	*9*	*10*	*11*
1. Total Exports	7288.9	5723.0	5261.6	5884.7	6038.5	6130.3	5845.2	5531.9	6299.0	6329.4
Commodity composition :										
2. Jute Manufactures	2697.3	1289.2	1137.6	1237.8	1182.5	1188.1	1109.2	1011.5	1090.0	1317.2
3. Tea	939.4	808.6	1021.6	1477.4	1091.4	1451.4	1136.5	1296.9	1290.9	1235.9
4. Cotton fabrics	521.5	620.6	636.4	633.1	566.3	629.6	584.7	454.8	641.5	576.5
5. Vegetable oils	236.1	255.4	48.9	200.2	343.5	155.9	105.9	63.7	148.1	85.4
6. Iron ore	10.0	37.0	58.2	42.1	62.7	93.1	118.6	96.5	145.9	170.3
7. Manganese ore	156.9	217.6	242.7	129.2	107.2	258.1	297.0	136.4	119.9	140.6
8. Mica	132.1	90.1	79.9	67.2	83.7	87.7	86.6	95.8	100.4	101.5
9. Unmanufactured tobacco	161.4	130.3	110.2	117.6	106.5	124.8	146.3	146.8	135.3	146.1
10. Coffee	5.5	13.9	14.6	76.4	14.9	66.9	67.3	78.9	63.3	72.2
11. Cashew kernels	90.5	129.8	109.9	107.0	129.2	145.3	151.6	158.5	160.5	189.1

12.	Manufactured leather	250.2	201.1	249.7	205.8	225.2	209.7	209.2	188.6	304.5	248.5
13.	Spices	291.7	205.9	162.0	104.3	93.1	78.0	80.1	80.1	144.6	166.4
14.	Coir yarn and manufactures	102.8	71.6	81.5	84.5	89.4	96.9	82.8	82.1	88.6	90.0
15.	Raw cotton	136.7	193.3	94.0	101.9	296.9	134.6	90.8	166.2	100.6	70.0
16.	Lac	148.7	74.4	67.6	105.5	117.1	94.6	68.5	57.0	62.9	63.2
17.	Raw wool	49.0	84.1	58.7	86.1	97.3	104.0	110.8	96.6	122.1	77.2
18.	Sub total (2 to 17)	5929.8	4422.9	4173.5	4776.1	4606.9	4918.7	4445.9	4210.4	4719.1	4750.1

Source : DGCI & S Monthly Statistics of Foreign Trade of India.

rate of imports was about 6 per cent, while that of exports was only marginal, about 1.3 per cent.

The stagnation in India's export during the first decade of India's planning (1951-61) was due to the fact that the export earnings from commodities like tea, jute manufactures, coffee, cotton textiles, vegetable oils, cahsew kernels, leather and leather manufactures and coir products which accounted for 70 per cent of India's total export earnings showed no strong upward trend. This is brought out by figures given in table 1.5. The markets for these commodities had been dominated by the traditional trading partners like UK, USA and Japan. Increasing competition in the international markets regarding tea, jute, coffee and cashew kernel had reduced India's importance in the export of these products. Ceylon in 1950s and South Africa in 1990s were the powerful competitors of India in the international market for tea. East Pakistan was the biggest competitor in jute. Dr. S.J. Patel[43] is an ardent supporter of the thesis of stagnant world demand for India's products. He used this thesis in explaining India's stagnant export-earnings over the first decade of Indian Planning (1951-61). Dr Manmohan Singh,[44] after a detailed analysis of earnings form India's principal export commodities through the 1950s has also come out in support of the view that world demand for Indian exportables has been stagnant. This is generally considered to be an extreme view. Dr. Anne Krueger, commenting on Dr. Patel's analysis has maintained that "the past behaviour of Indian exports can be more than adequately explained by the policies of the Govt. of India and the Planning Commission combined with internal demand and supply factors within India".[45] This view has also been corroborated by the GATT reports : "It is evident that the failure of semi-industrialized countries (India is one of them) to keep their share in world trade is due to the fact that their production of principal export commodities was not sufficient to meet domestic requirements and at the same time to maintain and adequate volume of export supplies. Not can there be any doubt that, given limited investment resources, this slow growth

43. S.J. Patel, "Export Prospects and Economic Growth India" Econ. Journal 1959.
44. Manmohan Singh, *India's Export Trends*, Clarendon Press, Oxford, 1964 (Chaps. 2-8).
45. Anne Krueger, Commet on Patel's articles, Econo-Jurnal, Jnue 1961, pp.436-42.

of primary production is closely connected with the rapid growth in their industrial activities".[46] It is true that India was unable to take advantage of whatever demand was there for her exports due to rapid growth in internal demand side by side with the slow growth of production of exportables. Over and above these factors, there were also high excise and export-duties, leading to positive blocking of exports, increase in cost of production without any improvement in quality to suit sophisticated foreign consumers; domestic inflationary trends making domestic markets more profitable compared to international market; and the protective tariff and quota system adopted by the importing developed countries. There was also the invasion of synthetics and other man-made substitutes affecting the world demand for jute and cotton textiles. All these factors point to the need of reorientation in India's export policy in the context of a growing need for export earnings for development purposes. Export earnings financed 83.4 per cent of India's total imports during the First Five-Year Plan (1951-56). But during the Second Five Year Plan (1956-61) the proportion of imports financed by current export earnings fell to 56.2 per cent.[47] In the context of these problems, India discovered a great opportunity in Soviet bilateralism for the expansion of her export trade.

Features of Indo-Soviet Trade

Indo-Soviet Trade is now organised largely within the framework of bilateral trade agreements. The agreements usually cover a five-year period and aim at a more or less self-balancing system of imports and exports. The first trade agreement was signed in 1953. This trade agreement was the outcome of a reassessment of Soviet approach towards the developing countries. India's role in Korea brought the two countries closer still.[48] All these events led to the signing of an agreement to set up Bhilai Steel Plant in early 1955. In 1947 when India became independent and established diplomatic and commercial relations with the USSR, few could have visualised that the trade between the two nations would grow so rapidly and at such a phenomenal pace. Total

46. GATT, International Trade, Geneva, 1957, p.17.
47. The Third Five Year Plan, Planning Commission, New Delhi, 1961, p.133.
48 P.J. Eldridge, The Politics of Foreign Aid in India, Vikas Publications, Delhi, 1969 p.52.

Indo-Soviet trade in 1950-51 was barely Rs. 0.22 crore while in 1975-76, it crossed Rs.700 crores. This spectacular growth in a span thirty years provides an example of fruitful trade and economic co-operation between the two countries with different social systems. At present, the USSR is one of India's major trade partners and one of the biggest importers of Indian goods. In 1947, almost all the foreign trade of India was directed towards Britain or countries where Britain had strong political and business influence i.e., mainly countries in West Europe and the USA The USSR was an unexplored and totally new territory so far as Indian foreign trade was concerned. Although immediately after independence in 1947, India had opened itself up for trade with the USSR, not much advance was made until the end of India's First Five Year Plan. In 1947-48, India's exports and imports to and from USSR were Rs. 287 lakhs and Rs. 32 lakhs respectively. The following table 1.6 gives the picture regarding India's exports and imports to and form the USSR during the period 1947-53, that is, before the signing of an trade agreement between the two countries. But this period was followed by exchange settlement phase since December 1953. From March 1956, a new phase in Indo-Soviet trade - Exchange settlement-cum-credit agreement period -- had started replacing the former. Then again a new trade and payments agreements in January 1956 marked the beginning of the off-set settlement-cum-credit arrangement phase which proved to be very significant in terms of its impact on India's trade expansion and economic growth.

Table 1.6

India's Trade with the USSR (1947-48 to 1952-53)

(Rs. lakhs)

	Exports	*Imports*	*Balance of Trade*
1947-48	287	32	+ 225
1948-49	536	312	+ 224
1949-50	336	1626	- 1290
1950-51	134	22	+ 112
1951-52	667	138	+ 529
1952-53	85	24	+ 61

Source : Monthly Statistics of the Foreign Trade of India : DGCI and S.

All the agreements prior to 1958 had a clause stating that payments relating to commercial and non-commercial transaction between India and the USSR and other East European countries were to be effected in Indian rupee or pound sterling. Any balance in the rupee account which is maintained in the authorised banks of either country, was to be converted into sterling on demand at the usual banks' selling rate for sterling. Since 1959, new bilateral trade agreement have been concluded between India and the Soviet Union. According to its payment clause, all payments of commercial and non-commercial nature between these two countries are to be effected in Indian rupees. Any balance in the rupee account of the bank can be used, upon the expiry of the agreement, during the ensuing six to twelve months for the purchase of Indian or Russian goods, as the case may be or would be settled as per further agreement between the two governments. It has also been agreed that if there was any change in the par value of the Indian rupee, the funds will be readjusted proportionately. In view of certain difficulties arising from changes in exchange rate, there has been as earnest desire to introduce gold clause in all transactions between India and USSR Article 8 of the Indo-Soviet Trade Agreement which came into force from January 1, 1959 has clearly pointed out "Any balance in the Rupee Accounts of the State Bank of the USSR in connection with the grant of technical credit will upon expiry of this agreement, be used during the ensuring six months for the purchase of Indian or Soviet goods, as the case may be, or will be settled in such other way as may be agreed upon between the two parties".

The expansion of exports and imports under the rupee trade system has helped India to have a more balanced international trade. The self-liquidation procedure of trade balances has added to the possibility of further expansion and growth of trade between India and the USSR.

In short, if there is any one area where Indian export promotion measures have justified themselves, it is in regard to the trade with the USSR and other East European countries. For a proper evaluation of the rupee-trade, we can advance the following criteria on which it may be judged : (a) Could India have established links with the Soviet Bloc to get an increasing share of its trade without rupee trade agreements? (b) Is the composition of trade to the advantage of both the parties? (c) Has India been able to get prices for her exports under this agreement comparable to what are obtainable in the world market? (d) Does rupee trade mean any diversion of India's trade? (e) Does rupee trade restrict the flexibility of commercial policy of the trading countries? (f) How far does rupee trade facilitate selling operations? (g) Is India limiting its exports to the essential commodities that the country needs for its economic growth?

These are important points which will merit fuller discussion in the subsequent chapters.

CHAPTER 2

INDO-SOVIET TRADE AGREEMENTS AND INDIAN PLANNING

In this chapter, our main objective is to assess the importance and role of bilateral trade and payments agreements between India and Soviet Union in the light of India's planning strategy which has sought to pay particular emphasis on "heavy" or "capital-goods" industries at least since 1955-56. One of the most important objectives of India's Second Five Year Plan (1 April 1956 to 31 March 1961) was to initiate "rapid industrialisation with particular emphasis on the development of basic and heavy industries".[1] It is generally agreed that the core of development lies in rapid industrialisation and diversification of the economy. For industrialisation to be rapid enough, basic industries like iron and steel, non-ferrous metals, coal, cement and heavy chemicals as well as industries which make machines for making machines have to be developed rapidly. In other words, India was to strive for the achievement of economic self-sufficiency by developing the basic and key industries. Since the USSR. had concentrated on the development of heavy industry since the Revolution, the internal cost structure in that country had changed in such a manner that it had become advantageous for her to increase exports of machinery and import raw material specially agricultural products.[2] India, on the other hand, being a Third world country would have some comparative advantage in the production and export of agriculture-based commodities. So, *prima facie*, there was some scope for expanding trade between India and Soviet Union. As the consumption of most agriculture-based commodities of Indian origin was below the saturation point in the USSR there were promising opportunities for increased Indian exports of tea, cotton and jute textiles, vegetable oils, tobacco as well as leather goods to USSR Thus an exchange of India's

1. Second Five Year Plan : Summary, Govt. of India, Planning Commission, 1956 p.11.
2. Allen, R.L. : *Soviet Economic Warfare*, Public Affairs Press, Washington D.C., 1960, Chap.3.

traditional exports for machinery and equipment from the USSR and the industrialised East European countries could open up possibilities of "fruitful and mutually beneficial trade on a substantial scale".[3]

Another relevant point which needs due consideration is that throughout at least the first three Five-Year Plans (1951-66) India's efforts at planned development have tended to increase her requirements of imports much faster than her earnings on exports. This posed a serious balance of payment difficulty. Since the late 1950s, India has increasingly relied upon inflow of foreign aid as she experienced a chronic shortage of foreign exchange. But the inflow of foreign aid has its own problems, for instance, (a) the cost of ties-loan was often higher than that of purchase through the expenditure of free foreign exchange and (b) debt service was bound to impose a burden on the economy. It is against this background that the new trade outlet provided by the USSR regarding India's traditional commodities should be judged. The mechanism under which such trade expansion took place was two fold :

(i) Bilateral trade and payments arrangements.

(ii) Repayment of loans in mutually agreed products of debtor countries or in the currency of debtor countries. The object of our study is to analyse the Indian experience in respect of the actual working of two-fold mechanism.

Stagnation of Indian Exports

Stagnation of export-earnings at an initially low level is as much a deterrent factor for economic growth as the fluctuation of export-income. Until Alasdair I. Macbean's statistical study[4] regarding export instability and economic growth, it was generally held that short-term instability of export-earnings would have adverse influence on the prospects of growth in underdeveloped countries. Fluctuations in the exports of underdeveloped countries tend to generate parallel fluctuation in their imports. Such import

3. M. Singh, *India's Export Trends*, Oxford University Press, 1964, p.225.

4. Alasdair I. Macbean: *Export Instability and Econ. Development*, George Allen and Unwin Ltd, 1966.

fluctuations must have their adverse effect on the demand for imported capital-goods which are necessary for economic growth in developing countries. Macbean's study has contended that for underdeveloped countries in general, export fluctuation has not been an important obstacle to their economic development; though it is possible to demonstrate that export instability may seriously reduce the ability of some underdeveloped countries to achieve high rates of economic growth. It has been established beyond doubt that stagnation of export-earnings at low level will have its adverse impact on the economic growth of all the developing economies.

In the light of the above observations the stagnant export earnings of India during the first decade of planning from 1951 to 1961 became a matter of serious concern. During the First Five Year Plan, the value of Indian exports had collapsed from its Korean War peak in 1951 and had been stagnant until 1961. India not only had a rather low ratio of exports to national income, her share in total world trade was also falling throughout the period. Table 2.1 brings out the changes in the value of India's exports and her share in total world exports.

The table reveals that after 1951 there was a definite downward trend in India's exports. In 1951 peak in export-earnings was reached due to Korean War boom. After that export earnings remained more or less stagnant. Indian exports declined from 2.2 in 1951 to 1.2.in 1961. This sluggishness of India's exports has to be studied against the background of the fact that over the same period world trade expanded rapidly from $ 74,800 mn. $ 118,600 mn.

Table 2.1

India's exports and share of total of world exports (1948-61)

Calendar year	*World Exports (U.S. $ million)*	*Indian Exports (U.S. $ millions)*	*Indian Exports as percentage of World exports.*
1948	53,300	1,363	2.6
1949	53,900	1,309	2.4

(Contd.)

1	2	3	4
1950	55,200	1,146	2.1
1951	74,800	1,611	2.2
1952	72,400	1,295	1.8
1953	73,400	1,116	1.5
1954	76,400	1,182	1.5
1955	83,200	1,276	1.5
1956	92,600	1,300	1.4
1957	99,300	1,379	1.4
1958	94,800	1,221	1.3
1959	100,600	1,308	1.4
1960	113,400	1,331	1.2
1961	118,600	1,387	1.2

Source : International Financial Statistics, I.M.F., Feb. 1952 (P.XVII-XVIII), May 1961 (pp.36, 38), Dec. 1962 (pp. 38, 40).

For the decade as a whole, there was stagnation both in average price and volume of export-commodities. Table 2.2 gives the picture regarding export price and volume index, assuming 1958 as the base-year.

Table 2.2

Export Earnings, Volume and price indices (1951-61)

Year	*Value of Indian exports (U.S. $ millions)*	*Export value index (1958 = 100)*	*Export price index (1958 = 100)*	*Export volume index (1958 = 100)*
1951	1611	132	143	96
1952	1295	106	117	89
1953	1116	91	100	92
1954	1182	97	102	94

(Contd.)

1	2	3	4	5
1955	1276	104	100	105
1957	1379	113	101	110
1958	1221	100	100	100
1959	1308	107	100	107
1960	1331	109	109	101
1961	1387	114	111	105

Source : International Financial Statistics, I.M.F. Dec. 1957 and Dec. 1960.

From the above table the significant fact emerges that the level of export values, prices and volumes were more or less stagnant over the period , if the Korean War boom is excluded.

The result is also demonstrated very clearly in terms of export performance of principal commodities through the decade. Table 1.5 in Chapter 1 shows in detail the breakdown of India's exports by principal commodities. If we examine the table carefully, we find that except for a few commodities like coffee, iron-ore and cashew kernel there was not strong upward trend in export-earnings. J. Bhagwati and P. Desai have also calculated this statistically with the help of the linear regression equation $X = a + bt$ fitted to data for 1951-61 (with X as the export value) and they have come to the conclusion that "there is no upward trend of statistical significance to be found in the export performance of any of the commodities" except for cashew kernel, iron ore and coffee. In five major export commodities which add upto over 50 p.c. of total export earnings tea, jute, cotton textiles, vegetable oilseeds and oils and unmanufactured tobacco there was no strong upward trend. Thus for jute textiles India's share in world exports continuously declined from 85.7 p.c. in 1951 to 73.3 p.c. in 1960. For tea the share declined from 49.4 p.c. on the average for 1948-50 to 42.8 p.c. for 1958-60. For cotton textiles, the share was 11.3 p.c. in 1948-50 but remained below that figure for most of the remaining years. For vegetable oilseeds and oils, the Indian share of groundnuts trade fell from 11.9 p.c. in 1948-50 to as low as 3 p c. during 1958-60. For unmanufactured tobacco, the share was 7.2 p.c. in 1948-50 and it was close to 5 p.c. in 1958-60.[5]

There has been some controversy whether the explanation of Indian stagnant export-earnings was to be found in terms of stagnant world demand for India's traditional products or in terms of India's supply elasticities. S. J. Patel analysing the long-term trends in Indian exports until the end of the First Plan in terms of volume, composition and direction of such exports has suggested the hypotheses of falling world demand for India's traditional exports as the main factor responsible for the relative stagnation of Indian exports, making export-promotion measures adopted by the Govt. relatively ineffective.[6] Now, if the rate of economic growth in underdeveloped countries like India is left at the mercy of growth of foreign demand for their exports the development process must necessarily remain slow.

Benjamin Cohen, commenting on patel's analysis of the problem pointed out[7] that the stagnation of Indian exports was more due to higher domestic production cost and rising domestic demand leading to higher relative prices of Indian exports in the world markets than due to the relatively inelastic (or falling) world demand for India's traditional exports. He pointed out that it was this reduced competitiveness of India's exports, primarily due to the price factor which was the reason for the statistically observed falling share of India's exports in the world market. Anne Krueger and Prof. P.T. Bauer have also maintained that "the past behaviour of Indian exports can be more than adequately explained by the policies of the Govt. of India and the Planning Commission combined with internal demand and supply factors operating within India".[8]

If one is not biased towards either of the two types of approach, discussed above, it has to be admitted that domestic

5. J. Bhagwati and P. Desai (1970) : *India : Planning for Industrialization*, Oxford University Press, pp.375-76.

6. S. J. Patel, *Export Prospects and Econ. Growth : India*, Econ. Journal, 1959.

7. Cohen, B., *The Stagnation of Indian Exports*, Quarterly Journal of Economics, March, 1964.

8. Anne Krueger's comment on S.J. Patel's article, Econ. Journal, June 1961, p.439.

policies of the Indian Govt. via export controls and quotas, export duties, inflationary pressures and other policies aimed at promoting domestic consumption were important factors in the explanation of stagnant export proceeds; no less important were the other factors like P.C. Mahalanobis strategy of planning for a closed economy, general sluggishness of world exports of raw materials and India's failure to make the best use of whatever trade possibilities were available.

Table 2.3

Average annual value of Indian Exports during 1st and 2nd Five Year Plans

(In million Rs.)

	First Plan (1951-55)	*Second Plan (1956-60)*
Exports	6,039	6,027
Imports	7,240	10,720
Export-Import ratio	83.4%	56.2%

Source : For exports - D.G.C.I. and S. : Monthly Statistics of Foreign Trade of India.

For imports - The Third Five Year Plan, Planning Commission, New Delhi, 1961, p. 133.

The fact, however, remains that whatever be the cause of the stagnation in India's export-income, it served as a limiting factor on the import-capacity of the country during the first decade of economic planning. The stagnation of Indian export-earnings at a low level has produced a wide gap between her export-income and import requirements. During the First Plan (1951-56), the country's export-earnings financed 83.4 p.c. of her total imports. During the Second Plan (1956-60), this percentage figure was reduced to 56.2. Table 2.3. provides the average annual value of India's exports during the first two plans with the export-import ratio. The sharply increasing requirements of imports as the plan investments increased had to be financed by a large-scale withdrawal from India's limited foreign exchange reserve and by a massive external assistance. Over the period 1951 to 1960, the country's sterling balances were drawn down by Rs. 7,360 million in addition to the country's utilization of external assistance worth about Rs. 16,944 million.[9] This situation imposed a serious constraint on the economic growth of the country since a small fall in export-earnings or in the expected amount of foreign aid could have disproportionately adverse effects on the economic health of the country.

It is against this background that the role of Indo-Soviet Bilateral Trade Policy should be judged in the matter of trade creation and expansion. Bilateral trade and payments arrangement with USSR and other Socialist countries provided India with opportunities for the creation of new markets for her products.

Nature of the Indo-Soviet Bilateral Trade and Payments Agreements

Even before 1959, India had negotiated several trade agreements with foreign countries on a bilateral basis. But these were not utilised by India as a deliberate instrument for increasing her exports. The trade agreements were designed only to demonstrate to the other country/countries that certain goods were available for export. the principle that trade should expand on a self-balancing basis was not recognised. Prior to 1959, the trade agreements which India concluded with USSR and other East European countries has little difference from other convertible currency agreements. Outstanding balances at the end of any such trade agreement period (which was general 3 to 5 years) were eligible to be converted into sterling on demand for the purpose of settlement. The actual volume of trade was still determined by the relative profitability of trade transactions.

After 1959 there was s distinct change. The new trade and payments agreement between India and USSR which came into force on January 1, 1959 and which was valid for a period of five years made a clean departure form the provisions of the old agreements. the outstanding trade balances at the end of the agreements period were to be settled by the export of mutually

9. Reserve Bank of India : Report on Currency and Finance (1960-61) Statement 90.

agreed products. This resulted in larger trade volume, since any trade-deficit could always be settled without convertible currency balances, a provision on which India had to place considerable emphasis due to the foreign exchange crisis that arose during the Second Plan period. In other words, the rupee balances held by the State Bank of the USSR in India were no longer convertible into sterling on demand, and it was agreed that any balance outstanding at the expiry of the agreement would be used for the purchase of Indian or Soviet goods or as agreed upon by the two parties. The export of goods form India to the USSR or from the USSR to India was to be carried out in accordance with the schedules of commodities to be agreed upon between the two Govts. for ever calendar year before the beginning of the year to which they referred. The new agreement was instrumental in expanding the volume of trade between two countries. Table 2.4 shows the position of Indo-Soviet trade five years before and after 1958-59 when the element of genuine bilateralism was introduced Indo-Soviet trade relations. It is clear that the value of total trade turnover (exports and imports together) had increased considerably after 1960.

Table 2.4

India's trade with the USSR

Year	*Exports*	*Imports*	*Balance of trade*	*Total (Rs. in cr. at post devaluation rates)*
1953-54	1.9	0.9	1.0	2.8
1954-55	3.3	2.8	0.5	6.1
1955-56	5.0	9.8	-4.8	14.8
1956-57	24.6	26.6	-2.0	51.2
1957-58	26.3	39.4	-13.1	65.7
1958-59	39.4	27.1	12.3	66.5
1959-60	47.9	27.1	20.8	75.0
1960-61	45.4	25.0	20.4	70.4
1961-62	50.7	62.8	-12.1	113.5
1962-63	60.2	92.3	-32.1	132.5
1963-64	82.1	107.9	-25.8	190.0

Source : DGCI and S . Monthly Statistics of Foreign Trade of India.

Bilateral trade and payments agreements are often a precondition of trade with USSR and other Central Planned East European Countries (CPEECs). The conditions involved in bilateralism, need not be unwelcome from the Indian point of view. In the first decade of planning, when India faced dismal export prospects for many of her traditional exports in their traditional markets, India's capacity to import machinery and equipments in the needed amount was severely limited with convertible foreign exchange. The opportunity of trade expansion through the instruments of bilateral trade and payments agreements was therefore an important factor in the subsequent growth of industrial capacities in India.

Trade of Centrally Planned East European Countries (CPEECs) in the Global Perspective

After the mid 1950's the trade of CPEECs emerged as a highly dynamic segment of world trade, though it appears from the figures that this dynamism slowed down to some extent exports after the mid 1960s. Table 2.5 shows the growth of CPEEC trade in relation to world exports, excluding East European countries.

Table 2.5

Growth of Trade (percentages)

Year	*World exports excluding East-European countries*	*Exports of East European countries*
1957-65	66.3	105.3
1965-74	310.5	232.3
1957-74	682.8	582.3

Source : Monthly Bulletin of Statistics, U.N.

During 1957-65, world exports increased by 66 per cent, whereas the exports of CPEECs went up by 105 per cent. This spurt in exports during this period can be attributed to the conclusion of bilateral trade agreements between CPEECs and the countries of the Third World. During the other sub-period, 1965-74 exports of Socialist countries have increased by more than 200 per cent, while the world exports have increased by about 300 per cent. In 1953, centrally planned economies contributed about 9 p.c. of world exports, developed countries 65 p.c. and developing countries only 26 p.c. for developing countries and 67 p.c. for developed countries.[10] Since the USSR is the most dominant partner in the group of CPEECs, India naturally aimed at capturing a rising share in the trade of the USSR by Indo-Soviet trade agreements.

During this period, there was also an appreciable expansion in the amount of economic assistance extended especially by the USSR that gave further stimulus to growth in trade between India and USSR and other East European countries. Closer political relations also helped to bring about an acceleration in trade in the last two decades between India and the USSR and other East European countries. India's exports to the USSR and other East European countries increased from less than 1 p.c. of India's total exports in the early 1950s to as high as 24 p.c. in 1972-73. The USSR has emerged as India's single most important trade partner among the East European countries with nearly 2/3rds of the exports directed to these countries being absorbed by the USSR However during 1973-76 India's exports to this region declined sharply as a proportion of its global exports. During 1974-75, they accounted for 20.6 per cent of India's total exports and this figure declined about 17.2 per cent in 1975-76. A similar trend is observed in case of imports also. India's imports from this region increased form less than one per cent of the India's total imports in the early 1950s to 12.4 p.c. in 1972-73 and further to 14.6 o.c. in 1974-75. But during 1975-76, this share is estimated to have declined to around 11 p.c. During 1975-76 India's export trade with USSR and other CPEECs declined in absolute terms and as a proportion of India's total trade. In case of trade with USSR alone, India's exports as a percentage of total exports were only 0.2 in 1950-51 it increased to 13.7, the figure further increased to 15.5 in 1972-73. After 1972-73, India's exports to USSR as a proportion of total exports began to decline. In 1974-75 India's exports to USSR as a percentage of total exports

10. World Bank Report on the Structure of World Exports, Eastern Economist, Annual Number 1974, p.1370.

declined to 12.7 which was further reduced to 10.5 p.c. in 1975-76. In case of India's imports from the USSR the figure was 0.2 p.c. of total imports in 1951-52, it increased to 10.9 in 1069-70 and declined to 8.5 p.c. in 1974-75, which further declined to a 5.9 p.c. in 1975-76.[11]

It may be argued that such short-term fluctuations are nothing exceptional in case of trade between two countries. It is quite possible that in the next few years this decline in trade may be reversed. Though it is too early to predict, it is likely that the developments that are now taking place in India's external sector will usher in significant changes in India's trade with this region.

Analysis of Indo-Soviet Trade Agreements

The trading pattern between India and the USSR is determined broadly by five year trade agreements. This five year period does not exactly correspond with India's Five-Year developmental plans; yet these agreement do take into account the likely requirements of each other so that they are normally expected to fit in with the two countries' development plans.

The First Trade Agreement which was signed for the period 1953-58 covered the last three years of Indian First Five Year Plan (1st April 1951 to 31st march, 1956) and first two years of the Second Five Year Plan (1st April, 1956 to 31st March, 1961). Both the countries accepted the rupee as the unit of account and trade was to be bilaterally balanced. However, if a surplus on either side developed in any year, the country concerned could demand settlement in sterling during the currency of the agreement as well as on the expiry of the agreement. The settlement in convertible currency was quite common during this period. Hence the payment arrangement was in effect multilateral.

In Trade Agreement of 1953, it has been specifically stressed that the main objective was to provide for "every possible development and strengthening of trade relations between the two countries on principles of equality and mutual benefit".[12] Table 2.6

11. Monthly Statistics of Foreign Trade of India : DGCI and S. Govt. of India.
12. Indo-Soviet Trade Agreement (1953-58). The text of the agreement is reproduced in an official publication, India's Trade Agreements as in force in 1955, Ministry of Commerce, Govt. of India, New Delhi.

Table 2.6

India's trade with USSR during the period of the First Bilateral Agreement : Exports, imports and balance of trade (Rs. in crores in post-devaluation rates)

Year	Indian total trade			Indo-Soviet trade			Imports from USSR as % of total imports	Exports to USSR as % of total exports
	Imports	*Exports*	*Balance*	*Imports*	*Exports*	*Balance*		
Pre-Agreement :								
1950-51	1025.1	946.7	-78.4	0.3	2.0	1.7	Neg.	0.2
1951-52	1378.9	1106.0	-272.9	2.2	10.5	8.3	0.2	0.9
1952-53	1001.5	872.7	-28.8	0.3	1.4	1.1	Neg.	Neg.
First Trade Agreement :								
1953-54	854.6	812.7	-41.9	0.9	1.9	1.0	Neg.	0.2
1954-55	997.7	918.4	-79.3	2.8	3.3	0.5	0.5	0.4
1955-56	1023.8	921.5	-102.3	9.8	5.0	-4.8	0.9	0.5
1956-57	1423.0	976.5	-446.5	26.6	24.6	-2.0	1.9	2.5
1957-58	1633.4	1001.0	-632.4	39.4	26.3	-13.1	2.4	2.6

Source : R.B.I., Report on Currency and Finance 1962-63 p.s. 128

gives a picture regarding the growth of trade during the First Agreement Period (1953-58).

From the table, it is found that while India's total exports and imports have increased by 1.2 and nearly 2 times respectively during the First Trade Agreement period (1953-58), India's exports to an imports from USSR have increased by about 14 and 39 times respectively during the same period. This increase in trade should be considered in the context of the generally growing trend of Soviet trade with developing countries. In 1953 Soviet exports to and imports from developing countries were 45 and 72 million roubles respectively at current prices, in 1957-58 at the end of the agreement period they increased to 327 and 373 mn roubles respectively at current prices.[13] In other words, Soviet export to developing countries as a whole increased by about 7 times, whereas Soviet exports to India, one of the chief Soviet partners in trade among the developing countries(i.e. Indian Imports from USSR) increased by about 39 times during 1953-58. During the same period, Soviet imports from developing countries increased by about 5 times and its imports from India alone increased by about 14 times.

From 1956 when the Second Five Year Plan was launched, there was considerable increase in the value of Indo-Soviet trade and India began to experience adverse balance of trade with USSR Because of the "heavy industries strategy" adopted in the Second Five Year Plan, India's import requirements from USSR went on increasing at a rate which could not be made good by the increase in export earnings from USSR Under the circumstances, India's demand for import of capital goods proved to be somewhat inelastic in nature. At the same time, Soviet Union by mid-1950s had achieved a high standard in the production of capital goods and the country enjoyed considerable economies of scale in the production of such goods. Naturally, India's import from USSR consisted mainly of machinery and equipment and industrial raw-material. The USSR Ministry of Soviet foreign trade indicated that during 1954-58 the early average of India's imports from Soviet Union was as follows : Machinery and equipment (59.2%), Rolled ferrous and non-ferrous metals

13. Vineshniaia torgovlia USSR : Statisticheskei sbornik, 1918-66, Moscow, 1967.

(33.1%), Fertilizers (0.4%), pulp and paper (1.4%).[14] India's exports to USSR were mostly made up of consumer goods. From early 1950s, the supply of consumer goods come to be regarded as constraints for the successful implementation of economic development plans in USSR Naturally, USSR Govt. was interested in exchanging capital goods for the import of consumer goods. This applied, first and foremost, to such goods as were not to be found in the USSR due to natural conditions : Jute, coffee, tea, spices, cashew nuts etc. which formed the major part of Soviet imports from India. In the circumstances, India was not required to pay for her imports either in terms of gold or hard currencies.

One of the distinctive features of the first and subsequent trade agreements has been that India for the first time was able to organise her foreign trade with USSR on a planned basis. Both sides determine lists and volumes of goods for mutual deliveries well in advance. The agreements provided further that the schedules of import and export attached to them would be revised every year.

An analysis of the schedules of exports and imports of India and USSR reveals that in the First Trade Agreements there were 39 items of Soviet export to India and 20 items of India's exports to USSR in the original agreement to which five more items (cashew nuts, hydrogenated oil, footwear, woollen fabrics and mica) were added as a result of exchange of letters between the two Govts. in January, 1957. The following was the schedule of goods for exports from USSR to India :

1. Foodgrains (wheat, barley).
2. Crude petroleum.
3. Petroleum products (benzene, kerosene, diesel fuel, mazut, lubricating oil).
4. Iron and steel manufactures.
5. Asbestos raw. 6. Carbon black. 7. Chemicals.

14. Ministry of Foreign Trade of USSR, Foreign Trade of the USSR, Statistical Handbook, Moscow, 1969.

8. Dyestuffs. 9. Timber. 10. Cellulose
11. Medicaments, raw materials for medicines, medical instruments.
12. Industrial plant and equipments.
13. Paper of different kinds, including newsprint.
14. Boring equipments.
15. Mining equipment, cutting machines, rock-loading machines, coal combines.
16. Road-building equipments : scrapers, bulldozers, ditchers, planers, rollers.
17. Building machines : concrete mixtures, solution mixtures, lime-slackening machines, electro-vibrators.
18. Single and multi-shovelled excavators, autocranes.
19. Heavy electrical plant and equipments.
20. Electrical equipments.
21. Compressor installation, locomobile, pumps.
22. Gas-cutting and electric welding equipments.
23. Textile machinery.
24. Polygraphical equipments : printing and type-setting machines.
25. Food-industry equipments.
26. Shoe-industry equipments.
27. Industrial sewing machines.
28. Machine tools, metal-cutting instruments.
29. Wood-working machines.
30. Hand pneumatic and electrical tools.
31. Testing machines, laboratory equipments.
32. Microscopes, optical apparatus, seismographic instruments.

33. Ball Land roller-bearing.
34. Tractor, agricultural machines.
35. Motor cycles.
36. Photographic and cinematographic equipments.
37. Tinned fish and caviare.
38. Cinematographic films (exposed).
39. Printed matters including books and periodicals.

The schedule for goods to be exported form India to USSR was as follows :

1. Jute manufactures. 2. Raw wool. 3. Tea. 4. Coffee.
5. Tobacco unmanufactured. 6. Shellac.
7. Spices, black-pepper, cardamom, ginger and others.
8. Hides and skins, tanned. 9. Calf skins, tanned.
10. Goat skins tanned. 11. Leather and leather manufactures.
12. Vegetable oils. 13. Essential oils - sandal wood oil, lemon-grass oil, palmrose oil.
14. Cordage and of vegetable fibre, including coir yearn and coir ropes.
15. Chemicals. 16. Raw materials for medicines.
17. Animals, living. 18. Cinematographic films (exposed).
19. Printed matters including books and periodicals.
20. Indian handicraft and cottage industries products.

A close scrutiny of Soviet exports to India shows that almost all the items were in the nature of capital goods and industrial raw materials which were necessary for the industrialisation of Indian economy. The exports of such items suited the economic development of Soviet Russia also. The list of Indian exports which includes mainly agricultural products, on the other hand provided an important outlet for many India's traditional items. Table 2.7. gives a picture regarding India's export of principal commodities to USSR during this period.

Table 2.7

Exports of principal commodities to USSR (Rs. lakhs)

		1955	1956	1957
1.	Tea	-	416	538
2.	Hides and skins undressed	113	160	268
3.	Wool, raw	-	153	200
4.	Jute manufactures	-	202	127
5.	Foot-wear	-	15	116
6.	Spices	89	77	105
7.	Cashew kernel	-	-	93
8.	Vegetable oils	-	-	84
9.	Tobacco, unmanufactured	-	Neg.	50
10.	Coffee	-	41	47
11.	Mica and Mica manufactures	-	1	23
12.	Shellac	39	81	20
	Total including other items	248	1233	1748

Source : DGCI and S : Monthly Statistics of Foreign Trade of India.

These commodities constituted the major portion of India's export trade with Russia. Since these were mostly consumer goods, it was likely that the demand for such goods would continue. Tea, for example being a more popular beverage than coffee unlike in most European countries, it was likely that there would be considerable scope for expansion of tea exports to USSR Again, in spite of the availability of substitute materials like Kenaf (a fibre comparable to mesta), hemp and ramie flax the USSR produced, it was thought that there was considerable scope for jute manufactures exports to USSR.

The First Trade Agreement was only a stepping stone for bigger co-operation in the economic field between the two countries. 1955, the Soviet Union offered the first long-term credit of Rs. 647.4 million for meeting the cost of importing machinery and technical know-how for setting up the first public sector steel plant at Bhilai in the Indian State of Madhya Pradesh. Soviet Union also agreed in 1955 to offer a gift of machinery for setting up a mechanised state farm in the public sector which is now the biggest in the country. During the same year, the USSR and UNESCO agreed to assist India to set up an Institute of Technology in Bombay. In 1955 both the countries decided to start also a regular shipping line between their ports using an equal number of Indian and Soviet ships.

Second Trade Agreement (1958-63)

This trade agreement between India and Soviet Union is important landmark in the history of the growth of Indo-Soviet trade. This agreement marked a clear departure form the payment provisions of the earlier agreement in so far as rupee balances outstanding in the central account were no longer convertible into sterling on demand but could be utilised for the purchase of Indian or Soviet goods as the case might be. With this trade agreement, the era of bilateralism in Indo-Soviet trade can be said to have really began. It covered three years (1958-61) of the Second Plan and the first two years (1961-63) of the Third Indian Five Year Plan. The increased tempo of industrialisation in India was reflected in the composition of goods exchanged between the two countries. Under the first trade agreement (1953-58) India's exports consisted of mainly 5 for 6 commodity groups and the Soviet exports to India were limited to separate items of machinery, raw materials and some goods of industrial use like rolled ferrous and non-ferrous metals, agricultural machinery etc. Under the Second Agreement India's exports to USSR rose to 40 groups of commodities in 1963-64. At the same time in the list of Soviet exports to India, as revealed in Indian commercial statistics the single item machines and equipments constituted 56.5 per cent of the total. The trade turnover between the two countries increased by more than 100 per cent from Rs. 66.5 crores (at post-devaluation rate) in 1958-59 to Rs. 152.5 crores (at post-devaluation rate) in 1962-63. Total value of Indian trade increased from Rs. 2,326.6 crores in 1958-59 to Rs. 2,851.9 crores in 1962-63. Table 2.8 depicts a picture regarding the growth of Indo-Soviet trade during the Second Trade Agreement period.

Table 2.8

India's Trade with USSR during the period of Second Trade Agreement (Rs. in crores at post devaluation rates)

Year	*Total value of Indian trade*	*Total value of Indo-Soviet trade*	*Percentage share of Indo-Soviet Trade to total Indian trade*
1958-59	2326.6	66.6	2.8
1959-60	2523.3	75.0	2.9
1960-61	2764.4	70.4	2.6
1961-62	2850.6	113.5	3.9
1962-63	2851.9	152.5	5.3

Sources : Monthly Statistics of Foreign Trade of India, DGCI and S.

Third Trade Agreement (1963-68)

This agreement was signed in 1963 and came into effect from the beginning of 1964. It was made valid for a period of five years ending in 1968. Subsequently letters were exchanged in New Delhi on 7th January, 1966, extending the validity of the Agreement for a further period of two years ending 1970. The text of the Agreement ran as follows : "The Govt. of India and the Govt. of USSR noting with satisfaction the successful development of trade relations and being desirous of further increase of the volume of trade between the two parties, have agreed upon the following"[15] (Third Trade Agreement). It gave a further impetus to Indian imports of Soviet capital goods for her industrialisation programme. In 1967-68 machinery and other capital equipments accounted for as much as 72 per cent of the total Indian imports from the Soviet Union. Among other imports, oil products and fertilizers were important which accounted for 5.8 and 5.6 per cent in 1967. This was largely due to the growing Indian capacity in producing steel in which respect Soviet

15. India's Trade Agreement with USSR (1963-68). The text of the agreement is reproduced in India's Trade Agreements with other countries, Ministry of Commerce, Govt. of India, New Delhi.

assistance towards the building of Bhilai Steel Plant was an important contributory factor. Between 1954 and 1958, imports of machinery, equipment and ferrous and non-ferrous metals accounted for about 70 per cent of India's annual imports from the Soviet Union. Imports of Fertilizers and oil and oil-products have increased progressively form the Soviet Union. Machinery, equipment, ferrous and non-ferrous metals, fertilizers, oil and oil-products constituted nearly 90 per cent of imports form USSR were made up of textile fibres, chemicals, medicinal and pharmaceutical products. Soviet Union is not necessarily the only country from which India imported these major items. If the imports from other countries were taken into account, these major items of Indian imports from the Soviet Union would constitute about 50 per cent of all the Indian imports.

Tea, jute manufactures, hides and skins, cashew kernels, cotton textiles (including yarn), coffee, oilseed cake and meal, clothing were the important commodities which constituted Indian export-basket. They constituted more than 60 per cent of India's exports to the Soviet Union. It is true that in India's trade with the USSR, the emphasis is still on traditional export commodities. However, there is a gradual change in favour of manufactures, especially those of the engineering industry replacing traditional "staple export" commodities. The exported manufactures are made up of footwear, clothing, chemicals, iron and steel and a number of engineering goods. The value of clothing exports to U.S.S.R. was Rs. 394 lakhs in 1966-67, it increased to Rs. 820 lakhs at post devaluation rates in 1968-69. The engineering exports to Soviet Union were of the order of Rs. 51 lakhs in 1966-67, it increased to Rs. 97 lakhs at post devaluation rates. Another major product of export to the Soviet Union is iron and steel. It was Rs. 271 lakhs in 1967-68 and it increased to Rs. 1768 lakhs in 1970-71.[16]

The Soviet Union constituted the single most important market for several Indian export-items. In the early 1970s, Soviet Union accounted for 55 per cent of India's total exports of men's shirts, 59 per cent of woollen hosiery, 52 per cent of fruit juices. Exports of canned fruits, juices and other fresh fruits to the

16. D.G.C.I. and S : Monthly Statistics of Foreign Trade of India, various issues.

Soviet Union increased from 300 tons in 1965 to 1900 tons in 1966 and to 3800 tonnes in 1967.[17]

The average export performance of Indian economy during the Third Plan was significant when compared with that of the Second Plan. One of the important factors behind this improvement was the increase in exports to Soviet-bloc countries, beginning about 1960-61. This accounted for an improvement by nearly Rs. 1 million between 1964-65 levels and 1960-61 levels.[18] Table 2.9 shows that 50 per cent of the improvement in average Third Plan export performance over the Second Plan came from the trade with Socialist countries.

Table 2.9

Indian Exports by Major Destinations 1956/7-1960/1 and 1961/2 - 1965/6 (in Rs.)

	Average		*Change*
	2nd Plan	*3rd Plan*	
Socialist countries	3,571	11,329	+ 7,758
(USSR therein)	(2,345)	(3,524)	(+ 3,524)
West Europe	23,233	23,832	+ 599
Asia and Oceania	15,962	19,003	+ 3,041
Africa	4,749	5,215	+ 466
America	12,857	16,791	+ 3,934
(US therein)	(9,276)	(13,114)	(+ 3, 838)
Total :	60,372	76,170	15,798

Source : Basic Statistical Material Relating to Foreign Trade, Production and Prices Vol. 13 (Part II) Govt. of India, 1967.

In 1963-64, the percentage share of Indo-Soviet trade to total

17. Attam Prakash : *Perspective of Indo-Soviet Trade*, in Vadilal and Dagli (ed) *Indo-Soviet Econ. Relations - A Survey*, Vora and Co., Bombay, 1971, p.72.

18. J. Bhagwati and P. Desai (1972) : *India, Planning for Industrialization*, Oxford University Press, (p.397).

Indian trade was 5.9, in 1969-70 at the end of the Third Trade Agreement the share increased to 11.6 per cent. Total value of Indian trade with the Soviet Union marginally declined from Rs. 3171.2 crores in 1963-64--the starting year of the Agreement to Rs. 2975.6 crores in 1969-70 when the Agreement came to an end after its extension by two-years in 1967-68.

The actual list of goods for exports from India to USSR during 1963-70 was as follows :

Mica; Raw Jute; Wool, raw; Goat skins, raw, semi-tanned and tanned; Tabacco; Essential oils; Shellac; Vegetable oils including castor oils; Jute bags; Jute cloth; Coffee; Tea; Spices (black pepper and cardamom); Bananas, fresh ; Cashew kernels; Cotton-piece goods; Woollen cloth; Leather footwear; Opium; Handicraft; Coir goods; Sheep casings; De-oiled cakes; Groundnuts HPS, drugs and pharmaceuticals including quinine, salts, strychnine/papavarine/ephedrine/steroid harmones and vitamin A- natural; various chemical products including insecticides, books, periodicals and postage stamps; exposed cinematographic films; Engineering products including metal cutting precision tools/pumps, compressors, components and ancillaries for chemicals and oil industries/textile machinery including hosiery machinery and needles/fans, air conditioners and other electro-technical appliances/zip fasteners/razor blades, woollen and cotton-knitted wear including hosiery, men's shirts; Fancy leather goods; Fruit juices and canned fruits; Spectacle frames; Linoleum and tarpaulins; other goods.

Schedule B : Goods for exports from the USSR to India.

1. Machine tools and other metal working machines.
2. Power and other electro-technical equipments.
3. Generating sets (diesel and petrol), turbines and generators.
4. Mining equipments.
5. Lifting and transport equipments : cranes and hoisting equipments including mobile and E.O.T. cranes.
6. Construction and earth-moving equipments including excavators, dumpers, crawler tractor, bull-dozers, scrappers, motor-graders.
7. Metallurgical equipments.

8. Geological prospecting and oil-drilling equipments and spare parts.
9. Machines for food industry.
10. Cotton/woollen textile machinery.
11. Printing machinery and polygraphic equipments.
12. Laboratory testing machines, optical and control measuring apparatus, metal-cutting instruments and abrasive grains.
13. Ball, roller and paper bearings.
14. Wheel tractors, components, agricultural machinery and spare parts.
15. Machinery repair and servicing equipments.
16. River transport, dredging, marine diesel engines and other equipments.
17. Air-crafts : helicopters and other equipments.
18. Spare parts, components, industrial materials etc. for HEC, Ranchi and Bhilai Steel Plant.
19. Steel Mill Rolls.
20. Other machinery and equipment.
22. Rolled steel products.
23. Tin Plates.
24. Pipes; 25. Pig iron, foundry grade; 26. Gas cylinders;
27. Zinc; 28. Lead; 29. Platinum; 30. Power cables;
31. Caustic soda; 32. Other chemicals;
33. Intermediates for dyes.
34. Raw film, photographic paper and materials.
35. Ammonium sulphate; 36. Muriate of Potash;
37. Asbestos, raw; 38. Refractories; 39. Wood pulp.
40. Newsprint; 41. Paper-craft packing and other materials.
42. Medicines and veterinary instruments and equipments.
43. Books and periodicals and postage stamps.
44. Exposed cinematographic films.

45. Industrial explosives; 46. X-ray films, raw materials; 47. Calculating machines; 48. Other goods.

An analysis of the commodity composition reveals that there has been some gradual change in the Indian export basket--agricultural products yielding place to engineering products including metal cutting precision tools/pumps, compressors, components and ancillary for chemicals and oil industries/textile machinery including hosiery machinery and needles/fans, air conditioners and other electro-technical appliances/zip fasteners/razor blades. This move may be regarded as a move in the desirable direction; since the establishment of industrial base in Indian economy by importing capital goods from USSR and other countries will generate capacities for production and exports of engineering goods and other manufactured products. Moreover, India's exports to USSR being mostly consumer's goods in all the previous trade agreements, it was unlikely that the demand for these goods would continue to grow at an equally high rate in the subsequent trade agreement periods.

Russian exports to India, on the other hand, from the Third Agreement period seemed to be weighted more in favour of industrial raw materials, spares and components for Soviet-assisted projects. Imports of the conventional types of plant and machinery have been on the decline on account of availability of indigenous production in India.

Fourth Trade Agreements (1971-76) :

This agreement came into force January 1, 1971 and was to remain valid for a period of five years. The Govts. of India and USSR, "noting with satisfaction the successful development of trade relations and being desirous of further increase in the volume of trade between the two countries" had agreed on concluding the Fourth Trade Agreement (1971-76). It was emphasized in Article 1 of the Trade Agreement that "both Govts. will, in every possible way, develop and strengthen the trade relations between the two countries on the principles of equality and mutual benefit. They will study and with utmost goodwill, take decisions on the suggestions which either of them could like to present for the consideration of other with the purpose of achieving closer trade and economic relations".[19] Such an Article was present in all the previous Trade Agreements between India and USSR.

The value of Indian exports to USSR in 1971 was of the order of Rs. 208.7 crores, it increased to Rs. 418.2 crores in 1974-75. Imports from USSR also increased from Rs. 87.3 crores to 402.5 cr. over the same period.[20] India during the Fourth Trade Agreement period was passing through her Fourth Five year Plan (March 1, 1069 to April 30, 1974). Having made considerable headway in the matter of industrial development, India was more in need of essential imports such as industrial raw materials, petroleum, non-ferrous metals and similar imports. So the schedule of Indian imports from USSR listed some 59 items on which considerable emphasis was given to such imports. The schedule of imports was as follows :

1. Machine tools and metal-working equipments, including welding equipment.
2. Power and electro-technical equipment for the following projects : Patraut, Hardganj and Balimela, mobile power stations (diesel and gasoline), turbines and generators and electro-technical equipments.
3. Mining prospecting, oil-drilling equipment and spare parts.
4. Lifting and handling equipment, lifting cranes including self-driven and bridge cranes.
5. Rolling equipment.
6. Steel mill rolls and partially machine rolls.
7. Metallurgical equipments, including equipments for foundry shops.
8. Ball and roller bearings.
9. Textile equipment for the manufacture of cotton, woollen and jute fabrics.

19. Indo-Soviet Trade Agreement (1971-76), India's Trade Agreements with other countries, Ministry of Commerce (as in force on Jan 1, 1973), Govt. of India, New Delhi.
20. D.G.C.I. and S : Monthly Statistics of Foreign Trade of India (various issues).

10. Printing machines, equipments and Rotoprint machines.
11. Abrasive grains and cutting tools.
12. Laboratory testing equipment, control-measuring and optical instruments, scientific apparatus and metal-testing machines.
13. Construction and earth-moving equipments including excavators, dumpers, crawler-tractors, scrapers, motorgrades.
14. Spare parts to construction and earth moving equipments.
15. Repair equipments for technical servicing.
16. Cinematographic and studio equipments.
17. Wheel tractors including "Belarus" T-40, T-25, components, agricultural machinery.
18. Crawler tractors for agricultural purposes.
19. Equipments and spares for mechanised farms.
20. Harvesting combines.
21. Miscellaneous agricultural machinery.
22. Spare parts for tractors and agricultural machinery.
23. Sea and river ships, dredgers, marine engines and other equipments including tankers "Valikij Oktja-braj" type 16300 DWT, cargo ship "Bejestsa", type 13600 DWT.
24. Air transportation means including helicopters, other equipments and spare parts.
25. Components and equipments needed for manufacturing programme of Soviet-assisted projects (completed and under construction) and replacement of the projects.
26. Spare parts to the equipments delivered for projects built with the USSR assistance.
27. Other machinery and equipments including the above-mentioned, equipment for chemical industries, food processing industries, crashing, grinding and dressing equipments, pumps and compressors and equipments for electronic industry.
28. Equipments for All India Radio.

29. Equipments for coal-based fertilizer plants.
30. Technical diamonds.
31. Kerosene.
32. Diesel oil.
33. Oil and lubricants.
34. Crude oil.
35. Asbestos.
36. Sulphur.
37. Ferroalloys.
38. Rolled Steel Products.
39. Galvanised steel sheets.
40. Steel pipes.
41. Zinc.
42. Nickel.
43. Copper and rolled copper products.
44. Rolled bronze products.
45. Platinum.
46. Palladium.
47. Chemicals including reagents and laboratory chemicals.
48. Dye intermediates.
49. Muriate of potash.
50. Ammonium sulphate.
51. Urea.
52. Refractories.
53. Wood pulp.
54. Newsprint.
55. Industrial paper.
56. Pharmaceuticals.

57. Medical and veterinary equipments and instruments including dental equipments.
58. Books and periodicals.
59. Miscellaneous goods (including pedigree sheep).

Schedule of goods for exports from India to the USSR was as follows:

Machinery and equipments manufactured at industrial enterprises built in India with the assistance of the USSR (including excavators, containers, cranes, gear boxes and others); Railway wagons; Automobile storage batteries, traction and other batteries; Electric motors ACP. 25-100 KWs.; Garage equipments; Small hand tools; Rolled steel products; Wire ropes; Mica; Jute, raw; Wool, raw; Goat skin, raw, semi-tanned and tanned; Tobacco; Cigarettes; Shellac; Castor oil; Essential oils; Wire enamel (lac terebac); Jute bags, jute cloth; Coffee, Instant coffee; Tea; Spices, Red chillies, Cardamom; Cashew kernel including consumer packs, HPS groundnuts; Deoiled cakes including rice-bran cakes and compound animal fed ; Fruit juices; Fresh and canned fruits; printed cotton cloth and other cotton piece goods; Woollen textiles, woollen knitwear; Readymade garments; Bed-linen towels and handkerchiefs; Leather shoes, sports footwear, chappals; Raw opium; Spectacle lenses and frames; Medicines; Raw materials for production of medicines; Surgical instruments; Surgical gloves; Vacuum flasks; Enamel ware; Handicrafts including scarves and kerchiefs (silk); Coir goods, machine-made carpet; Brushes; Aluminium power cables; Tyres; paints, Enamels and varnishes including marine paints; lemon chrone; Dye-stuffs, Anato-seeds; Miniature bulbs; Dry batteries; Cosmetic products; Books and periodicals; Miscellaneous goods.

An analysis of the commodity-composition in the latest trade agreement reveals that there has been considerable diversification of Indian exports to and imports from the USSR. If we compare the list of Indian export-goods during the Third Agreement period (1963-70) and the Fourth Agreement period (1971-76), we find that the change is more in favour of industrial machineries and equipments which are products of Soviet assistance, other important items are engineering goods and simple manufactures like ready-made garments, woollen textiles and knitwear, jute bags and cloth etc. The overwhelming predominance of traditional primary products in India's exports has been on the decline.

In Indian import-goods from the USSR now consist more of equipments, spare parts and industrial raw materials necessary for the industrial development of the country. The importance of turn-key projects has been reduced.

Exports of Indian engineering goods have increased from Rs. 233.08 lakhs in 1970-71 to Rs. 1095.28 lakhs in 1974-75. Table 2.10 gives details regarding the nature of these engineering products and their exports during 1970-75

Table 2.10

Export of Indian engineering goods to USSR (F.O.B. Value in lakh Rs.)

	Commodity	*1970-71*	*1971-72*	*1972-73*	*1973-74*	*1974-75*
1.	Malleable castings	-	-	0.15	8.83	6.7[illegible]
2.	P.A.Equipment	-	-	-	8.44	
3.	E.P.N.S. Ware	33.87	43.52	75.39	47.84	74.3[illegible]
4.	Sanitary Fittings	-	-	5.81	12.15	
5.	Hoisting and pulling machines	-	-	8.74	8.68	1.0[illegible]
6.	Garage Equipments	-	0.11	84.49	148.30	132.9[illegible]
7.	Hand , small and cutting tools	20.40	36.40	21.57	22.00	39.6[illegible]
8.	Air compressors and parts	-	-	-	-	46.[illegible]
9.	Elec. power machinery	-	-	-	-	12.[illegible]
10.	Wire Ropes	6.51	19.72	38.61	69.90	7.[illegible]
11.	Cutlery	-	0.33	1.29	5.43	
12.	Instruments Surgical & Medical	21.63	50.78	40.50	17.82	

1	2	3	4	5	6	7
13.	Diesel engines and parts	-	-	-	2.64	-
14.	Washing machinery	-	-	-	5.70	-
15.	Refrigerators, air-conditioners etc.	0.59	-	0.01	-	-
16.	Aircraft and parts	-	-	0.01	-	17.00
17.	Auto and auto-parts	-	-	-	-	11.50
18.	Batteries-storage	44.01	81.46	92.98	118.13	292.30
19.	Batteries - dry	-	0.90	17.55	-	0.98
20.	Elec. Wires and cables	105.65	256.08	346.01	331.42	450.66
21.	Others	0.42	0.78	0.26	5.74	1.59
	Total :	233.08	490.08	733.37	813.02	1095.28

Source : Handbook of Export Statistics 1974-75, Engineering Exp. Council, Cal. India.

To sum up : A careful study of the trade agreements between India and USSR over the period reveals that for the first time India now has opportunity to organise her foreign trade with the Soviet Union on the basis of a fairly long-period plan. It is well in advance of the actual transaction that both sided can determine lists and volumes of goods for mutual deliveries. These agreements provide at the same time for the development of balanced trade and for reciprocal application of the most-favoured nation treatment in trade. Moreover, technical credit facilities make possible an even flow of trade, and for orderly Soviet purchases of Indian goods. All commercial transactions between these two countries are, of course, effected through the use of Indian rupees.

Beginning from the Third Trade Agreement in 1963, one can see the change in the commodity-composition of Indo-Soviet trade. Engineering products including metal-cutting precision tools/ pumps, compressors, components and ancillary for chemical and oil industries/textile machinery including hosiery machinery and needles/fans, air conditioners and other electro-technical appliances, Zip fastners and razor blades were included in Indian export list to the USSR Simple manufactures like woollen and cotton-knitted wear including hosiery, men's shirts, fancy leather goods were also included.

In the Fourth Agreement from 1971 there has been some notable change in India's exports to the USSR Machinery and equipment built in India with the Soviet assistance such as excavators, container cranes, gear boxes, railway wagons, automobile storage batteries, traction and other batteries, electric motors AC P.25-25-100 KWs, garage equipments, small hand tools rolled steel products, wire ropes etc, are some of the important export-goods to USSR.

On the other hand, so far as India's imports from USSR are concerned, it is not difficult to see the change. In the first two trade agreements, there was much emphasis on the import of "turnkey type of projects" among other items like raw materials, power and oil-drilling equipment, equipment for coal mining industry, equipments for irrigation projects. In the Third and Fourth Agreements, the change is more in favour of industrial components and spare parts, essential industrial raw-materials like crude petroleum and petroleum products like benzine, kerosene, diesel, fuel, mazut, lubricating oils etc.

The general observation of Prof. Kidron regarding the East European Bloc trade with the developing countries indicate that the block exports to developing countries consisted mainly of manufactures, armaments in particular; while raw-materials, food and beverages from the developing countries still accounted for 85 per cent of their exports to the Bloc countries. Thus, in Kidron's view the commodity composition of such trade has remained firmly within an "imperialistic mould".[21] This observation does not seem to apply to India's trade with USSR. It may be true that in the early years India's exports consisted mostly of primary tropical products and her imports also consisted of products manufactured in the USSR. But when we take into account the evolution of the two countries' trading pattern upto the Fourth Agreement period, we find that the products manu-

21. M. Kidron (1972) : *Pakistan's Trade with Eastern Bloc Countries*, New York, Praeger Publishers, p.9.

factured in India had almost edged out exports of primary commodities. The interchange between primer products and manufactures which was the hall-mark of "imperialist" trading links, is no longer a characteristic of Indo-USSR trade.

CHAPTER 3

COST-BENEFIT ANALYSIS OF INDIA'S TRADE WITH THE U.S.S.R. AND EASTERN EUROPE

A cost-benefit analysis of India's trade with the USSR and the Eastern Europe has to be undertaken within the frame work of certain guiding principles. These principles are somewhat different from those generally followed in case of trade with convertible currency, since India's trade with the USSR and Eastern Europe is guided by the principle of bilateral trade and payments agreements in terms of "rupee payment".

For the calculation of possible costs, the criteria to be adopted are (i) how far the rapid increase of Indian exports to USSR and Eastern Europe has displaced its exports to the convertible currency areas. If there is any evidence of such displacement, it would be harmful from India's point of view. Firstly, India will face an immediate loss of free foreign exchange due to physical diversion of Indian goods from convertible currency markets to East Europe. Secondly, this diversion of goods carries with it the risk of selling at a premium in the markets of West Europe, thus disrupting India's normal trade relation with its traditional partners. In other words, the cost element depends upon how far these exports have been truly additional or not. (ii) The second important criterion for the measurement of cost whether the "import purchasing power" of India's exports to the USSR and Eastern Europe is lower than that of her exports to other areas.

On the benefit-side, the important criteria to be followed are (i) whether India's exports to the USSR and Eastern Europe are truly additional or not, (ii) whether India is receiving satisfactory prices for her exports in East European markets, (iii) whether India has received from these countries high-priority goods at competitive prices in relation to world prices, (iv) whether India has received the benefits of diversification with respect to non-traditional items in accordance with the trade agreements.

Let us, first, take up the question of possible diversion of

India's exports and related problems.

Diversion of trade in the context of Indo-Soviet/East European trade is described as switching supplies to the USSR and East Europe by disregarding market opportunities elsewhere. It can take place under different conditions : (i) When the domestic production constraint exists, and the country being unable to take advantage of the opportunities in all markets switches the supplies to USSR and East European countries re-export the commodities imported from India to the West European markets. The existence of this switch trade is an indication that India could have sold these commodities on its own in West European markets. Possible reasons for re-export may be as follows : (i) USSR and Eastern Europe can make little use of the imports Indian goods, and at the same time, they are badly in need of free foreign exchange, (ii) the re-exported products have good markets in convertible currency areas of Western Europe.

In order to establish diversion of the first type, it is necessary to establish the fact that India was losing her share in other markets due to increased exports to USSR and East Europe. But the loss of share may also be the result of other factors like the lack of competitiveness of Indian goods in terms of price and quality, the restrictive trade policies of the importing countries. So in order to measure trade diversion, the impact of these factors should be isolated from the main component. The other important factor in the measurement of diversion is the rate of growth of domestic consumption, if the supply elasticities are low both in short and long-run.

The starting point in the calculation of trade diversion should be to verify whether the relative rate of decline of India's market share in other markets was greater in 1961-70 than in 1950-60 and if it is so, how much is the contribution of the "other factors" discussed above. The amount of loss of market, thus obtained should be deducted from the total amount of decline. The rest of the decline can then be properly attributed to increased exports to USSR and Eastern Europe.

In order to establish the significance of export diversion of this nature, a study of each principal export commodity separately will be useful.

Tea : Tea is one of the most important contributors to India's export earnings. India accounted for about 43 per cent of the average annual world production and world exports in the period 1958-60.[1] But in 1960s, this share shows a falling trend. It is a misfortune for countries like India that their exports are dominated by such commodities in which international trade has grown relatively slowly. Between 1938 and 1960 the volume of world trade in all commodities went up by over 100 per cent.[2] But the volume of world trade in tea over the same period increased by only 38 per cent. Because of this background it appears plausible that exports of tea to East Europe cannot be considered as diversion. Between 1957 and 1960, average annual exports of tea to the Socialist countries was 10.8 mn. kg. export to Socialist countries were 20.4 mn. kg. and to the rest of the world it was 188.8 mn. kg. annually. India's share of tea imports into USA and UK has steadily declined. Table 3.1 shows India's share in imports of tea into select developed countries.

Table 3.1

India's share in imports of tea from select developed countries

(percentages)

Country	*1963*	*1964*	*1966*	*1968*	*1969*
U.S.A	26.0	22.6	18.6	18.4	16.5
U.K.	54.3	53.2	46.2	44.8	35.6
E.E.C.	24.7	34.0	31.1	23.5	25.8
Canada	28.8	29.9	21.4	20.4	16.7
Japan	-	1.02	3. 8	10.1	6.7

Source : Reserve Bank of India, Report on currency and finance (Bombay, 1971); Office of the Econ. Adviser, Govt. of India, Foreign Trade Statistics with special reference to rupee payment countries.

At the same time, India's exports of tea to the East European countries have increased from 20 mn. kg. in 1963 to 36 mn. kg. in 1970. Although production has increased, the aggregate exports have declined. Table 3.2 shows India's production and exports of tea over the period.

1. This world production excludes the production of mainland China and USSR.
2. U.N. Statistical Year Book, 1961, Table 151, p. 426.

Table 3.2

India's production and exports of tea (Qty. in mn. kg.)

Year	*Production*	*Aggregate exports*	*Exports USSR*	*Exports to East Europe*
1961	354.4	206.3	11	13
1963	346.4	223.5	16	20
1965	366.4	199.4	23	26
1967	384.8	213.7	20	24
1969	394.5	176.7	29	34
1970	421.0	208.0	32	36

Source : Reserve Bank of India, report on currency and finance (Bombay, 1971); Office of the Econ. Adviser. Govt. of India, Foreign Trade Statistics with special reference to rupee payment countries.

The faster rate of decline of India's exports to Western markets in the sixties may be explained by the sharply upward movement of Indian tea-prices as compared to the prices of her competitors like Ceylon and Kenya. Benjamin Cohen has argued that the correlation coefficient between relative export market share is significant (0.90) for UK imports of tea from India over the period 1951-60,[3] assuming the commodities exported by two competitors--tea from Ceylon and India--have equal income elasticities of demand and equal cross price elasticities of demand for all other commodities. But the Table 3.3 shows that Indian prices were not out of tune from those of her competitors and relative price did not change significantly after 1960.

Thus the relative price movement cannot explain the loss of India's relative market share in the 1960s. But the emergence of East African countries in a tea export market was certainly a factor. India was losing to East African countries in 1950s and the trend continued in 1960s. So far is India's production of tea is concerned about 60 per cent of her total production and export is mainly in terms of common teas.[4] Competition from

3. B. Cohen : *The stagnation of Indian Exports* Q.J.E., March, 1964, pp.610-611.
4. H. Roy : *Tea price sabilisation*; The Indian case, Calcutta, 1965, p.120.

East African countries in this line of production was more serious than from Ceylon. The share of the East African countries in total world imports increased form about 5.3 per cent in 1959-60 to an average of 6.8 per cent in 1960-65. In terms of volume it amounts to about 16/17 mn/kg. annually. Thus most of this increase in trade was at India's expense.

Table 3.3

Average unit prices of tea : India, Ceylon and Kenya (per 100 lb. in U.S. $)

Country	*1960*	*1961*	*1962*	*1963*	*1964*	*1965*
India	59.20	57.50	55.63	56.53	56.53	55.71
Ceylon	56.13	54.94	53.30	52.42	52.62	51.32
Kenya	51.48	51.21	48.99	48.14	46.42	48.55

Source : IMF International Financial Statistics.

If one could establish that USSR and Eastern Europe were customers of common-quality tea during this period the question of diversion would lose its importance since the West European markets for such tea was all the time declining. But a closer scrutiny of India's exports of tea to USSR and East Europe reveals that India was exporting mainly high-quality tea to these countries. So far as the production of this tea is concerned, India produced only 40 per cent of her total production in terms of high grade variety.[5] A large part of additional production was a result of coarser plucking rather than of new planting during 1950-60. This was a factor behind quality-deterioration. According to the findings of the Plantation Enquiry Commission of 1956 about 30 per cent of the total area under tea in India was in need of immediate replantation, having been planted before 1900. 79 per cent are of Darjeeling which produces some of the finest quality of tea in India was in need of immediate replantation.[6] But the actual pace of replantation has been less than 1 per cent a year in the postwar years. The demand for this good quality tea was quite high in the international markers. Prof. Richard Stone's

5. *Ibid.*
6. Vide their report, Vol.1, New Delhi, 1956, p.62.

finding that income elasticity of demand for tea at high income levels is negligible[7] cannot apply to the case demand for high-grade tea taken separately. So the supply being limited, if it is exported from India to USSR and Eastern Europe, thereby neglecting demand elsewhere, there is strong evidence of diversion in tea-trade. Of course, in the meantime there will be some demand for the good quality tea in the domestic market and this should be deducted to find out the magnitude of diversion. According to A. Datar's calculation domestic consumption of good quality tea cannot be more than Rs. 25 mn. per year and the magnitude of diversion in the 60's was in the neighbourhood of Rs. 55 mn. annually.[8]

Jute : Jute manufactures is one of the most important foreign exchange earners for India. It normally accounted for over 20 per cent of total annual export proceeds during 1950s; in 1960s the contribution of Jute manufactures in total foreign exchange earnings approached 16 per cent.

Imports of jute textiles have increased in all the important markets quite steadily. In USA, the most important purchaser of

Table 3.4

India's share in Jute Textiles import from select developed countries

(Percentages)

Country	*1963*	*1964*	*1966*	*1968*	*1969*
USA	84.9	82.4	79.0	77.8	77.2
UK	79.4	83.3	65.2	49.6	27.6
EEC	51.9	39.4	28.8	27.2	14.7
Canada	83.1	83.2	82.6	86.3	80.5
Japan	-	99.5	-	64.5	79.9

Source : DGCI and S : Monthly Statistics of Foreign Trade of India.

7. Rechard Stone, *Measurement of Consumer's Expenditure and Behaviour in the UK during 1920-38,* Cambridge, 1954, Vol.1, p.145. (His study of consumer's expenditures in UK for 1920-38 suggested an income elasticity of demand of 0.04 and a price elasticity of 0.3 for tea in the UK market).
8. Asha L. Datar: India's Econ. Relations with the U.S.S.R and East Europe, 1972, Cambridge University Press (P. 142).

jute textiles, the rate of growth of import has been of the order of 28 per cent during 1960s, in Japan, the rate is as high as 320.5 per cent and in EEC the rate is 246 per cent. So far as India is concerned, she is losing her relative share in all the important markets. Table 3.4 gives India's actual share in these markets during selected years in the 1960's. One of the reasons for this decline may be explained in terms of Pakistan's vigorous competition since 1957 and the competition from synthetic substitutes. Pakistan adopted an aggressive policy relating to the exports of Jute manufactures. Its advantages, according to R.K. Singh, included among others "supply of abundant, cheap and better quality jute, relatively low wages, and far by far the most important, the Export Bonus Scheme which alone gives the industry a cost advantage of Rs. 140 per ton" in the industry in that country.[9] G.M. Adamjee an ex-President of Pakistan Jute Mills Association estimated that after the introduction of the Bonus Scheme in January, 1959 exports of jute manufacture increase by about 62 per cent per year. On the other hand, as India's reactions were slow, she was bound to lose some ground to Pakistan. Pakistan's exports of sacking bags increased from 60.4 thousand tons in 1957 to 123.8 thousand tons in 1960; while hessian cloth increased from 29.7 thousand tons to 61.9 thousand tons during the same period.[10] Pakistan from 1960 emerged as important competitor in the export of sacking bags produced out of ordinary quality jute. But both hessian cloth and carpet-backing which have got good demand in other markets need good quality jute in their manufacture. Since it is true that India's capacity of producing good quality jute is limited, exports of hessian cloth or carpet backing to USSR or Eastern Europe is diversionary. So far as carpet-backing is concerned, USA is the most important purchaser and Eastern Europe is not counted in this matter. But Eastern Europe has emerged as an important buyer of Indian Hessian cloth and sacking bangs. As the Hessian cloth has good market elsewhere and its availability is constrained in nature. Table 3.5 gives an idea of exports of jute manufactures to East Europe.

9. Singh, R.K. : Prosperity through Exports, Engineering Export Promotion Council, Calcutta, 1965 (P. 154).
10. Pakistan's Foreign Trade Statistics.

Table 3.5

India's exports of jute manufactures to East Europe (in Rs. Million)

	1961-62	*1962-63*	*1963-64*	*1964-65*	*1965-66*
Hessian cloth	42.2	46.3	57.6	64.5	82.0
Sacking bag	60.9	58.0	92.0	158.5	231.7

Source : DGSI : Monthly Statistics of Foreign Trade.

In the 60s, India was exporting hessian cloth to Eastern Europe whose value was of the order of Rs. 58 mn. annually. These exports were diversionary.

Table 3.6

India's production, consumption and exports of jute manufactures

(Qty. in '000 tons)

Year	*Production*	*Consumption*	*Aggregate exports*	*Year end stocks*	*Exports to East Europe*	*Exports to USSR*
1961	997	278	760	56	52.0	25
1962	1231	303	874	83	60.0	31
1963	1324	333	875	1212	88.4	69
1964	1272	378	931	105	132.0	102
1965	1336	378	929	122	159.0	129
1966	1120	405	746	123	190.8	104
1967	1157	388	769	129	147.4	112
1968	1085	435	673	126	133.0	103
1969	893	380	579	70	102.0	76
1970	995	441	539	539	143.0	105

Source : Reserve Bank India, Report on currency and finance (Bombay, 1971); Office of the Econ. Adviser, Govt. of India, Foreign Trade Statistics with special reference to rupee payment countries.

So far as sacking bags are concerned, India's powerful competitor is Pakistan and so India's exports of sacking bags worth

Rs. 100 mn. annually may be regarded as largely additional in nature. During this period Indian exports of jute manufactures to Eastern Europe were in the range of 7-22 per cent of total exports and only 4-12 per cent of total production. The growth of stocks of jute manufactures over the year ends is also an indicator that exports to East Europe had little to do in the matter of any loss of markets in convertible currency areas. Table 3.6 shows India's production, consumption and exports of jute manufactures.

Table 3.7

Production, Consumption and Exports of Coffee in India.

(Qty. in '000 tons)

Year	*Production*	*Consumption*	*Aggregate exports*	*Exports the rest to the world*	*Exports to East Europe*	*Exports to USSR*
1962-63	56.2	34.7	22.4	15.0	7.4	2.3
1963-64	69.3	33.6	33.0	22.14	10.26	8.8
1964-65	61.0	35.2	23.0	16.8	17.2	9.0
1965-66	63.9	36.9	28.8	12.1	16.7	8.6
1966-67	78.3	35.6	35.0	18.3	16.7	6.4
1967-68	70.5	36.5	29.8	11.2	18.4	7.1
1968-69	73.0	35.8	32.0	12.3	19.7	7.3
1969-70	63.1	39.1	31.2	7.5	23.5	9.1
1970-71	110.0	33.6	31.9	7.5	24.4	8.4

Source : (i) Reserve Bank of India, Report on currency and finance, (ii) Office of the Econ. Adviser, Govt. of India, Foreign Trade Statistics.

Coffee : Coffee is a minor item in India's exports. Earnings from this commodity formed barely 1 per cent of India's total export earnings during 1950s. The situation did not changes much during 1960s. During 1958-60 exports formed only 33 per cent of the total production of coffee in India. Average production during 1958-60 was to the tune of 47.3 thousand tons, while exports were 15.2 thousand tons. Domestic consumption has increased much--between 1948-50 and 1958-60 it has increased by about 71 per cent. As a result, the exportable surplus of coffee has not been because of inelasticity in the supply.

In 1960s production fluctuated with its resultant fluctuations in exports to both convertible currency areas and Eastern Europe. Table 3.7 gives an idea about production, consumption and exports of coffee in India.

The share of export to East Europe has varied between 31 per cent and 62 per cent. the USSR has been important purchaser, absorbing nearly 37-40 per cent of export to Eastern Europe.

Indian coffee is well-known for its special aroma and it has its own markets. So even after reducing domestic consumption, it was not possible to serve all markets equally due to the existing production constraint. Accordingly, (Table 3.7) when we see that during 1960's exports to East Europe had increased, this was bound to have been at the cost of other convertible currency markets. Table 3.8 shows India's share in coffee imports form selected development countries.

Table 3.8

India's share in coffee imports from selected developed countries

(percentages)

Country	*1963*	*1964*	*1966*	*1968*	*1969*	*1970*
USA	0.09	0.03	0.01	0.04	0.05	0.9
UK	0.01	2.2	0.05	0.08	0.2	-
EEC	0.07	1.0	0.04	0.04	0.3	-
Canada	Neg.	0.3	Neg.	Neg.	Neg.	-
Japan			Neg.	Neg.		

Source : DGCI and S: Monthly Statistics of Foreign Trade of India.

Right through the decade, India's share in coffee imports into convertible currency areas negligible. This poor performance can be attributed partly to the failure of production coupled with steady demand in domestic market (cf. Table 3.7). Restriction on exportable surplus has also been imposed as a result of increased exports to USSR and Eastern Europe.

According to a study made by the Indian Institute of Foreign Trade the most important constraint on Indian exports after 1962 was the quotas imposed by the International Coffee Agreement rather than domestic supply. India's export quota which varied from 18 thousand tons to 22 thousand tons, was determined on the basis of Indian production.[11]. India very often had not been able to completely fulfill her quota (cf. Table 3.7). It is estimated that she had fulfilled only 72 per cent of the quota assigned to her. So it is not correct to assume that quota imposition was the real effective constraint on India's coffee exports. The fact is quotas can also be revised; these were only provisional. Had she fulfilled her quota in the first 6 months of the year, she could have requested a revision of the initial quota as has been done by many countries. India could not do so because of the limited availability of supply and the increasing exports to East Europe and USSR Moreover, the East European countries (including USSR) were re-exporting Indian coffee. Some of the East European countries like GDR, Yugoslavia, Bulgaria which are bound by International Coffee Agreement had exceeded their share of exports to quota countries by about 50 per cent in the later years of 1960s.

Cashew Kernel : It is an export-oriented product because nearly 90 per cent of production is meant for export. From 1951 to 1960, India's exports of cashew nuts increased from 21.6 thousand tons to 42.7 thousand tons.[12] Over the same period, the value of exports increased from Rs. 90.5 mn. to Rs. 189 mn. If adequate supplies were available, according to market survey, it would be possible to raise the level of exports to the extent of doubling the amount in 1960s over the level reached on 1950s. In fact, India's total exports of cashew increased very rapidly in 1960s. Table 3.9 gives in idea about this.

11. Indian Inst. of Foreign Trade : India's Trade with Eastern Europe, New Delhi, 1966, Ministry of Finance, p.32.

12. Manmohan Singh : *India's Export Trends*, Oxford, 1964, p.213.

Table 3.9

India's Exports of Cashew Nut Kernels to Selected Markets
(in Rs. million)

Year	*Total*	*UK*	*USA*	*Australia*	*Canada*	*EEC*	*USSR*	*Total Eastern Europe*
1958	152.1	9.4	109.4	4.1	5.5	3.5	20.0	20.3
1959	160.0	7.8	106.0	2.7	5.5	4.3	18.2	20.4
1960	189.1	13.4	125.3	5.9	6.8	5.4	22.5	25.1
1961	181.7	12.5	105.5	6.5	7.4	6.0	27.8	35.7
1962	192.7	9.4	108.7	6.8	6.0	10.5	21.3	44.1
1963	214.3	10.7	119.3	7.2	6.9	9.6	42.5	52.1
1964	290.3	17.5	146.8	10.7	9.5	9.2	77.0	86.2
1965	274.0	12.3	147.5	8.2	9.0	9.0	69.1	78.1

Source : DGCI and S.: Monthly Statistics of India's Foreign Trade.

From the above table, the trend is clear that Eastern Europe had emerged as an important market for cashew kernels in 1960s. Indian exports to UK, Australia, Canada and EEC countries were smaller than her exports to the East European countries during the period 1958-65.

Cashew nuts generally belong to the class of luxury goods and it is argued that India should have curbed domestic consumption for increasing the quantum of exportable surplus. It is true that this might have increased the amount of exportable surplus but only marginally and the real problem lies in the availability of raw cashew, Table 3.10 shows the level of domestic production and imports of raw cashew.

From the above table, it will be fairly obvious that India did not produce enough cashew to meet the entire demand from all sources. From table 3.9, we have seen that India's exports to UK, Australia, Canada and the E.E.C. Countries were smaller than her exports to the USSR and Eastern Europe. If we take into consideration the growth of per capita income and consumption of these countries, it is difficult to believe that these countries could not have absorbed the amount exported to Eastern Europe. According to M. Singh's estimate there was a vast potential market for edible nuts in all the above countries, offering scope for further increasing India's exports of cashew nuts.[13] Moreover, all evidence shows that East European countries have re-exported considerable amount of cashew nuts to the Western markets. If the East European countries could sell the commodity in the markets, India could have done the same thing and thus exports to Eastern Europe was not a net gain to India.

Table 3.10

Total Availability of Raw Cashew in India ('000 tons)

Period	*Imports*	*Domestic production*	*Total*
1955-56	62	80	142
1956-57	51	81	132
1957-58	101	95	196
1958-59	122	103	231
1959-60	97	113	210
1960-61	112	122	240
1961-62	102	129	231
1962-63	155*	157	312
1963-64	157	161	318
1964-65	192	171	363
1965-66	162	135	336

* From 1962-63 onwards the figs. are not comparable with figs. or earlier years because the coverage increased in that year.

Source : (a) DGCIS, Monthly statistics of Foreign Trade of India.
(b) Ministry of Agriculture : Production, Area yield and production of principal crops.

The above analysis is confined to the period ending in 1965-

13. M. Singh (1962) : *India's Export Trends*, Oxford University Press, p.213.

66. After 1966 also we find that Eastern Europe was emerging as a relatively more important market, as compared with the rest of the world. Table 3.11 will show the division of India's export of cashew nuts between Eastern Europe and the rest of the world.

Table 3.11

India's Exports of Cashew Kernel to East Europe and the Rest of the World (Qty. in metric ton)

Year	*Aggregate exports*	*Exports to Europe*	*Exports to the rest of the world*
1966-67	50,756	18,841	31,915
1967-68	51,039	13,961	38,078
1968-69	63,661	22,970	40,691
1969-70	60,662	29,333	31,329
1970-71	50,300	19,000	31,300

Source : Cashew kernel Export Promotion council Report.

Pepper : Black pepper is a commodity in which world trade is dominated by a few countries including India. In the late 50s, India, Indonesia and Sarawak accounted for nearly 85 per cent of total world exports of black and white pepper. In 1960s Eastern Europe had emerged as an important market for pepper. Indian exports to this market had increased from 30 per cent to 80 per cent of total exports during the period 1960-61 to 1970-71. As a percentage of production, India's exports to East Europe as well as to other countries increased from 21.4 in 1961-62 to nearly 60.0 in 1970-71. Table 3.12 shows the production and exports of pepper to East Europe and to the rest of the world in 1960s.

The above table shows that India's exports of pepper to East Europe had increased at the cost of export to the rest of the world. This increase in exports to East Europe might be regarded as diversionary in character because India could have captured other markets at the expense of Indonesia. Indonesia during most of 1960s was suffering from problems of expending export of black pepper. Table 3.13 shows how Indonesia's exports dropped significantly from the peak reached in 1959 and reached that level again only in 1963. India could not capitalize on the fluctuation of Indonesian exports because she had a limited export surplus and had commitments to export a certain amount to U.S.S.R. and East Europe.

Table 3.12

Production and Exports of Pepper.

(Qty. in '000 tons)

Year	*Production*	*Exports*	*Europe to East Europe*	*Exports to the rest of the world*
1961-62	28,390	21,620	6,200	15,420
1962-63	26,110	20,868	7,086	13,776
1963-64	24,500	18,938	9,645	8,293
1964-65	21,310	17,381	9,251	8,130
1965-66	23,250	26,305	12,696	13,707
1966-67	22,980	21,785	11,299	10,486
1967-68	30,785	24,868	18,021	6,847
1968-69	32,000	25,500	13,877	11,623
1970-71	26,200	15,200	10,100	5,100

Source : Ministry of Food and Agriculture Govt. of India, Agricultural Situation in India.

Table 3.13

Indonesia's Exports of Black Pepper (in thousand tons)

1959	*1960*	*1961*	*1962*	*1963*	*1964*	*1965*
28	13	19	11	28	23	12

Source : BAPPENAS (Planning Organisation of Indonesia).

Cost statistics of pepper demonstrate that Indian pepper is more expensive than Indonesian pepper, but because of the high quality of Indian pepper it is much in demand in the US market. A survey of India's export potential of spices shows that USA, West Germany, Canada and Japan registered an impressive growth rate of spice import to the extent of 8-12 per cent per annum.[14] The NCAER report on black pepper shows that large amount of purchase by USSR in the open market at higher prices might have led to the price rise of the commodity in the domestic market[15] and this was an indication that producers would be unwilling to exports of pepper to USSR, USA and Canada will reveal that since a modest beginning in 1953, USSR has emerged as the most important market for pepper in 1960s. Table 3.14 will elucidate the point.

Table 3.14

India's Exports of Pepper.

Value : Rs. in lakhs. Quantity : Kgs. in Lakhs.

Year	*To USSR*		*To USA*		*To Canada*	
	Quantity	*Value*	*Quantity*	*Value*	*Quantity*	*Value*
1953-54	10	93	74	745	7	61
1954-55	7	56	97	473	9	37
1955-56	40	146	67	231	7	23
1956-57	34	55	65	159	8	16
1957-58	48	98	50	80	7	14
1958-59	22	43	36	78	8	16
1959-60	36	141	92	405	11	43
1960-61	49	244	37	171	5	23
1961-62	28	103	90	329	11	41
1962-63	30	93	65	200	13	41
1963-64	56	179	23	70	12	36
1964-65	50	201	22	96	10	37
1965-66	80	341	58	245	12	50

Source : DGCI and S: Monthly Statistics of Foreign Trade of India.

Raw Wool : India is only a minor exporter in this field. So she had to accept export prices as given from outside and the only course open to her was that she could adjust her export supplies.

14. USAID, Survey of India's Export Potential of spices, Vol. 11A (of three), (MTCE, New Delhi), pp 1-5 and A 135.
15. National Council of Applied Econ. Research, Export Propects of Black Pepper, New Delhi, 1965, p.84.

India is a producer of special type of raw wool which was used for making carpets, besides other things. So India never faced any difficulty in the matter of its exports. The only problem was the problem of limited supply. Moreover, after, the internal demand for raw wool had increased due to increased defence requirement and consequently the exportable surplus had been reduced. The major burden of this reduced surplus had fallen on the markets of western economies; since India had some firm commitments of exports to USSR and other socialist countries. So diversion of trade took place in favour of USSR and Eastern Europe at the expense of UK and USA Table 3.15 makes the point clear.

Table 3.15

India's Exports of Raw Wool.

Quantity : Kgs. in million. Value : Rs. in lakhs.

Year	*To USSR*		*To USA*		*To Canada*	
	Quantity	*Value*	*Quantity*	*Value*	*Quantity*	*Value*
1956-57	2	173	4	277	6	389
1957-58	3	193	4	98	7	429
1958-59	4	219	4	241	6	289
1959-60	3	169	5	329	6	327
1960-61	3	163	2	144	5	269
1961-62	7	405	1	86	5	249
1962-63	5	322	0.5	29	3	159
1963-64	3	170	2	121	4	250
1964-65	6	366	1	78	4	236
1965-66	7	404	Neg.	10	3	167

Source : DGCI and S : Monthly Statistics of Foreign Trade of India.

Hides and Skins (raw) : India is only a marginal exporter of hides, skins and leather in the world. So the question of limited international demand does not stand in the way of India's expansion of exports of these commodities. Of course, it is generally true that the export prospects growing competition of synthetic leather and rubber. According to a study by The Economists' Intelligence Unit, the consumption of sole-leathers in the UK market fell by more than 20 per cent between the late 40s and late 50s and the consumption of other heavy leathers fell even more markedly.[16] However, India being a marginal exporter, international demand fluctuation were not important for her. The real problem in the matter of raising the quantum of exports was to be found in the inelasticity in the supply of raw hides and skins in the country. In India there is widespread prejudice against animal slaughter and many State Governments have passed anti-cow slaughter legislation. Naturally the country largely depends upon the natural death rate among animals in spite of the fact that India has one of largest cattle population in the world. So far as the slaughter of goat is concerned, there is practically no inhibition. But the size of the exportable surplus has been affected adversely because of the growth of internal demand as a result of increasing income and urbanisation. There is a special market for Indian hides and skins among the manufactures of shoes and handbags, because Indian hides and skins are smaller and free of fat. USSR and other East European countries paid a higher price in 1960s for Indian raw skins and hides and thereby diverted supplies from other markets. Table 3.16 gives a picture of India's exports of hides and skins to USSR, USA and UK.

Table 3.16 above shows that India being a marginal exporter, increase in exports to USSR had taken place at the expense of USA and UK.

Tobacco Unmanufactured : The bulk of India's exports consists of Virginia flue-cured tobacco. For this variety USA and the Federation of Rhodesia and Nyasaland are the major exporters. USA supplies about 60 per cent of total world exports of Virginia flue-cured tobacco. Moreover, the USA in order to get rid of tobacco surpluses, has been selling tobacco in exchange for local currencies of the importing countries, under various concessional terms and schemes such as PL 480 etc. Indian tobacco is the cheapest relative to American, Canadian and Rhodesian tobacco; yet there has been only limited demand of it because of its inferior quality. According to an official classification the top grades of Virginia form only about 27 per cent of the total Indian exports of

16. The Economists' Intelligence Unit, The Commonwealth and Europe, London, 1960, pp. 227-28.

that variety.[17] Exports to the East Europe and the rest of the world had fluctuated considerably over 1960s, although production had increased. Table 3.17 gives a picture regarding Indian production and exports of unmanufactured tobacco.

Table 3.16

India's Exports of Hides and Skins.

Quantity : Kgs. in lakhs. Value : Rs. in lakhs.

Year	*To USSR*		*To USA*		*To Canada*	
	Quantity	*Value*	*Quantity*	*Value*	*Quantity*	*Value*
1	2	3	4	5	6	7
1953-54	1	4	56	259	17	126
1954-55	19	120	52	258	15	116
1955-56	19	128	49	248	11	83
1956-57	28	197	33	161	12	57
1957-58	30	228	51	207	11	55
1958-59	49	384	45	213	6	42
1959-60	60	602	30	198	4	37
1960-61	56	438	31	203	4	26
1961-62	41.7	243	36	229	5	46
1962-63	71.7	479	31	197	3	56
1963-64	62	511	30	200	4.5	51
1964-65	83.3	512	17.6	140	3.4	31
1965-66	71	540	18	147	5	65
1966-67	89	1050	8	107	4.3	87
1967-68	52.6	432.6	5	75	1.2	17.4
1968-69	35	256	4	49	3.9	30.7
1969-70	48.8	531	7.4	116	2.7	14

Source : DGCI and S : Monthly Statistics of Foreign Trade of India.

17. "Types and Grades of unmanufactured tobacco exported from India in 1957", Deptt. of Marketing, Ministry of Food & Agricuture, Govt. of India, 1960.

Table 3.17

India's Production and Exports of Unmanufactured Tobacco.
(Quantity : '000 tons)

Year	*Produ-ction*	*Aggregate exports*	*Exports to East Europe*	*Exports to the rest of the world*
1963-64	307	63.2	32.4	30.8
1965-66	293	56.1	28.4	37.7
1966-67	353	37.4	7.7	29.7
1968-69	434	54.0	8.0	46.6
1969-70	357	57.7	12.1	45.6

Source : Tobacco Export Promotion Council.

The share of Eastern Europe in India's exports had gone up from between 15 per cent and to 50 per cent. This high percentage generally strengthened the fears of diversion. But looking at the prospects of exports to convertible currency areas there was no evidence of any planned diversion towards the countries of Eastern Europe. The USA did not provide much scope for increased exports from Indian point of view because USA itself is a major producer and exporter of tobacco. Indian share in the tobacco imports into USA was negligible even before the bilateral trade and payments agreement with USSR and other countries of East Europe. The share of India in the UK market had increased from 9.3 per cent in 1963 to 10.8 per cent in 1970. This increase took place in the face of severe competition by Rhodesia. So far as E.E.C. markets are concerned, India's share declined from 1.5 per cent in 1963 to 0.4 per cent in 1969-70. If these factors are taken into account exports to USSR and East Europe could very well be regarded as an welcome addition. Table 3.18 shows India's exports of tobacco to USSR, USA and UK.

The other important commodities are mica, raw jute, groundnuts, castor oil, woollen manufactures, lac, manganese ore which together accounted for 10 per cent of India's exports to East Europe. For Castor oil in the 1950s India was one of the main exporters in the world and USA and UK were the two principal markets. But India started losing ground to Brazil in the late 50s. The main point was that Brazilian oil was of superior quality and price was relatively lower than Indian price. Moreover, USA preferred to rely on the nearer source of oil like Brazil. Thus India was not in a position to compete. The question of diversion does not arise here.

Table 3.18

India's Exports of Tobacco Unmanufactured

(Qty : Kgs. in million)

Year	*To USSR*	*To USA*	*To UK*
1956-57	1	1	15
1959-60	5	1	17
1963-64	19	Neg.	16.5
1967-64	4.8	6.6	24.5
1969-70	10	0.9	20

Source : DGCI and S : Monthly Statistics of Foreign Trade of India.

So far as the exports of raw jute and groundnuts are concerned, it may be pointed out that these two fall in the category of undesirable exports. Throughout most of 1950s, India banned the export of raw jute. In the 1960s there was shortage of production of groundnuts and therefore it was mistake to export these commodities. It may be argued that India was forced to export these commodities to make up the shortfalls in other commodities to USSR and Eastern Europe.

As regards the exports of mica, it may be pointed out that its exports fluctuated in the 50s and 60s. The only change was that the share of East Europe increased could not be regarded as diversionary because India was going to lose the US market anyway. US authorities favoured the emergence of Brazil as a producer of mica by raising the price paid by 25 cents in 1955.[18]

19. Asha L. Datar : India's Econ. Relations with USSR and Eastern Europe, Cambridge, 1972, p.155

USA did not renew its contract with India regarding stock piling for defence in 1960s.

Woollen manufactures and leather footwear had become promising export items to USSR and Eastern Europe upto 1970. Table 3.19 shows the share in value of India's total exports of selected commodities to East European countries in the context of India's total export of such commodities.

Table 3.19

India's Total Exports Selected Commodities to East Europpean Countries as a Share of India's Total Exports of Such Commodities

(per cent)

	Commodities	*1960-61*	*1967-68*	*1971-72*	*1972-73*
1.	Jute manufactures	3.4	18.0	17.2	26.9
2.	Tea	6.5	12.7	25.7	25.9
3.	Coffee	29.5	57.9	57.3	46.1
4.	Cashew kernel	13.4	25.8	32.9	39.4
5.	Leather	0.7	26.7	34.5	25.7
6.	Tobacco (unmanufactures)	4.9	15.2	41.4	49.7

Source : DGCI and S : Monthly Statistics of Foreign Trade of India.

Thus exports to the East European countries of India's traditional items such as jute goods, tea and leather rose from a negligible share in 1960-61 to around 26 per cent in 1972-3. At the same time, these countries also lifted an increasing share of India's non-traditional exports, which rose sizeably during this period viz., clothing from 9 per cent to 78 per cent, cashew kernel from 13 per cent to 39 per cent and tobacco (unmanufactured) from 5 per cent to nearly 50 per cent. During most of this period this was brought about by an increase in absolute amounts of exports of these commodities and was not always at the cost of exports to India's traditional markets.

During the period from 1960-61 to 1972-73 there was an overall secular increase in India's exports to almost all regions and this was marked in case of some of her traditional as well as non-traditional export commodities. The countries which lifted substantial amount of India's increasing exports were, besides USSR and other East European countries, Japan, USA, ECM countries, EFTA countries excluding UK. The only major country where India's exports remained at around the same level was the UK (Rs. 173 crores), while in case of exports to countries like Australia, New Zealand, Kenya and Tanzania, there was only a moderate rise and in the case of Pakistan (West), Srilanka, Burma and China there was a fall. This showed the tendency for India's trade pattern to shift away from its colonial association with commonwealth countries and/or British dominated countries to new trade partners in the Far East (Japan, Hong Kong, Singapore and Philippines), North America (USA), Europe (USSR, France, West Germany, Italy etc.), Africa (UAR, Sudan, Zambia etc.), Middle East (Iraq). Thus it cannot be readily concluded that India's exports to USSR and other East European countries has taken place at the expense of trade with convertible currency markets.

The above discussion on commodity diversion shows that there had not been any large scale diversion to USSR and Eastern Europe. Again there was the natural cost for opening new markets in socialist countries. One may not be in disagreement with A. Datar's estimate that 21 per cent diversion (or nearly Rs. 340 million in terms of 1965-66 prices) might be treated as a necessary cost for opening Socialist countries' markets. But it is an undisputed fact that USSR and Eastern Europe re-exported some of the commodities imported from India and this was an additional cost in the sense that India was thereby being deprived of free foreign exchange earnings.

Re-export of Indian Commodities : An Economic Analysis

It has been observed that part of Indian exports of select traditional products to Eastern Europe is re-exported to the West European markets. Transactions of this type will obviously reduce the quantum of India's convertible currency earnings. Not only that, such transactions will disrupt the market for Indian goods by re-exporting goods at a lower price than could be realised by India in the ordinary course of trade. The basic reason for this is that Eastern Europe including USSR is very much in need of free foreign exchange as these countries also suffer from severe adverse balance of payments with convertible currency areas. So the sale of Indian products to the West European markets even at a lower price will bring the much needed foreign exchange to these countries. But an element of puzzle in the situation is : how to ascertain that USSR and Eastern Europe were indeed re-exporting goods of Indian origin. If it is found that a particular country is exporting a commodity which it does not produce the issue is clear regarding re-export. But in most cases re-exports fall within categories of good that are produced domestically. In such cases determination of re-export becomes rather difficult.

A wider interpretation of re-exports is that when a country exports domestically produced goods but at the same time the country also imports these goods from other countries, re-exports can be said to take place. Thus it can be pointed out that when the USSR's imports of tea from India are not meant for increasing domestic consumer demand, but enable the USSR to increase her exports of tea, this constitutes a case of re-export of Indian tea. Accepting this interpretation of the term 're-exports', many developing countries, besides India which have trade intercourse with the Socialist countries have registered their protests in Algiers meeting of the "Group of 77" and in Lima Conference. In these meeting there was a consensus of opinion among the members that socialist countries should "refrain from re-exporting the goods purchased from developing countries, unless it is with the consent of the developing counties concerned".[19] In the Committee of V of UNCTAD III, the developing nations again pressed their demand regarding limiting re-export. The Socialist countries have agreed on this point. But in fact the question of re-exports cannot be tackled properly unless one has full knowledge about domestic production and consumption, over and above figures relating to trade. Here also some difficulties crop up. (1) Unless a socialist country is an important exporter of the commodity concerned, there will be no mention of the country in the import statistics of the countries of Western Europe. (2) The other difficulty that arises is that many commodities are often re-exported through third countries. In order to solve all these

19. H. D. Shourie, UNCTAD II. A step forward (Indian Inst. of Foreign Trade, New Delhi, 1968), Chap. 10.

problems a full scale study concerning trade, production, consumption of all the Eastern and West Europe would be necessary.

It is accepted in official circles that there is some amount of diversion for commodities like tea, coffee, spices and jute goods. According to A. Dater, the percentage of diversion is between 5 and 10.[20]

M. Goldman provides an example of cahsew re-export. When the cashew nuts are placed on a ship destines for Eastern Europe, they are diverted midway to Rotterdam or sent directly to New York. These goods are then sold at a 5 per cent discount on the world price. These are violations of Indian trade agreements with Eastern Europe. According to Indian customs officials, of all East European countries only Rumania has come to terms with India in the matter of distribution of the commission-benefit[21] on such re-exporting trade.

Studies made by the Indian Institute of Foreign Trade[22] and S. Dave[23] have revealed that there is some re-export of oilcakes and coffee. The 11th Report on Utilisation of External Assistance[24] (4th LokSabha) provides a list of commodities such as cashew nuts, de-oiled cakes, goat skins, coffee which were re-exported to other countries by the East European countries. These diversion-resales are stated to have been a common practice with almost all the East European countries. However, the USSR is the single exception about whom few complaints have been received. The GDR and USSR are the most important importers of cahsew kernel among countries of Eastern Europe. In 1961-62, USSR imported cahsew kernel to the extent of 6008 thousand kg., in 1970-71, it rose to 14,400 thousand kg. Over the same period the G.D.R's import of cahsew increased from 1,850 thousand kg. to 3,200 thousand kgs. The domestic demand in

20. A. Datar : *India's Econ. Relations with the U.S.S.R and Eastern Europe*, 1972, Cambridge University Press, p.161.

21. M. Gokeman : *Soviet Foreign Aid*, New York, 1967, pp.110-11.

22. Instt. of Foreign Trade : India's Trade with Eastern Europe, New Delhi, 1966.

23. S. Dave : *India's Trade Relations with the East European Countries* 1952-53 to 1959-60, Indian Econ. Journal, July, 1961.

24. Utilisation of External Assistance (4th Lok Sabha), 11th Report, pp.222-34.

these countries for these commodities is expected to rise at the rate of not more than 5 to 6 per cent per annum. In the circumstances, the above-noted almost dramatic growth of exports certainly calls for some enquiries about possibility of re-exports.

In the offtake of coffee from India, USSR tops the list of importers form the Eastern European region. In 1961-62, the import of coffee was 2,007 thousand kg., it increased to 9,100 thousand kg. in 1969-70. Such an increase in imports may raise doubts about re-exports. Tea imports were to the extent of 11,917 thousand kg. in 1961-62 to USSR from India. It rose to 31, 930 thousand kg. in 1970-71. This significant increase in import may have something to do with the question or re-export. So far as oilcakes are concerned, the Soviet import figure was only 4 thousand tons in 1963-64, it increased to 63 thousand tons in 1970-71. In oilcakes import the roles of Czechoslovakia, Poland and East Germany are also important. It may not be irrelevant to argue that these countries have been often singled out as re-exporters of oilcakes. The East European countries have also re-exported commodities whose demand was not so favourable in the markets concerned, for example grey cotton or tea. That is why they had to sell these commodities at a fairly heavy discount thereby disrupting India's markets, Moreover, if the volume of resale is large enough, these countries may even be successful in forcing price downward and when the commodity demand is not price-elastic, India does not stand to gain by lowering prices.

Diversification of India's Exports to USSR : A Survey

The assessment of gains from Indo-Soviet trade is also linked up with the issue whether India's exports to USSR and other East European countries have resulted in diversifying India's exports in accordance with the trade agreements. It is necessary to emphasize the fact that the trade between India and East Europe cannot grow on rupee-payment basis unless the share of non-traditional goods is enhanced substantially. In so far as the traditional goods are concerned, the East European countries work under limitation in regard to their consumption. So the attempts to buy more of these traditional goods largely to balance the exports to India is bound to result in excessive purchases leading to 'switch trade'. To reduce the quantum of this "switch trade", it is desirable that the proportion of non-traditional goods in India's exports to rupee-payment countries should be on the rise and ultimately India's sales to these countries should be confined to what these countries can really consume. In the case of USSR, Indian exports of primary commodities and traditional textile goods was nearly 3/4ths of the total exports. It is because of this that the recent trade agreements with the USSR have specially stipulated that the share of manufactured goods would be enhanced in the coming years taking it upto 60 per cent of the total by 1975. In 1953-54, the share of traditional commodities in India's exports to the East European countries was more than 90 per cent; it is reported to have declined to nearly 45 per cent in recent years indicating that there has come about a remarkable shift in the structure of India's export trade.

The period of 1965-70 has witnessed some determined effort to include increasing number of non-traditional goods for exports under the trade plans. But a review of actual export figures and provisions under the trade plans makes it clear that exports of traditional goods, specially cashew kernel, coffee, oilcakes and pepper have been either within the trade plan provisions or exceeded it; while the exports of non-traditional goods have generally failed to reach the targets. In some cases only one-third of the targets has been achieved. Nevertheless, there is some progress in the matter of export of drugs and pharmaceuticals, knit-wear, ready-made garments etc. in keeping with the trade plan provisions. But taking these developments into considerations the conclusion remains true that exports have not been diversified adequately. Primary commodities and semi-processed goods such as tea, coffee, oilcakes, cashew, hides and skins, raw wool, raw jute and raw cotton still constitute a sizeable part of Indian exports. If traditional textiles, jute, cotton and coir are taken into consideration, their total share goes upto more than 65 per cent.[25] According to the report prepared by the Estimates Committee of the LokSabha the same pattern holds true in case of USSR, where the effort to diversify exports is intense.[26] Table 3.20 gives

25. Indian Instt. of Foreign Trade : India's Trade with East Europe, New Delhi, 1973, p. 34.

26. Estimates Committee 14 the Report, 1971-72, LokSabha Secretariat, New Delhi, 1972, p. 100.

a picture of share in value of India's total exports of selected commodities to East European countries. Analysing the table, it is observed that the share of engineering goods begins to be recorded only from 1967-68. In 1967-68 the percentage share was 17.8 of India's total exports of engineering goods, in 1971-72 it had declined to 11.2 and in 1972-73 it was 13.7 of India's total exports of engineering goods.

It is still largely true that the standard of living in these countries is much lower than that in the countries of the West. In recent years these centrally-planned economies are found to have thrown their doors open to West European business firms. Even in the case of USSR, foreign companies are being encouraged to set up big industrial outfits. The Italians have been invited to set up a joint plant for the manufacture of 'Fiat cars'.

Table 3.20

India's total exports of selected commodities to East European countries as a share of India's total exports of such commodities

(per cent)

	Commodities	*1960-61*	*1967-68*	*1971-72*	*1972-73*
1.	Jute manufactures	3.4	18.0	17.2	26.9
2	Tea	6.5	12.7	26.7	25.9
3.	Leather	0.7	26.7	34.5	25.7
4.	Oilseed cake and meal	16.4	74.0	65.2	60.9
5.	Clothing	9.4	60.0	54.2	78.0
6.	Cahsew kernel	13.4	25.8	32.9	39.4
7.	Iron ore and concentrates	38.8	17.0	15.C	15.2
8.	Tobacco (unmanufactured)	4.9	15.2	41.4	49.7
9.	Coffee	29.5	57.9	57.3	46.1
10	Engineering goods	-	17.8	11.2	13.7

Source : DGCI and S : Monthly Statistics of Foreign Trade in India.

Surely India can also undertake to manufacture some of the ancillary products in which the country has specialised over the past years and because USSR is currently contemplating vast expansion in the motor car industry, it is for India to extend her trade by offering manufactured ancillaries for the expanding motor car industry.

The bilateral trade and payments agreements will become meaningful only if the partners try not only for export diversification but also import diversification. Many of the East European countries, specially the USSR and Czechoslovakia, two most important trade partners of India in the bloc have all along maintained large supplies of capital goods. In 1963, imports of machinery and equipment from the Soviet Union exceeded the target by 43 per cent. In 1984, machine tools and other metal working machinery exceeded the target by 205 per cent, transport, and lifting equipment by 242 per cent, machinery for food, cotton and woollen industry by 1016 per cent. In case of Czechoslovakia, machinery including electrical machineries increased much above the target-figure. In 1963, iron and steel products increased by 250 per cent and "capital goods n.e.s." by 182 per cent. But an analysis of commodity composition of imports from USSR indicates that the share of machinery imports has gone down from 1967-68. The share of machinery other then electrical increased from 18.6 per cent in 1960-61 to 55.0 per cent in 1964-65; but the percentage declined to 40.79 in 1968-69. In 1969-70, there has been seen some marginal increase to the extent of 42.82 per cent. The reason for this decline is that India has been able to develop considerable infrastructure and productive capacities so as to be in a position to supply the needed machines and equipments to satisfy largely the domestic demand. Moreover, increasing exports to the East European bloc have forced India to a large extent to import more of those goods which have hitherto been imported from the convertible currency areas. There has been a re-orientation of trade because of increased imports of raw meterials and spare parts. Similarly, there is an increase in the imports of fertilisers, non-ferrous metals, sulphur and mercury. The share of fertilisers increased from 0.7 per cent in 1964-65 to 1.50 per cent in 19970-71, of zinc from 0.9 per cent in 1964-65 to 1.50 per cent in 1970-71. Another factor partly responsible for dampening the demand for capital goods is the fall in investment activity in India.[27] Trade agreement entered into between India and East European countries from 1970 onwards have provided for imports of increasing quantities of fertilisers. Since a majority of the plants in these countries are based on gas and not on naptha (which is in short supply consequent upon the cut of oil by the Middle East countries), the supply of fertilisers is ensured. On the contrary the production of fertilisers in the West European countries is likely to suffer curtailment because of (1) reduced supply of naptha (ii) high labour costs and (iii) increasing domestic consumption. Table 3.21 gives an idea of shipment of fertilisers from East European countries to India during (1970-72).

Table 3.21

Shipment of Fertilizers from East European Countries

(Qty : in thousand tons)

	Commodity	*Country*	*Shipment made during*		
			1970	*1971*	*1972*
1.	Fertilizers	Bulgaria	90	190	116
		Poland	80	111	119
		Romania	34	40	-
		USSR	22	38	63
		Hungary	-	-	-
			226	389	298
	Ammonium	Romania	45	142	185
	Sulphate	USSR	93	-	60
			138	142	245
II.	Muriate of	USSR	5	24	28
	Potash	GDR	19	40	115
			24	64	143
Total fertilizers actually shipped :			388	595	686

Source : "The World Fertilizer Situation in 70s" paper read by Mr. S. Ramachandran Chairman, MMTC, at the FAI Seminar, 1973.

27. Institute of Foreign Trade (1973) : "India's Trade with East Europe : Prospects for Diversification", Foreign Trade Bulletin Vol. I, No, Jan. 1971, pp. 3-5.

In this context, it is necessary to examine the argument that the East European countries buy mainly those non-traditional goods which have high import content involving high convertible currency expenditure by India. But the machinery, equipment and chemicals which India imports from this region also has a certain amount of import content from the West European countries. Therefore, it is difficult to calculate the net advantages/disadvantages of such exchange. India receives payments in rupees for export of cahsew kernel to East European countries, but she has to incur expenditure in foreign exchange. The extent of this will be clear from Table 3.22.

Table 3.22

India's Foreign Exchange Outgo in Respect of Cashew Export to East Europe.

(Rs. Crores)

		1970-71	*1971-72*	*1972-73*
1.	Rupee receipts from exports of cashew kernel to East Europe	18.5	20.0	26.1
2.	Important payment in convertible foreign exchange for cashew nuts for (1)	10.4*	8.7*	12.1*
3.	Foreign exchange for import replenishment on (1)** (a)	1.1	0.8	1.2
4.	Total foreign exchange payment incurred on (1) [2+3]	11.5	9.5	13.3

* Estimated roughly on the basis of proportion of the value of total cashew nuts imported by India, to the value of total cashew kernels exported by India, for respective years.

** Estimated approximately on the basis of the rate of import replenisnment allowed.

(a) This could be also a part of the total import for imports of packaging material etc.

An answer to switch trade in third countries in such commodities would be to intensify the sales drive in these countries for Indian cashew which can be more easily indentified as compared with other Indian exports.

The idea of co-operation between USSR and India for the purposes of starting production in certain new lines assumes considerable importance in the context of trade diversification. the surplus capacities in Soviet-aided projects in India have been used to produce items which could be used in the Soviet economy. The Soviets have evolved the concept of "compensation" in production co-operation. This implies that whenever a joint production unit is set up, production from it should be shared by the partners, the contribution by either side being paid for in this way. While the concept itself is not altogether novel and is in fact practised by multinational companies, especially in the field of oil--India is hoping to use it to the Soviet Union in favour of the non-traditional items. The scope for joint production programme has been defined as follows : Co-operation in setting up enterprises on (in Soviet parlance) compensation basis; mutual supplies among the units of machinery equipment and services, units and parts, within the framework of the co-operation ; co-operation in the supply of equipment for industrial projects in third countries; and conversion deals-depending, of course, on the capabilities and the availabilities of capacities or their planned expansion. The Soviet side offered assistance in the production of mica in India--a part of which would go to the Soviet Union in payment of Soviet assistance. The Indian side accepted this if the projects encompassed fabricated mica. The Soviet side similarly showed interest in setting up production capacities, on the same basis, for caustic soda, fluorspar, flourine chemicals and non-ferrous metals. The question of setting up in the USSR on compensation basis a pulp and paper plant was also considered. The Indian side offered to supply some of the equipment, including complete plant with a capacity of upto 200 tons per day, as well as the structurals and other auxiliaries. The Indian side seemed very keen on a conversion deal in cotton. Capacity was proposed to be reserved for the manufacture of textiles an dready-made garments for supply to USSR and some textile units in the public sector proposed to be selected for this purpose. It was suggested that, besides cotton, equipment to modernise and renovate machinery would also be obtained from the USSR.

The Tying of Imports

As per trade agreement, India will have to utilise its export-earnings for the purchase of goods and services from the partner country. So one should consider not only the partner's ability to supply the goods but also its willingness to import goods from India. The important questions in this respect are : (i) whether India had the necessary freedom of choice in placing orders for goods and (ii) the prices and quality of goods available compared to other sources of supply. A study of trade agreements between India and USSR and other socialist countries reveals that there is a wide variety of goods but none of these are special in the sense that only USSR or other East European countries could have provided them. Table 3.23 shows that the commodity composition of imports from the USSR and other East European countries has been similar to that of imports from the rest of the world. It cannot be said that India was importing these commodities only for the purpose of using up its earnings from exports. In 1960s the share of machinery-import was quite high--about 50 per cent of total imports from the East European countries because all the credits utilised upto 1966 were for imports of machinery. Moreover, countries like USSR and Czechoslovakia specialise in exports of "turnkey plants".

Table 3.23

Commodity Composition of India's Major Imports from USSR (Rs. in lakhs) (percentage in bracket)

Commodities	1960-61	1967-68	1970-71	1971-72	1972-73
1. Electrical machinery, apparatus and appliances	92 (5.7)	441 (3.9)	628 (5.9)	809 (9.3)	1381 (13.1)
2. Iron and steel manufactures	505 (31.8)	620 (5.5)	804 (7.6)	686 (7.9)	826 (7.8)

(Contd.)

	Commodities	1960-61	1967-68	1970-71	1971-72	1972-73
3.	Machinery other than electric	290 (18.2)	5774 (51.5)	5045 (47.5)	3054 (34.9)	2208 (20.9)
4.	Transport equipment	7 (0.4)	105 (0.9)	216 (2.0)	282 (3.2)	780 (7.4)
5.	Fertilisers manufactured	105 (6.6)	508 (4.5)	422 (3.9)	217 (3.2)	540 (5.1)
6.	Organic chemicals	12 (0.7)	130 (1.2)	74 (0.7)	192 (2.2)	276 (2.6)
7.	Petroleum products	15 (0.9)	318 (2.8)	562 (5.3)	792 (9.1)	- -
8.	Paper and paper boards	4 (0.2)	283 (2.5)	520 (4.9)	557 (6.4)	555 (5.2)
9.	Medicinal and pharmaceutical products	8 (0.4)	42 (0.4)	76 (0.7)	51 (0.6)	10 (0.1)
10.	Inorganic chemical	16 (1.0)	7 (0.1)	19 (0.2)	12 (0.1)	2 (0.02)
11.	Zinc and zinc alloys	53 (3.3)	147 (1.3)	344 (3.2)	223 (2.5)	552 (5.2)
12.	Professional, scientific and controlling instruments	9 (0.5)	104 (0.9)	167 (1.6)	117 (1.3)	185 (1.7)
13.	Manufactures of metals	63 (3.9)	96 (0.9)	98 (0.9)	20 (0.2)	105 (0.9)
14.	Cinematographic materials	1 (0.06)	1 (0.01)	1 (0.01)	3 (0.03)	2 (0.02)
15.	Asbestos	2 (0.1)	146 (1.3)	226 (2.13)	285 (3.3)	453 (4.3)

(Contd.)

	Commodities	*1960-61*	*1967-68*	*1970-71*	*1971-72*	*1972-73*
16.	Special transaction*	6 (0.3)	421 (3.7)	642 (6.0)	7 (0.08)	27 (0.3)
17.	Others	399 (25.1)	2079 (18.5)	769 (7.2)	1425 (16.3)	2670 (25.3)
	Total :	1587	11222	10613	8732	10572

* Relates to samples, defence stores etc. not classified according to kind.

Source : DGCI and S : Monthly Statistics of Foreign Trade of India.

India's commodity composition with respect to major imports remained more or less the same with other East European countries as with USSR Table 3.24 shows India's imports from East European countries.

Table 3.24

India's Imports from East European Countries.

(Rs. in Lakhs)

Year	*USSR*	*Bulgaria*	*Czechoslovakia*	*GDR*	*Hungary*	*Poland*	*Rumania*	*Yugoslavia*	*Total*
1960-61	1587	54	876	331	202	442	495	444	4431
1967-68	11222	193	2734	2157	1179	2378	459	1998	22320
1970-71	10613	1548	2020	1863	1495	2803	1658	765	22765
1971-72	8732	1381	1017	2029	868	5045	1329	545	20945
1972-73	10572	875	1552	1882	1428	3448	1344	679	21780

Source : DGCI and S : Monthly Statistics of Foreign Trade of India

Table 3.25 shows how the total imports from East European countries as percentage of India's total imports have varied over the years.

Table 3.25

India's Imports from East European Countries

(Rs. in crores)

Year	*India's total imports*	*Imports from East Europe*	*3 as % of 2*
1.	*2.*	*3.*	*4.*
1960-61	1122	44	3.9
1967-68	2008	223	11.1
1970-71	1634	228	14.0
1971-72	1824	209	11.5
1972-73	1797	218	12.1

Source : Compiled from DGCI and S figures.

It is generally true that there are some difficulties involved in the matter of locating and importing the goods from the East European countries because of their different economic and political system. Foreign trade is a part of the plan in these economies. Orders from foreign countries are to be incorporated in the production targets while the plans of these countries are being formulated. So domestic production remains unresponsive to changed demand conditions abroad. On the other hand, the general character of private firms is that they do not plan their purchases in advance. So the difficulties on obtaining imports from the East European countries are to some extent unavoidable.

Another problem is that when import licences are issued for commodities included in the trade agreements, partner countries are not consulted about their ability to deliver these goods within the specified time limit. Moreover, these countries generally produce goods meant for large-scale production. So small producers of India find it difficult to meet their requirements from these countries.

Imports form USSR pose a special difficulty. The USSR does not have any marketing organisation in India. Sometimes, importers from India are not even aware of what the Russians have to offer. On the other hand, Czechoslovakia and Hungary are sufficiently active in establishing contacts with Indian importers. So the importers of India first try other East European countries because import licences are issued for the rupee-payment area as a whole. Thus the whole question of import becomes time consuming, involving long negotiations. Public sector imports have also suffered from long delivery dates. In this respect it should be made clear that India is not an exception in the matter of facing difficulties regarding imports from the East European countries. R.L. Allen has pointed out that "In 1955, the Soviet Union imported $ 92 mn. more than it exported. In 1956, imports were $ 112 mn. more than exports and this disparity increased to $ 139 mn. by 1957. Some of the purchase were covered by convertible currency payments, as in the case of Cuban sugar. Many countries, however, are tied to Soviet Union by trade and payments agreements which specify bilateral balancing of trade (expect for Soviet credits) and hence some of the export surplus of developing countries is in fact short-term credit granted unwillingly by them to the Soviet Union. Argentina felt this most acutely when in early 1958 a delegation toured the Soviet Union and Eastern Europe to try to buy enough goods to settle accounts.[28] In late 1950s India had also difficulties in obtaining goods from the USSR.

The Estimates Committee of LokSabha inquiring into import licence tied to particular countries has observed that where the import licence has been tied to Czechoslovakia, the Indian Company has been obliged to wait two and a half year for delivery and even then has been offered less than half the original order. Similar difficulties were also experienced when the import licence was tied to USSR and the actual user in India had only received delivery of one model of the original order.[29]

Thus it is not possible to conclude that India had absolutely free choice with respect to its purchase from Eastern Europe.

28. Allen, R.L. : *Soviet Econ. Warfare*, Public Affairs Press, Washington D.C., 1960 (p.3).

29. Ministry of Finance : Utilisation of External Assistance (4th LokSabha) 11th Report.

Similarly, regarding the question of buying low priority goods, it is possible to argue that since India's imports are regulated by import licensing, the Govt. should grant a license only when the good is necessary. But on the otherhand, it is possible that the Govt. was willing to issue a license for something else, but because of the trade partner's willingness to provide certain goods importing country had no choice. Only the negotiators regarding commodity composition of import can throw some light on this question.

Conclusions regarding quality of imports must remain open because the most important imports from Eastern Europe are machinery and equipment. No comparison becomes meaningful unless the goods that are imported are identical or at least similar in all important respects to goods from other sources. As the Indian Govt. representative before the Estimates Committee pointed out "About quality one can only compare like with like. As India imported specialised machinery and equipment from the East European countries it is not possible to compare it with imports from other countries".[30] In private discussions Govt. officials seemed to accept the view that East European products are not good enough to compete with Western products. [31]

The Terms of Trade

The benefits derived from trade with Eastern Europe depend upon the net increase in exports, the commodity composition of export and import and the terms of trade obtained. Trading under bilateral trade and payments agreements does not normally subject itself to the laws of supply and demand. So there is a tendency of prices to be set to the advantages of the stronger party. It is possible that countries like India with limited bargaining power might suffer on two counts -- buying at a higher price and selling at a lower price than the international price.

Authors like J.R. Carter, J. Berliner, M. Goldman, Vassil

30. Ministry of Finance : Utilisation of External Assistance (4th LokSabha), 11th Report , pp.222-23.

31. A.L. Datar: *India's Econ. Relations with the USSR and Eastern Europe*, Cambridge, 1972 , p.167.

Vassilev and Kurt Muller[32] have all charged that the Soviet Union sells its products at 15 to 20 per cent higher than the world prices and purchases primary commodities from the developing countries at 15 to 20 per cent lower than world market prices. Horst Menderhausen has also explored the possibility that Soviet bilateral trade has resulted in higher prices for Soviet exports and lower prices for Soviet imports than when the Soviet Union purchased or sold similar goods for hard currency.[33]

J.R. Carter is of the opinion that the Soviet Union practises price discrimination in all its trade relations with developing countries including India. He has collected data to prove his point. His analysis covers 80 common commodities entering into Soviet trade with the developed and developing countries. The data are for two years -- 1958 and 1965. Here we have selected some commodities studied by Carter and put them together in Table 3.26.

The Less Developed Countries (LDCs) bought 1843 tractors from the Soviet Union in 1958 for 11.82 mn. roubles, while the industrial West paid only 7.02 mn. roubles for the same number of tractors. There is a difference of 4.80 mn roubles showing that the former paid about 2500 roubles more for every tractor bought in the Soviet Union. In 1965, the difference was reduced. Newsprints which are generally imported by countries like India in huge quantities cost the LDCs 13.39 mn. roubles for 24500 tons, while the same quantity cost the industrial West only 12.98 mn. roubles in 1958. The developing countries paid 17 roubles more per ton of newsprint than the industrial West. The Soviet Union sold 5400100 tons of crude petroleum for 55.36 mn roubles to the LDCs in 1965, while the same quantity was sold for only

32. J.R. Carter: "The Net cost of Soviet Foreign Aid", F.A. Fraeger, New York, 1971.
    J.R. Berliner, "Soviet Economic Aid", F.A. Praeger, New York, 1958. Marshall, I Goldman : "Soviet Foregin Aid", F.A. Fraeger, Washington, 1967.
    Kurt Muller: "The Soviet Bloc and the Developing Countries", Indian Ed. Thacker & Co., Bombay, 1970.
33. Horst Menderhausen : Terms of trade between the Soviet Union and the smaller communist countries: 1955-57, Review of Econ. and Statistics XLI, 2 (May, 1959), pp.106-118.

47.72 mn roubles to the industrial West. The developing countries thus paid about 14 roubles more per ton on crude petroleum than the industrial West. Similar comparisons for other commodities confirm J.R. Carter's conclusion that there has been price discrimination against the less developed countries.

Table 3.26

Soviet Exports of Selected Commodities to the Less Developed Countries as well as to the Industrial West

(in '000 rouble)

Particulars	*1958*			*1965*		
	Quantity	*Value at less developed countries prices*	*Value at industrial West prices*	*Quantity*	*Value at less developed countries price*	*Value at industrial West prices*
Bulldozers	-	-	-	586 pcs	9275	7325
Bicycles	9313 pcs	652	466	9555 pcs	77	53
Motor cycles	186 pcs	111	165	2484 "	448	401
Tractors	1843 "	11182	7019	4440 "	5315	1993
Coke	10000tons	947	716	8000 tons	122	130
Crude Petroleum	2193800."	130935	129873	5400100 "	55360	47719
Kerosene	305700 "	34372	32863	-	-	-
Diesel fuel	602800 "	56640	59858	1806900 "	30782	28525
Structural steel	-	-	-	10400 "	1177	1056
Zinc	3208 "	2301	2259	12039 "	3646	3347
Aluminium	3600 "	7085	6548	1600 "	727	520
Urea	-	-	-	314 "	30	23
Newsprint	24500 "	13388	12978	46825 "	5325	4762

Sources : J.R. Carter, "The Net cost of Soviet Foreign Aid", pp. 124-25; based on Ministry of Foreign Trade, Planning and Economic Administration, "USSR Foreign Trade in 1958 and 1965".

One of the reasons for the discriminatory price phenomenon in Soviet trade lies in the fact that prices are generally pegged around the world market prices which are on the whole more remunerative for machinery and equipment than for primary commodities and basic materials. Such standardisation cannot possibly be precise in case of machinery and equipment. So they are likely to command higher prices. Hence in general the primary-producing developing countries are likely to lose against the machine-selling developed countries like the Soviet Union.[34]

The world market prices of the commodities which are in the same category as Soviet exports will be higher than would have been the case in a world market that included Soviet exports. Similarly, the world prices of goods which are akin to Soviet imports are lower than would have been the case in a world market that included Soviet demand for such goods.

Raymond F. Mikesell and Jack N. Behrman have stated this in another way when they said : "If the bloc countries were to make all their purchase of primary commodities in free world markets, market prices would in some case be higher than the prices which they offer their agreement partners. And if they sold on a competitive basis, they would in some cases have to make substantial price concessions in order to sell their own exports on world market and to overcome the preference for western goods. Thus bilateralism undoubtedly provides "means of obtaining more favourable terms of trade for bloc countries especially in purchasing primary commodities, even though apparently they may be offering more favourable "terms of trade."[35]

There may be another explanation for the discriminating prices. The Soviet Union and all other East European countries being very much short free foreign exchange, are only too willing to undersell their goods in the developed countries where competition is stiff and quality standards are very high.[36]

34. Alic Nove : "East-West Trade" in P.A. Samuelson (ed.) "International Econ. Relations : Proceedings of the Third Congress of International Economic Association", Macmillan & Co., St. Martin's Press, New York, 1969 (p.106).

35. Raymond F. Mikesell and Jack N. Behrman, *Financing Free World Trade with the Sino-Soviet Bloc*, Princeton, N.J. Princeton University 1958 (p.70).

36. Alic Nove : "East-West Trade" in P.A. Samuelson (ed.) *International Econ. Relations Proceeding of the Third Congress of International Economic Association, New York*, 1969 (p.107).

While not challenging Carter's data, one cannot fully agree with his conclusion that there exists a planned price discrimination by Soviet Union against the less developed countries. Though the prices charged to the LDCs are higher than those charged to the developed countries, they need not be higher than the ruling world market prices; because the general guiding principle in annual trade talks relating price fixation of goods is to peg the prices commodities around the world market prices.

The important question now is to ask whether there is any discriminatory pricing by the Soviet Union is its trade relations with India. In other words, whether the bilateral character of India's trade with these countries compels her to accept less favourable prices for her exports and imports as compared with what she can get from other countries, with which trade is conducted inconvertible currencies. This can be studied from a comparison of the unit value indices of India's exports to and imports from these countries and other countries over a number of years. Such comparison suffers from several limitations. First, the difference in unit prices which arise from difference in quality or type of goods make a sustained comparison very difficult. This is because trade data available from the DGCIS, group several items with varying quality, size or type in on code group and any further details of the same are not available for different countries. Secondly, prices are influenced by several other internal and/or external factors which affect demand/supply conditions. These include, among other things, the existence of alternate sources of supplies in other countries, the extent of demand in convertible currency countries and the size of the product surplus generated in Indian industries which, together, would influence the international prices. Even in the case of few selected export/import commodities, the extent of surplus or deficit in India of some of the goods for which there is a strong/weak, international demand would influence prices differently in convertible currency areas and in rupee payment countries. This was noticed particularly in the case of export goods like cashew kernel, leather, oilseed cake and meal, tea, jute goods and tobacco.

In order to study the effect of relative prices, a detailed examination of 7 major export commodities constituting 60-70 per cent of India's export to East Europe has been made. The selected commodities are oilcakes, coffee, tea, jute textiles, coir and coir manufactures, cashew kernel, spices and tobacco (unmanufactured) (Table 3.27). The table provides the unit values, unit value index and the ratio of export prices to the East European countries and the rest of the world during 1962-63 to 1969-70. It reveals two strikingly important features regarding prices : (1) there has been a remarkable similarity in the movement of unit value index of exports to the rest of the world and East Europe. (2) The unit values derived by India for spices, tea, oilcakes and coffee sales in the East European countries have been more often higher than what India received from the rest of the world. In other commodities like cashew kernel, jute fabrics, tobacco (unmanufactured), coir and coir manufactures, the unit values that India has received for its exports to the East European countries are less than the unit values received from the rest of the world. A study conducted by the Institute of Foreign Trade points out that the major explanation for this divergence can be found in the differences in quality of products supplied to the East European countries and to the rest of the world, the quality of products supplied to the former being inferior. The East European countries have imported more of broken cashew kernel than the cashew kernel whole. The average share of East Europe in the import of cashew kernel whole is only 10 per cent whereas their share in the import of cashew broken is as high as 51 per cent (cashew broken is assumed to be of inferior quality). Similarly, in case of tobacco (unmanufactured) the purchases made by the East European countries are of different grades receiving lower unit values. The difference in the unit value of exports of jute textiles can be explained by the larger share of sacking cloth and bag in the East European purchases, while the sales to the rest of the world consist of carpet backing with higher unit value. So the above data suggest that the prices received by India are not less than those received from the rest of the world. In fact, in some cases they are higher.[37]

Table 3.28 provides also a picture of unit value of 21 selected commodities exported from India to East European countries from 1968-69 to 1971-72. The table reveals that while in the case

37. *India's Trade with East Europe*: Indian Institute of Foreign Trade, New Delhi, 1973.

[illegible] ... are less than the [illegible] in the [illegible] part of the world [illegible] ... [illegible] East Europe [illegible] ... The East Europe [illegible]

Table 3.28

Unit value of selected commodities exported from India to East European Countries (in Rupees)

	Commodities	Unit of quantity			1969-70		1970-71		1971-72	
			East European countries	Other countries	East European countries	Other countries	East European countries	Other countries	East European countries	Other countries
	1.	2.	3.	4.	5.	6.	7.	8.	9.	10.
1.	Cashew kernal whole	Kg	10.53	10.16	10.12	10.15	11.07	11.03	10.77	10.88
2.	Coffee Arabica Plantation 'A'	Kg	6.81	6.46	6.69	6.04	8.28	7.84	6.66	6.31
3.	Tea Black leaf in bulk	Kg	8.92	7.69	7.98	6.97	8.14	7.34	8.06	7.37
4.	Tea black dust in bulk	Kg	5.37	6.96	-	6.34	-	-	7.46	7.05
5.	Black pepper garbled	Kg	5.12	5.27	7.44	7.06	8.56	8.63	7.73	7.96
6.	Solvent extracted oil cake	Ton	626.31	577.53	660.81	613.82	674.97	667.17	572.00	552.00

7.	Solvent extracted cotton seed oil cake decorticated	Ton	506.41	462.62	533.95	441.62	529.35	508.81	571.52	432.32
8.	Virginia flue cured tobacco	Kg	5.85	7.60	6.18	7.32	7.29	7.62	8.01	7.97
9.	Bengal Deshi raw cotton	Ton	3700.95	3937.29	4117.01	4115.25	4561.33	4296.49	4982.00	5228.86
10.	Mica (Bihar and Rajasthan good stained block)	Kg	119.81	72.09	102.49	55.20	108.63	116.32	110.35	41.84
11.	Mica (Bihar ahd Rajasthan stained block)	Kg	81.52	24.30	59.44	27.44	62.44	30.91	55.31	31.57
12.	Iron ore	Ton	60.66	55.38	62.03	55.56	62.31	54.01	64.33	49.94
13.	Sandal wood oil	Kg	268.55	252.48	257.28	252.62	229.05	240.06	212.59	224.30
14.	Sheep and Lamb skin veg. tanned (unfinished)	Kg	32.12	34.95	39.03	39.82	37.25	39.54	48.95	43.96
15.	Goat and Kid skin bark tanned (unfinished)	Kg	38.16	32.94	45.07	37.03	32.42	31.52	27.11	37.12

(Contd.)

1.		2.	3.	4.	5.	6.	7.	8.	9.	10.
16.	Cotton yarn and thread singles carded	Kg	6.05	6.24	6.25	5.88	7.00	6.49	8.60	7.47
17.	Coir yarn	Kg	2.17	2.07	2.19	2.17	2.34	2.25	2.41	2.34
18.	Sheeting carded yarn (unbleached)	Sq.m.	1.28	1.13	1.55	1.21	1.58	1.32	2.09	1.30
19.	Hessian cloth	Ton	2930.22	3089.11	2905.75	3110.13	3347.20	3398.45	3786.24	3670.86
20.	Sacking cloth	Ton	1940.39	2269.62	-	2479.77	2500.99	2639.36	-	3048.95
21.	Jute sacking bags	Ton	1994.49	2038.63	2382.18	1968.98	2722.56	2503.26	2984.99	2797.85

Sources : Monthly Statistics of Foreign Trade of India : DGCI and S

Table 3.29

Unit Values of Some Important Exports to East Europe and other Markets

	1953/4	1954/5	1955/6	1957	1958	1959	1960/1	1961/2	1962/3	1963/4	1964/5	1965/6
Raw wool												
East European countries	-	-	-	7.69	5.80	5.79	6.07	5.91	6.16	6.53	6.55	6.25
Others	6.31	5.19	6.39	6.26	5.64	5.39	5.34	5.71	5.51	6.06	6.31	5.54
Raw skins and hides												
East European countries	7.00	5.46	5.80	9.10	6.62	9.28	8.82	7.25	7.50	8.59	6.56	8.60
Others	5.89	6.09	7.54	4.06	5.32	5.96	5.63	6.81	7.42	7.78	9.33	9.91
Tobacco unmanufactured												
East European countries	-	-	-	1.52	1.29	1.77	1.59	1.40	1.98	2.50	2.36	2.56
Others	3.46	3.07	2.65	3.53	3.20	3.64	2.54	3.68	3.99	4.11	3.94	4.19
Cashew nut kernels												
East European countries	-	-	-	3.66	3.90	3.92	5.22	4.41	3.90	4.12	5.10	5.20
Others	4.05	3.08	4.11	4.19	3.75	3.95	3.26	4.33	3.99	4.22	5.27	5.39
Tea												
East European countries	-	-	-	7.54	7.65	7.47	5.69	7.12	6.97	6.32	6.40	6.72
Others	4.90	7.16	6.02	5.87	5.85	5.43	6.60	5.86	5.73	5.82	5.80	6.27

(Contd.)

	1953/4	1954/5	1955/6	1957	1958	1959	1960/1	1961/2	1962/3	1963/4	1964/5	1965/6
Jute manufactures												
East European countries	-	-	-	129.6	148.2	86.2	195.3	198.4	173.2	168.2	170.0	200.00
Others	161.3	145.9	137.8	148.0	123.0	116.2	157.1	180.1	174.6	166.7	178.3	204.7
Iron ore												
East European countries	479.3	412.2	477.2	202.0	533.4	495.2	666.4	495.0	488.7	438.3	442.6	417.3
Others	433.9	427.5	457.3	320.9	524.3	522.4	474.2	296.2	376.5	351.4	331.0	328.2
Coffee												
East European countries	-	-	-	6.55	5.56	5.89	4.76	3.03	3.85	3.67	4.39	5.20
Others	6.55	7.39	5.30	5.04	4.70	3.45	3.28	3.04	3.24	3.47	4.25	4.30
Black pepper												
East European countries	9.9	9.16	3.52	2.04	2.12	1.96	5.09	3.57	3.20	3.23	3.94	4.27
Others	9.83	4.14	3.64	1.36	1.76	3.22	4.33	3.67	3.11	2.38	3.85	4.17

Source : DGCI and S : Monthly Statistics of Foreign Trade of India (various issues).
Note : Blanks indicate that India's export during these years were negligible.

of some export commodities, prices realised from the East European countries were favourable in all the four years, in case of a few others, they were higher in most part of this period, as compared to those realised from all other countries. In the former category were coffee, tea (black leaf), solvent extracted cotton seeds cake, coir yarn and sheeting carded yarn, while the latter category included goat and kid skin, cotton yarn and thread and jute sacking bags. On the other hand, 5 out of 21 commodities realised mostly lower unit value on their exports to the East European countries : these were jute sacking cloth, hessian, black pepper, sheep and lamb skin and tobacco. Cashew kernel was the only commodity in respect of which the difference was negligible in all these years.

Tables 3.29 and 3.30 show the unit values of important export commodities to the East European countries as a group and to other markets and the unit values of India's exports to the USSR and other important markets. Table 3.27 shows that Eastern Europe paid consistently higher prices for raw wool and coffee land paid higher prices in all out on or two years for black pepper, tea, raw skins and hides and jute manufactures. They paid lower prices for cashew nut kernels and iron ore in some years. Table 3.30 provides a comparison of unit values of certain important exports to the UK, the USA and the USSR and shows that the unit values of exports to the USSR are higher than those to the UK or the USA for tea, coffee and raw wool and higher in all years except one for black pepper, goat skins (undressed), groundnut meal and castor oil. the comparison of average unit values of India's exports to the East European countries and other markets shows that the former are higher in most cases than the latter.

Table 3.31 and 3.32 show the index of India's exports to the USSR and the rest of the world during the period 1960-61 to 1964-65 to 1969-70. From Table 3.31. it becomes clear that the unit value fluctuations of exports to the U.S.S.R. were confined within narrow limits of 2 points -- the unit values fell from 100 in 1960-61 to 98.2 in 1962-63, rose again to 101.4 in 1963-64 and then levelled down to 99.7 in 1964-65.

Table 3.30

A comparison of unit values of selected commodities to major markets

(Rs. per Kg)

	1958	*1959*	*1960/1*	*1961/2*	*1962/3*	*1963/4*	*1964/5*	*1965/6*
Tea								
UK	5.9	5.9	6.2	6.1	5.8	6.3	5.9	5.3
USA	6.1	5.7	6.1	6.3	5.7	5.7	5.5	6.0
USSR	7.2	7.3	7.2	8.6	7.5	6.6	6.3	6.8
World	5.9	5.8	6.2	5.9	5.8	5.8	5.8	6.4
Coffee								
UK	4.7	4.9	4.1	3.2	3.80	3.78	4.47	3.55
USA	3.92	3.92	3.60	3.04	2.33	3.19	4.20	3.8
USSR	4.9	4.4	4.34	3.7	5.5	4.2	4.5	5.6
East Germany	6.2	4.4	4.8	2.1	3.3	3.3	7.3	5.2
World	4.98	4.16	3.66	3.04	3.73	3.58	4.32	4.93
Tobacco unmanufactured								
UK	4.92	5.35	4.52	5.78	5.76	5.90	5.79	5.22
USSR	1.61	1.62	1.89	1.06	1.94	2.54	2.34	2.51
World	2.99	3.45	3.32	3.62	2.87	3.31	3.15	3.57
Goat skins undressed								
USA	4.3	6.0	6.9	6.3	6.5	8.1	9.0	8.2
USSR	7.3	8.9	7.8	5.9	6.7	8.3	9.4	7.6
World	-	-	8.0	-	-	7.7	6.8	8.0
Black pepper								
USA	2.12	3.04	3.70	3.66	3.10	3.00	4.36	4.11
USSR	2.00	2.72	4.88	3.77	3.20	3.17	4.08	4.26
World	1.49	1.42	4.93	3.73	3.15	3.11	3.26	4.23

(Contd.)

	1958	*1959*	*1960/1*	*1961/2*	*1962/3*	*1963/4*	*1964/5*	*1965/6*
Raw wool								
USA	6.2	5.8	5.7	5.5	5.5	6..0	7.0	9.0
USSR	5.7	5.8	6.0	5.9	6.1	6.7	6.5	6.1
UK	5.1	5.3	5.2	5.0	5.8	6.1	6.5	Neg.
World	3.8	5.7	6.0	5.9	6.1	6.7	6.5	6.1
Cashewnut kernels								
USA	3.9	4.0	4.1	4.3	4.2	3.6	5.3	5.8
UK	3.4	3.5	4.4	4.0	3.9	4.1	4.9	5.7
West Germany	3.7	3.0	4.4	4.3	4.0	4.1	4.8	6.0
Canada	4.2	4.3	5.3	4.8	4.2	4.6	5.5	6.0
East Germany	-	3.3	3.9	3.8	3.5	3.7	4.1	5.0
U.S.S.R.	3.9	4.0	5.4	4.6	4.1	4.3	5.4	5.9
World	3.5	4.1	4.3	4.3	3.9	4.2	5.2	5.7
Castor oil								
UK	14.0	13.3	18.8	15.3	13.4	12.7	13.9	20.0
USA	9.8	13.3	13.0	-	10.0	-	20.0	20.0
USSR	15.3	14.6	15.8	16.1	14.2	13.4	18.5	17.1
World	-	-	14.3	16.0		13.5	16.3	17.3
Groundnut meal								
UK	-	-	-	3.59	3.66	3.75	4.16	4.06
Czechoslovakia	-	-	-	3.37	3.96	3.72	4.37	4.11
Hungary	-	-	3.25	3.69	3.70	4.40	4.20	4.34
Poland	-	-	3.33	3.89	3.86	4.38	4.24	4.24
East Germany	-	-	3.33	3.83	3.69	4.49	4.28	4.28

Sources : Computed from volume and quantity figures. DGCI and S. Monthly Statistics of Foreign Trade of India, (various issues).

Table 3.31

Unit value index numbers of export to the USSR and the rest of the world

Year	*Unit value index no. exports to the USSR*	*Unit value index no. of exports to the rest of the world*
1960-61	100	100
1961-62	99.1	81.9
1962-63	98.2	80.1
1963-64	101.4	78.8
1964-65	99.7	83.9

Source : DGCI and S : Monthly statistics of Foreign Trade of India.

In contrast to unit value fluctuation within a narrow limit in case of the USSR, the unit value index numbers of exports to the rest of the world declined continuously. It is clear that the range of all in the unit value index numbers of export to the rest of the world was as wide as 21.2 points against 2 points in case of USSR thus the unit values of a number of items which form a sizeable part of India's exports to the USSR, were relatively steadier than those secured by India from the rest of the world.

During 1965-66 to 1969-70, the unit value of exports moved favourably for India, as shown in Table 3.32. Column 2 of the table gives the unit value index of commodities constituting nearly 96 per cent of India's exports to the USSR Columns 3 and 4 give the index numbers of unit values of select commodities exported to the USSR and the rest of the world. By the end of the period the unit value index of exports to the Soviet Union was slightly lower than rest of the world during this period.

The reason for the slightly lower unit value index of exports to the USSR are (i) the adjustment after devaluation in case of U.S.S.R was only 47 per cent whereas it was 57 per cent in case of the rest of the world. (ii) USSR is a large purchaser of cashew kernel and jute fabrics of lower unit values, whereas exports to the rest of the world consisted of some high unit value items. In order to take into consideration the changing composition of trade, 1965-66 has been taken as the base year in Table 3.32.

Table 3.32

Unit value index of India's exports to USSR and the rest of the world

Year	*Unit value index of exports to USSR (general)*	*Unit value index of export of select commodities to USSR*	*Unit value index of export to the rest of the world**
1	*2*	*3*	*4*
1965-66	100.00	100.0	100.0
1966-67	142.50	146.3	160.4
1967-68	103.07	123.7	156.7
1968-69	124.07	145.3	157.0
1969-70	122.50	148.0	158.7

*Consists of the same commodity groups as exports to the USSR.

Source : DGCI and S : Monthly Statistics of Foreign Trade of India.

It is true that unit prices paid by Eastern Europe are not significantly higher than those which India received from other countries, but the timing of purchase and its method may have their impact on domestic and thereby export prices. This impact may or may not be beneficial. If the East European countries purchase at a time when there is large surplus with too many exporters making the situation worse by undercutting each other, the impact may be a stabilising one. The stability hypothesis has been examined in Appendix (2) of the same chapter. It is argued in official circles that in the late 1950 the bulk purchase from the USSR helped to stabilise the prices of tea and particular varieties of unmanufactured tobacco. But the pressure of East European demand may be harmful also when India is a price-taker in the world market. Indian products become too expensive in other markets as result of increased demand from the East European countries. This situation depends on the supply elasticity and so may not last very long. The NCAER report on black pepper points out that "when large scale purchases are made by the USSR and other countries in that region, price in India goes up. This is an important reason for higher prices on exports to the USSR and for the wide fluctuations in the domestic prices. When the USSR in the Indian market, sometimes the Indian prices non-competitive in other markets".[38] Similarly the domestic supplies of raw wool were limited in the 1960s while the demand was increasing. The higher price from the USSR helped in both increasing the domestic prices of raw wool and diverting supplies from other markets. Ahuja, while discussing India's trade with East Europe in the 1950's, says that this trade "has been largely responsible for an artificial raising of prices. This is especially so in the case of tea, coffee, as well as hides skins".[39] She goes on to suggest that higher prices are instrumental in diverting limited supplies. "It will be seen that for commodities where supplies are limited, the price divergence is vide and for commodities for which supply conditions were easier, the gap is narrow".[40]

The following qualifications should be noted before concluding that Eastern Europe paid higher prices for India's exports (a) As pointed out by Dave, India exported better qualities of tea and coffee to the East European countries.[41] This is probably true of black pepper, raw wool and raw skins and hides as well.

(b) The Unit value is also influenced by the broadness of the commodity group. For example, the category of "jute manufactures" is very broad and the average unit value would depend on the share of the individual items in the category. Eastern Europe paid a higher price for gunny bags but not for hessian cloth. Since they imported more gunny bags than hessian cloth, the average unit value of exports of jute manufactures to East European countries was higher than to other markets.

38. National Council of Applied Econ. Research : Export Prospects of Black Pepper, New Delhi, 1965, p.84.

39. Ahuja, K : *India's Trade with Eastern Europe,* Indian Econ. Journal, Jan., 1962 pp.361-65.

40. Ibid, p.362-63.

41. Dave, S : *India's Trade Relations with the East Europe,* Indian Econ. Journal, Jan., pp. 362-63.

(c) An important reason why unit values of exports to other markets appeared lower could be that Indian exporters under invoiced their exports. Indian exporters have preferred to keep a part of their proceeds as investment abroad. There has been no incentive to under state the export earnings from Eastern Europe because the proceeds cannot be transferred elsewhere.

(d) Since they buy in large quantities and make payment in rupees, the East European countries may have to pay higher prices to purchase goods in the open market. This is not so when the STC is responsible for exporting certain items like unmanufactured tobacco etc.

(e) 50 per cent of India's exports is required to be shipped in Indian vessels. So the East European countries may not have paid anything extra for transport and so they have no objection to paying higher prices for imported goods in the market.

To conclude the discussion on export prices of Indian goods, it is probably true that India obtained slightly higher prices for her exports to the USSR and other East European countries for some commodities, but it is not possible to say whether these prices were significantly higher than elsewhere because of quality differences.

Comparison regarding the unit values of India's imports from Eastern Europe and other countries is ever more difficult to undertake. Goods imported from various conclusion, comparable unit values may be used for the assessment of price-differences. Such a comparison should necessarily be supplemented by detailed investigation of individual commodity prices. Table 3.33 shows that the USSR is not charging higher prices. Even in respect of zinc, where the world market prices higher in the years concerned, there is no evidence to show that the USSR charged more than the other countries.

The major items of imports from the USSR have been machinery, iron and steel, fertilisers and newsprint which constitute over 10 per cent of India's total imports. They are also imported from traditional markets of the West. Fertiliser import from the USSR started in 1959 and increased more than 10 times between 1968-69. Table 3.34 provides information regarding India's imports of manufactured fertilisers form the USSR and other Western countries.

Table 3.33

Unit values of India's select import products (in rupees)

Country	*1960-61*	*1961-62*	*1962-63*	*1963-64*	*1965-65*
Caustic soda per Kg.					
USSR	0.51	0.51	0.35	0.25	0.31
USA	-	1.27	0.54	0.54	0.50
UK	0.53	0.27	0.65	0.42	0.48
Centri-pump-elect. motor operated No.1					
USSR	-	5296.4	2243.0	2289.0	3972.0
USA	7712.8	5565.5	6389.5	23116.0	17478.0
UK	4512.7	6446.4	5703.0	9312.5	7636.1
Copper tubes per kg.					
Yugoslavia	4.66	4.88	6.60	-	-
USSR	-	-	-	4.30	4.83
USA	8.52	7.73	8.12	7.01	6.69
UK	6.44	5.85	7.65	6.72	7.32
Zinc or speller ingot cakes per kg.					
USSR	1.25	1.16	0.91	1.08	1.69
USA	1.21	1.16	1.14	1.24	1.65
UK	1.30	1.23	1.04	1.28	1.78

Source : DGCI and S : Monthly statistics of Foreign Trade of India.

Comparing the unit values of fertiliser imports from the USSR, the USA and the UK no consistent trend of higher or lower unit values is observed for any country. By calculating the average annual unit values from 1958-59 to 1968-69 for USA, UK and USSR the figures are Rs. 281.61, Rs. 281.98 and Rs. 264.67 respectively at predevaluation rates.

Table 3.34

India's imports of manufactured fertilisers

Year	Unit	From USA Unit value (Rs)	From UK Unit value (Rs)	From USSR Unit value (Rs)
1958-59	Per ton	231.82	-	415.39
1959-60	"	190.48	-	212.00
1960-61	"	270.00	-	177.00
1961-62	"	216.66	-	276.59
1962-63	"	256.85	285.71	244.11
1963-64	"	377.49	257.89	194.54
1964-65	"	323.88	129.27	-
1965-66	"	285.29	242.86	269.44
1966-67*	"	454.49	376.66	452.67
1967-68*	"	533.00	696.12	456.25
1968-69*	"	500.86	593.33	440.92

* at post devaluation rates.

Source : DGCI and S : Monthly Statistics of Foreign Trade of India.

Table 3.35

India's imports of Newsprint

Quantity : Kgs. in lakhs. *Value : Rs. In lakhs.*

Year	*From West Germany*			*From Sweden*			*From USSR*		
	Quantity	*Value*	*Unit value (Rs.)*	*Quantity*	*Value*	*Unit value (Rs)*	*Quantity*	*Value*	*Unit-Value (Rs)*
1	*2*	*3*	*4*	*5*	*6*	*7*	*8*	*9*	*10*
1961-62	12	10.8	0.90	219	184	0.84	189	142	0.75
1962-63	4	4	1.00	191	154	0.81	186	142	0.76
1963-64	6	5	0.83	192	144	0.75	174	122	0.70
1964-65	2	2	1.00	139	103	0.74	242	170	0.70

(Contd.)

1	2	3	4	5	6	7	8	9	10
1965-66	0.68	0.49	0.72	78	58	0.74	302	215	0.71
1966-67	3.7	4.4	0.78 (1.19)	1.23	1.56	0.80 (1.27)	451	503	0.70 (1.11)
1967-68	2	2.38	0.75 (1.19)	34	43	0.80 (1.26)	251	280	0.71 (1.12)
1968-69	6.35	7.35	0.73 (1.15)	33	37	0.71 (1.12)	538	587	0.69 (1.09)
1969-70	1.98	2.46	0.79 (1.24)	-	-	-	481	595	0.88 (1.40)

Figures in brackets are at post-devaluation rates

Source : DGCI and S : Govt. of India, Monthly Statistics of Foreign Trade of India.

Table 3.36 shows that the unit values of imports from the USSR for iron and steel were lower than the unit values of imports from the UK and the USA in all the years between 1954 and 1965. Iron and steel imports are made up of many categories like bars, plates and sheets and tubes and pipes. A study of the unit values of these goods from 1966 to 1960-70 also shows that the Soviet unit values were definitely lower than the unit values of the USA, the UK and West Germany.

Table 3.36

India's imports of iron and steel

Quantity : '000 ton. Value : Rs. in lakhs.

Year	*From USSR*			*From USA*			*From UK*		
	Quantity	*Value*	*Unit value (Rs.)*	*Quantity*	*Value*	*Unit value (Rs)*	*Quantity*	*Value*	*Unit-Value (Rs)*
1	*2*	*3*	*4*	*5*	*6*	*7*	*8*	*9*	*10*
1954-55	17	66	388.3	42	245	583.3	82	824	1004.9
1955-56	61	310	508.2	134	908	677.6	162	1336	824.7
1956-57	85	824	969.4	295	1463	495.9	257	2196	854.5

(Contd.)

1	*2*	*3*	*4*	*5*	*6*	*7*	*8*	*9*	*10*
1957-58	304	1992	955.3	135	1087	805.2	180	1823	1012.8
1958-59	233	1253	537.8	93	643	691.4	152	1556	1023.7
1959-60	213	1002	470.4	91	623	687.9	211	1951	924.7
1960-61	69	505	731.9	139	1337	961.9	294	2646	900.0
1961-62	85	755	888.2	133	1395	1048.9	160	1924	1202.5
1962-63	98	688	702.0	207	2008	970.0	135	1599	1184.4
1963-64	51	412	807.8	280	2725	973.2	141	1414	1002.8
1964-65	158	880	557.0	211	2544	1205.7	230	1441	626.5
1965-66	120	813	677.5	170	2227	1310.0	93	1234	1326.9

Source : DGCI and S : Monthly statistics of Foreign Trade of India.

Table 3.37 and 3.38 give the general index numbers of Unit Value of imports form the USSR with 1960-61 and 1965-66 as respective base years.

Table 3.37

General index numbers of unit value of imports form USSR.

Year	*Chain index number*
1960-61	100.0
1961-62	102.3
1962-63	78.1
1963-64	97.1
1964-65	65.6

Source : DGCI and S : Monthly Statistics of Foreign Trade of India.

The general index numbers of unit value after a small rise of 2.3 in 1961-62 fell to 78.1 in 1962-63. They increased to 97.1 in 1963-64 land fell steeply to 65.6 in 1964-65. The inference that can be drawn from this is that the Soviet Union has to made attempts to increase the prices during the period. the marginal rise in the price during 1961-62 may be explained by the fact that the USSR increased its prices after establishing itself in Indian market and when the India Govt. brought this fact to the notice of the of the USSR such attempt was abandoned in the subsequent years.

Table 3.38

General unit value index numbers of imports from USSR

Year	Index number
1965-66	100.00
1966-67	133.00
1967-68	93.81
1968-69	91.35
1969-70	130.37

Source : DGCI and S : Monthly Statistics of Foreign Trade of India.

The movement of import prices has been favourable in two years and unfavourable in two years.

According to Surendra Dave "A study of about one hundred unit values of imports of chemicals, fertilizers, newsprint 'nd iron and steel products from these countries for the three years 1957-59 suggests that no higher prices were charged". But he points out that "the commodities for which the prices are higher, according to the information provided by some traders, consist largely of re-exports of West European goods" and "capital goods are not taken into account because of the obvious difficulties involved".[42]

The survey conducted by the Indian Institute of Foreign Trade relating India's trade with the Eastern Europe arrives at a similar conclusion : for comparable items there is no evidence that the USSR charged higher prices than other countries.[43] The survey is careful to point out that goods imported from various

42. S. Dave : *India's Trade Relations with East European Countries 1952/53 to 1959/60*, Indian Eco. Journal, July, 1961 (pp.479-88).

43. Inst. of Foreign Trade : India's Trade with Eastern Europe, New Delhi, 1966, pp.69-76.

countries are not identical and that a comparison of unit prices should be supplemented by detailed investigation of individual commodity prices.

There is little information available on the prices of machinery and equipment which constituted 60 per cent of India's imports from these countries. It has been admitted even by Govt. Officials that the prices of machinery and equipment have sometimes been higher by 10 to 30 per cent, compared to the cheapest sources of supply. But it is not possible to say whether imports were more expensive than other credit-financed imports. A significant proportion of the imports of machinery and equipment form the East European countries is financed by tied credit and so it is not fair to compare these prices with prices from non-ties sources. Michacl Kidron has suggested that "Indian might normally be paying anything between 6 and 15 per cent, sometimes as much as 20-30 per cent, above ruling prices for aid-supported imports".[44]

To sum up : The USSR and other East European countries have paid higher prices for some of India's exports but in some cases the prices for exports were lower, as far as merchandise trade was concerned. So far as prices of current imports (specially imports of raw material) are concerned, they are not generally higher. But this applies to only 25-30 per cent of India's total imports from these countries. From available evidence it appears that the prices of machinery and equipment from the East European countries were higher then prices offered by other countries. Machinery-import constituted at least 50 per cent of India's total imports from these countries. So taking into account all imports and exports, India's net terms of trade were perhaps worse with the East European countries than with the rest of the world. It is true that excluding the imports of machinery, India's net barter terms of trade are probably comparable to or at least not significantly inferior to its terms of trade with other countries. In fact, the machinery imported from these countries is of special kind and it is not possible to assess whether the prices are reasonable.

44. Michael Kidron : (1965) *Foreign Investment in India*, Oxford University Press, p.122.

Conclusions

The available evidence regarding a commodity wise study indicates that the major portions of India's rapidly expanding exports to the USSR and Eastern Europe have constituted a net addition to India's export earnings. The extent of diversion of commodities varies between 15 and 25 per cent of India's exports to these countries, in the sense that they could have been sold in hard currency markets. This diversion is no doubt a cost from Indian point of view since this reduces the amount of free foreign exchange. But the capture of a market should involve some cost in the form of price reduction etc., so if it is judged in the above light, the obvious conclusion is that India's exports to Eastern Europe are largely additional to, rather than in replacement of, exports elsewhere. Although there are instances of re-exports of Indian goods by the Socialist countries of Eastern Europe, this does not seem to have taken place on large scale.

An analysis of comparative prices of Indian exports and imports to and from Eastern European and the rest of the world indicates that Eastern Europe offered higher prices for some export items and lower prices for others and as far as industrial raw materials are concerned the prices from these two sources are comparable. Therefore, it seems that India's net barter terms of trade for merchandise trade alone are comparable or at least not significantly inferior to what it obtained from the rest of the world. But here the role of machinery-imports which constitute more than 50 per cent of India's total imports from these countries has not been taken into consideration. According to knowledgeable business circles prices of machinery supplied by these countries are generally higher, in some cases upto 25 per cent higher than international prices. Not if all imports and exports are taken into account, it is difficult to conclude that the terms of trade would remain favourable towards India. But one cannot agree with J.R. Carter's conclusion of planned price discremination on the part of the Soviet Union as far as its trade with India is concerned.

A decade of expansion of India's trade with the East European countries under bilateral trade and payments agreements has amply justified the calculations and expectations of the architects of bilateral trade and payments agreements regarding creation of import capacity through export expansion when this instrument was first used in 1959. Export to these countries increased from 0.9 per cent in 1953-54 to 22.9 per cent in 1970-71 and imports from them correspondingly increased from 0.4 per cent to 14.0 per cent. In other words, these countries did provide additional outlets for India's traditional exports and because they purchased in large amounts, it helped to stabilise, on certain occasions, the domestic prices of some commodities such as tea. In Calcutta auction of tea, the manner and timing of tea purchased by these countries have played a useful role in stabilising the prices of tea.

Besides these benefits, India has also managed to secure high priority goods from these countries and those too generally (with the exception of a few commodities) at satisfactory prices. So it may be concluded that this trade has been beneficial to India during the period under study (1953-74). But the future depends upon so many big "ifs" including the trade policies of East European countries. There are two major sources of uncertainty regarding India's weaker bargaining position -- India is not an indispensable supplier of any commodity to Eastern Europe, whereas India depends upon Eastern Europe for essential supplies. The second source of uncertainty is that if Sino-East European relations improve India may not be needed so much because at one stage India replaced communist China as a supplier.

In so far as question of burden of repayment in kind is concerned, it may be concluded that since by and large India's exports to these countries are additional in nature with terms of trade not significantly worse than elsewhere the burden of repayment in kind is not possibly higher than the burden of repayment in convertible currency.

Rupee-Rouble Exchange Rate

Cost-benefit analysis of Indo-Soviet trade would remain incomplete without any discussion on rupee-rouble tussle.

According to the long-term trade and payment agreements between India and the Soviet Union, the exchange rate between the rupee and the rouble is determined by the gold contents of both currencies. In purely legal terms, the gold content of both currencies have remained constant for the past several years. With the breakdown of the Briton Woods system after 1971, the official gold content almost all the world currencies has become a fiction since the exchange rate between any two currencies is quite different from the rate worked out on the basis of their respective official gold contents. With the Indian rupee linked to the sterling, which is floating on the foreign exchange markets, it is meaningless to talk of the official gold content of the rupee.

The gold content of the rouble is an equally fictitious concept. Before the breakdown of the Briton Woods system it made some sense when one talked about the gold content of the pound sterling, the French franc or the US dollar as the exchange rate worked out on the basis of their respective gold contents has some correspondence with their actual exchanges rates on the markets. But the rouble has never been a currency freely traded on the world markets and its gold content has been even more of a fiction than in the case of Indian rupee.

It is easy, therefore, to dismiss the argument of the Russian side that the gold content of the rupee *vis-a-vis* the rouble declined just because the rupee, linked as it was to the sterling, depreciated against other prominently traded currencies. The exchange rate of the rouble *vis-a-vis* other major world currencies is determined by the Soviet Union quite arbitrarily to suit exigencies of its foreign trade. Thus the cross rates of the rouble *vis-a-vis* other prominent currencies are rarely in alignment and one gets varying cross rates for the rouble depending on the particular foreign currency chosen for working out the cross rates.

The gold content of the rupee and rouble are thus meaningless entities; but what about the rupee-rouble exchange rate ? Russians are experts in fixing rates arbitrarily. All trade transactions between India and the Soviet Union are invoiced in rupees. If the Russians enjoy a payment surplus with India the Russian account is credited to the extend of that amount; and in case of a deficit, the Russian side is granted a technical credit. Since both Russian and Indian prices are quoted in rupees, the exchange rate between the rouble and the rupee is not of direct relevance in trade transactions. It is only for invisible transactions that the rupee-rouble exchange rate of relevance. The exchange rate is also of great relevance for repayments of principal and interest by India in respect of loans received by it in the past. When the rupee was devalued in 1966, the outstanding due to Russian were revalued by nearly one-half.

The gist of the Russian argument in the current negotiations is that since the rupee has got devalued *vis-a-vis* the rouble, current invisible payments as well as servicing of previous debts should be settled in terms of the devalued rate for the rupee. Acceptance of this contention would mean upvaluation of the outstanding loans to be repaid to the Soviet Union. A point could be raised here about the justification for such an upvaluation when the loan contracts are expressed in terms of rupees. But the Russian argument is that the gold parities of the rouble and the rupee form the basis of payments agreements between the two countries and since the gold content of the rupee has declined such an upvaluation is long overdue. Since 1971, the Soviet Union revalued the rouble unilaterally from 11.39 roubles to 100 rupees to 8.66 roubles to 100 rupees, there was an upward revaluations of credit repayments for past commercial and defence transactions by about Rs. 400 crores. Thus India would be a losing partner in Indo-Soviet argument has no basis now. The value of Indian rupee has gone up. Further, India has severed her link with sterling. Therefore, the Soviet argument has lost its force. India has got strong case for seeking an upward revision of the value of the Indian rupee. The matter is purely is bilateral issue to be settled according to the mutual satisfaction of both countries. Given India's relatively weak balance of payment position, it dependence on foreign loans and its reliance on the Soviet Union, in particular for supply of arms and for political support, any compromise that is reached on the rupee-rouble exchange rate is likely to favour the Soviet Union.

APPENDIX -I

Index Numbers of Unit Values of Exports and Imports :

Index numbers which show the relative changes in a variable compared with the particular base involve many problems in their computation. the following three are very important among them

: (a) choice of data (b) choice of average (c) choice of the base year.

Choice of Data :

The entire data have been collected from only one publication of India's trade statistics - Monthly Statistics of the Foreign Trade of India, a publication of the Department of Commercial Intelligence and Statistics, Govt. of India. Thus there is consistency in data.

Choice of Weights :

The simple arithmetic mean has the defect of giving equal weight to all the commodities even if they have varying importance. The weighted arithmetic average is an improvement over the simple arithmetic mean in the sense that it gives weights to commodities according to their importance in the total trade. Despite the theoretical superiority of Fisher's geometric average, it is not used since in involves extra ordinary difficulties regarding times and money in calculating index numbers. Hence we have used arithmetic mean (weighted) for the construction of index numbers. Paasche formula for current year index numbers

$$\frac{p_1 q_1}{p_o q_1} \times 100 \; (\quad = \text{select commodities})$$

has been used in the construction of index numbers. This formula registers more correctly the changes in the composition of trade and thus makes easy the task of current comparison.

Unit Value Versus Prices :

The important question is : whether one should take into account the unit value or prices of commodities while constructing index numbers. Index numbers are based on price quotations and they reflect more accurately changes in prices. Hence they are sometimes better than those using unit values. Unit value is derived by dividing total value reports in trade statistics by the quantity. If the commodity class is not homogeneous, changes in unit value may indicate only changes that may have occurred in the commodity composition of the group. Since the Monthly Statistics of Foreign Trade of India does not provide detailed information regarding price data reliance is to be placed on unit values.

Base Year Selection :

Looking at the commodity composition of India's of India's export goods to the Soviet Union, we should select the base year for exports. Since upto mid 1960s, there is not much structural change of India's exports to the Soviet Union, we may use 1960-61 as the base year for calculation. But after mid 1960s there had been some changes in the commodity composition. The year 1965-66 has been used as the base year.

For imports, a chain base year method has been used, since there were rapid changes in the structure of imports. In the commodity groups of imports, various items did not appear in one year but appeared in another. For example, chemical, sodium nitrate, sodium compounds and sodium benzoate did not figure in India's imports from the Soviet Union in 1960-61 whereas they figured significantly in 1962-63.

Coverage :

It is not possible to take all the commodities entering into Indo-Soviet trade. We will have to select commodities. As there is not much difficulty in data collection for India's exports, the coverage has been about 90%. But in the matter of imports, the coverage has been less than that of exports. The quantative data for many import items such as machinery are not available.

Trade Statistics from the Reserve Bank of India and the Director General of Commercial Intelligence and Statistics

The discrepancy between import figures from DGCI and S. and the RBI is much wider than discrepancy between export figures and this particularly due of imports from the Soviet Union and other East European countries. The discrepancies are due to differences in valuation, coverage and timing, methods of valuation etc.[1]

Both the sources - the DGCI and S and the RBI use the

1. A. Datar : *India's Econ. Relations with the USSR and Eastern Europe,* 1953 to 1969, Cambridge, 1972, p.109.

same data i.e. the shipping bill submitted by the exporters. But the valuation and the time of entry is different in the two cases. The RBI generally accepts the original bill of exports since it is interested in the actual flow of funds; but the DGCI and S. makes adjustments for any unrealistic values. It records only on the data of passing the shipping bill but the RBI records exports after the goods had actually been shipped.

Regarding imports, it is observed that DGCI and S records imports on the basis of "bill of entry" when the goods arrive. The RBI figures relate to the timing of payments, and the figures for imports are based on the outflow of foreign exchange. But DGCI and S. does not follow a uniform pattern. Sometimes it accepts tariff values and sometimes markets prices for imported goods.

For the East European countries. the most important items which account for difference between the RBI and DGCI and S data are the treatment of some technical assistance payments, inclusion/exclusion of defence imports and incomplete coverage due to Note Pass System.

RBI import figures include some payments for technical services with the imports of complete plants from the East European countries since these countries including payments for technical services in their invoice of imports. But these payments are excluded from the DGCI as S trade data.

In case of Indo-Soviet trade, we find that the discrepancies between data relating to India's imports from the Soviet Union are greater than those relating to India's exports to the Soviet Union.

So far as export-data are concerned, we find that since India's exports and Soviet union's imports are on f.o.b. basis, they are comparable. But there are wide discrepancies between India's imports (c.i.f.) from the Soviet Union as recorded in that country's trade statistics and Soviet export figures as recorded in that country's statistics. These discrepancies are largely attributable to inclusion of combatant defence equipment in Soviet trade statistics and the exclusion of the item in India's trade data. The fact that the difference between Indian and Soviet statistics is much greater from 1963 (after the Chinese invasion in 1962) onwards than before substantiates the above line of argument

APPENDIX - II

Sometimes it is argued that India's trade with the Soviet Union and other East European countries was instrumental in stabilising India's export-earnings in internationally trade commodities. The stability hypothesis can be examined by studying the degree of instability in India's export-earnings. Export instability has been defined as short-term fluctuations in export-earnings corrected for the trend.[1] For measuring this instability we can use Coppock's Instability index. It is defined as :

$$V.\log = \frac{(\log \frac{X_{t+1}}{X_t} -- m)^2}{N - 1}$$

Where X_t = value of India's exports in the year t,

N = Number of years,

m = arithmetic mean of the differences between the logs of X_t and X_{t+1}, X_{t+2} etc.

V.log = the logarithmic variance of the series.

The instability index is : [(anti-log V.log - 1) x 100] Such an index is considered to be the close approximation of the average year to year percentage variation.

The commodities selected for such an examination are tea, coffee, jute manufactures, cashew nuts, pepper and hides and skins. We know that these constitute important items in India's export list to the Soviet Union. The exercise has been carried out for the period 1961-62 to 1972-73.

Table-I provides Coppock's instability indices for the USSR and the world.

1. Macbean, A.T. : *Export Instability and Econ. Development*, George Allen and Unwin, London, 1966, p.34.

World value indices are lower than the value indices of the USSR. A relatively high instability index of India's export earnings from the USSR may reduce instability in overall trade in those commodities due to compensatory movements of exports to the USSR.

Table - I

Coppock's instability indices (1960-61 to 1972-73)

Commodity	*Value*	
	USSR	*World*
1. Tea	157.9	82.8
2. Jute manufactures	32.6	19.2
3. Coffee	35.9	27.6
4. Cashew kernel	39.0	29.1
5. Pepper	33.3	25.0
6. Hides and skins	25.3	47.3

Table 2 shows instability indices for East Europe (including USSR) and the world.

Table - 2

Coppock's instability indices (1960-61 to 1972-73)

Commodity	*Value*		
	East Europe	*Rest of the world*	*World*
1. Coffee	64.3	105.00	33.0
2. Tea	36.4	17.4	15.5
3. Oilcake	88.0	65.0	48.4
4. Cashew kernel	70.2	30.8	33.0
5. Unmanufactured tobacco	132.7	25.8	36.0

(Contd.)

1	2	3	4	5
6.	Castor oil	146.6	574.8	295.5
7.	Black pepper	41.9	54.3	28.9
8.	Jute manufactures	78.2	20.4	18.3
9.	Combined index for 8 commodities	49.2	14.1	16.6

The world indices of value for coffee, tea, oilcake, pepper, castor oil and jute manufactures are lower than for the rest of the world, indicating the fact that India's trade with East Europe has stabilized the value of India's overall trade in these commodities. For commodities like unmanufactured tobacco, the overall world index is higher than that of the rest of the world; while in respect of commodities like cashew kernel, the world index and the index of the rest of the world are almost identical. The broad conclusion that one may draw from the study is that trade with the East Europe was instrumental in stabilising the export-earnings of India's traditional commodities.

CHAPTER 4

CONTRIBUTION OF SOVIET TRADE TO THE GROWTH OF INDIAN INDUSTRIES

India's trade with the USSR and other East European countries can be looked upon as a part of its credit arrangement with them. India's advantage in this arrangement is that she can repay the credits by exporting her own products and no element of foreign exchange is involved. The arrangement also meets the East European countries in a better way in the sense that the repayment in kind is a "guarantee" of timely repayment of India's debt. In the East European countries credit is considered to be the only correct method of expanding foreign trade with the developing countries.[1] As Kidron points out, by the early 1960s, Soviet bloc countries were "clearly beginning to count and reject the cost of purely political trade"[2] and concentrating more on the trade-creation aspects. The trade and credit arrangements had their repercussions on the development of industrial infra structure in India.

The Soviet bloc countries looked upon the Co-ordination between trade and aid policies as a means of finding markets for machinery and obtaining raw materials from developing countries like India. At the same time, India was striving hard to achieve economic self-sufficiency and economic independence. Development of the basic and key industries was one of the basic factors in strengthening this economic independence. In India's First Five Year Plan (1951-56) the industrial targets were relatively few in number. In fact, this plan was very much a collection of a number of separate overhead projects, since the notion of planning for consistency at an inter-industrial level was still absent from the Indian planning scene.[3] The Second Plan (1 April 1956 - 31 march 1961) unlike the First Plan had an explicit theoreti-

1. Kidron, M. 1972 -- *Pakistan's Trade with Eastern Bloc Countries,* New York p.6.
2. *Ibid* p.7.
3. Bhagwati, J and Desai, P. (1970) : *India : Planning for Industrialization,* Oxford University Press, p.233.

cal frame and called for a marked shift in favour of capital goods industries. It was precisely during this period that an element of genuine bilateralism was introduced into India's trade with the Soviet Union. The non-convertible rupee payment agreement was concluded on Nov. 14, 1958 for a period of five years from 1959.

A decade of expansion of India's trade with the USSR and other East European countries under bilateral trade and payments agreements has amply justified the calculation and expectations of the architects of bilateral trade and payments agreements regarding creation of import capacity through export expansion, when this instrument was first put to use in 1959. Exports to the USSR and other East European countries increased from 0.9 per cent of total exports in 1953-54 to 22.9 per cent of the total in 1970-71 and 24 per cent in 1972-73. Imports from them correspondingly rose from 0.4 per cent of the total to 14.0 per cent, but fell to 12.1 per cent in 1972-73. This meant a substantial increase in the share of the East European countries in India's major commodity exports. In case of tea, the share of East European countries increased from 1 per cent of total tea exports in 1953-54 to 13 per cent in 1964-65 and to 20.6 per cent in 1970-71. Similarly in case of jute textiles, their share in India's total exports rose from 0.01 per cent in 1953-54 to 13 per cent in 1964-65, to 15 per cent in 1969-70 and to 24 per cent in 1970-71. In cashew kernel, their share was 29 per cent of the total in 1964-65 35 per cent in 1970-71.[4] A somewhat trend could be observed in coffee and tobacco.

India's imports from these countries have mainly consisted of petroleum and petroleum products, chemical elements and compounds, caustic soda, dyeing and tanning and colouring materials, fertilisers, rubber manufactures, paper and paper-board, newsprint, base metals, machinery, including electrical machinery and transport equipment. Table 4.1 gives the commodity composition of India's imports form the East European countries.

The East European countries are emerging as important suppliers of many commodities. Their share in imports of chemical elements and compounds steadily increased from 9.3 per cent in 1961-62 to 31.0 per cent in 1969-70. Similarly, in machinery

4. DGCI and S : Monthly Statistics of Foreign Trade of India.

other than electric, the share increased from 13.0 per cent in 1961-62 to 39.5 per cent in 1969-70 but slightly declined to 33 per cent in 1970-71. In electrical machinery too, their share has been sizeable. In non-ferrous metals and fertilizers, their share has fluctuating. Table 4.2 gives the share of East European countries in major imports to India.

Table 4.1

Commodity composition of India's imports from East European countries

(percentages)

		1964-65	*1967-68*	*1968-69*	*1969-70*	*1970-71*
1.	Chemicals	3.2	5.90	4.30	7.37	7.30
2.	Fertilizers	0.9	7.71	6.85	4.62	7.10
3.	Iron and Steel	13.0	11.18	6.16	7.73	11.80
4.	Zinc	0.9	1.11	0.65	0.74	1.50
5.	Machinery other than electric	54.0	53.54	39.79	39.22	37.10
6.	Copper	Neg.	0.29	0.03	0.08	0.01
7.	Transport equipment	1.9	3.38	2.73	1.89	2.80
8.	Lead	Neg.	0.03	0.20	0.16	Neg.
9.	Aluminium	Neg.	0.23	0.02	0.07	Neg.
10	Petroleum	4.5	2.46	2.17	4.79	2.90
11.	Others	21.6	24.17	37.10	33.59	24.49
		100.0	100.0	100.0	100.0	100.0

Source : Based on statistics issued by the Office of the Economic adviser, Govt. of India.

The commodity-composition of India's imports from USSR and other East European Countries reveals that India received important capital goods and other industrials essential for the industrial development of the country. Moreover, the bilateral trade and payments agreement has enabled India to obtain these goods in substantial quantities at a time when her free foreign exchange resources were scarce. Since under the arrangement imports are to be paid for by exports, this trading system has provided for a built-in mechanism for export promotion of Indian goods to the USSR and other East European countries.

Table 4.2

Share of East European countries in major import to India

(percentages)

	1961-62	*1964-65*	*1968-69*	*1969-70*	*1970-71*
Chemical elements and compounds	9.3	13.0	16.3	31.0	23.0
Fertilizers	17.2	5.0	14.8	19.4	24.0
Zinc	12.0	13.0	9.9	25.3	18.0
Machinery other than electric	13.0	25.0	32.7	39.5	33.0
Electrical Machinery	8.6	13.3	18.6	15.7	19.0
Iron and Steel	17.2	18.0	21.5	26.3	18.0
Copper	1.0	1.0	0.2	0.5	Neg.
Lead	5.0	11.0	1.1	0.6	Neg.
Aluminium	Neg.	Neg.	3.9	2.4	Neg.
Transport Equipment	3.4	4.0	12.7	10.1	10.9
Dyeing, tanning & colouring materials	4.5	6.0	13.9	5.0	4.4
Professional and scientific instrument	15.9	19.0	24.3	25.9	21.9
Paper and paper board	12.4	15.0	34.3	24.0	17.0

Source : Based on statistics issued by the Office of the Economic Adviser, Govt. of India.

The foreign exchange situation became very serious with the start of the programme of industrialisation during the Second Five Year Plan in India. Table 4.3 brings out how foreign exchange requirements rose much faster than foreign exchange requirements rose much faster than foreign exchange earnings. It is observed from Table 4.3 that from 1950-51 to 1960-61 imports rose from Rs. 65000 mn. to Rs. 11400 mn. or by 75 per cent and further to Rs. 19040 mn. in 1968, or by 67 per cent. During the same years, exports were Rs. 6010 mn. Rs. 6600 mn. and Rs. 13600 mn. respectively. In 1950-51, while savings and investment as a percentage of net domestic product were equal, domestic investment exceeded domestic savings by 3.7 per cent in 1960-61, by 2.8 per cent in 1965-66 and 2.5 per cent in 1968-69 and this gap was filled by external resources. In other words a good part of new investment with a foreign exchange component could be financed by external capital inflows.

Table 4.3

Domestic product, saving, investment and foreign trade, 1950-51 to 1973-74

	1950-51	*1955-56*	*1960-61*	*1965-66*	*1968-69*	*1973-74*
Net domestic product at factor cost (thousand million rupees)	159.6	188.1	208.6	259.7	290.7	383.3
Growth rate	-	3.4	4.0	2.6	3.9	5.7
Mid-year population (in million)	357	390	433	487	527	596
Growth rate	-	1.8	2.1	2.3	2.7	2.5
Investment-income ratio (%)	5.0	7.6	11.5	13.6	11.3	14.5
External resources income ratio (%)	·	0.6	3.7	2.8	2.5	1.3
Saving-income ratio (%)	5.0	7.0	7.8	10.8	8.8	13.2
(1) Household	3.1	5.1	5.3	6.3	6.4	7.6
(2) Corporate	1.1	1.2	1.0	1.2	1.0	1.1
(3) Govt.	0.8	0.7	1.5	3.3	1.4	4.5
Imports (thousand mn. Rs)	6.5	6.8	11.4	14.1	19.0	22.2
Exports (thousand mn.Rs.)	6.0	6.0	6.5	8.1	13.6	19.0

Source : RBI Bulletin, July 1970.

Role of Soviet Co-operation in the Development of Heavy Industry in India

The First Indian Five Year Plan (1 April 1951 to 31 March 1956) had relatively few industrial targets. In the draft outline of the First Plan issued in July, 1951, the Planning Commission described the objectives of the First Plan in the following terms: "The problem before the country is, firstly, to rectify the disequilibrium in the country caused by the warned partition and secondly, to initiate the development of certain basic resources so as to lay the foundation of more rapid economic growth in the future.[5] The essential objective of the Second Plan (1 April 1956 to 31 march 1961) was to secure "rapid advance along democratic and egalitarian lines". Within broad approach, the Second Plan was formulated with the following detailed objectives in view :-

(i) a sizeable increase in national income so as to arise the level of living in the country;

(ii) rapid industrialization with particular emphasis on the development of basic and heavy industries;

(iii) a large scale expansion of employment opportunities; and

(iv) a reduction of inequalities in income and wealth.[6]

The Mahalanobis two-sector model which formed the basis of the Second Five Year Plan emphasized high rates of capital formation putting high priority on building up of heavy industry in the public sector. the Mahalanobis model indicated that the rate of development in the long-run would depend upon the pattern of investment. The capacity to invest (without import of capital goods) in any one year would be determined by the pattern and volume of production of capital goods in the previous year. The rate of expansion of the basic industries, therefore, would set a limit to the rate of growth of the economy as a whole and might also constitute a limiting factor.[7] The strategy of

5. The First Five Year Plan, Planning Commission, Govt. of India, New Delhi, 1951.
6. Second Five Year Plan, Planning Commission, Govt. of India, New Delhi, 1956.
7. Mahalanobis, P.C.: *The Approach of Operational Research to Planning in India,* ISI Statistical series No. 18, Calcutta, 1963.

import substitution was this adopted with special emphasis on investment programmes in heavy industries. Rosenstein-Rodan has described this as a Soviet-type industrialization.[8] As has been suggested, the adoption of this strategy might have been partly due to the fact that Mahalanobis had close contacts with Russian economists and the impressed by Soviet thinking on industrialisation.[9]

The important question still remains whether the decision to develop heavy industries in India was taken after fully exploring the possibilities of "exchanging goods" through foreign trade. From Mahalanobis' speeches, articles and discussions of the plan frame it appears that foreign trade played a secondary role in his thinking. His two-sector model was basically a model of a closed economy. He took for granted the fact that world demand for India's traditional exports was stagnant and therefore import substitution was regarded as the more efficient strategy. As Bhagwati and Chakrabarty have pointed out, the Second Plan did not explicitly state the rationale of the shift to heavy industries in terms of foreign trade constraints so that later justification of this strategy by alluding to "stagnant world demand" for Indian exports was somewhat of an *ex post facto* rationalisation. According to them such a crucial assumption, if made, should have been thoroughly examined, whereas in face the Second Plan made only cursory references to the problem.[10]

Perhaps the reason why India's long-term export prospects or alternative strategies were not discussed in the Second Plan was as Nurkse has pointed out that "stagnant world demand for traditional exports of primary producers" was a part of the accepted orthodoxy, not only in India but among development economists in the West also.[11] However, it is important to mention that the preceding Five Year Plan's experience with the balance of payments and exports was comfortable and it is

8. Rosenstein-Rodan in *The Economics of underdevelopment* ed. by Agarwala, A.N. and Singh, S.P., Oxford University Press, New York, 1963 p.245.
9. Bhagwati, J. and Chakravarty, S .: "Contributions to Indian Econ. Analysis : A Survey" American Econ. Review, Suppliment, Part 2, Sept. 1969, p.7.
10. Ibid
11. Nurkse, R : *Patterns of Trade and Development* (Wicksell Lectures, Stockholm, 1959) Blackwell, Oxford, 1962.

somewhat baffling that India's export prospects could have been viewed with such pessimism as they apparently were.[12]

Still, it would be a case extreme over simplification to conclude that Indian planners adopted the strategy of development of heavy industries due to the USSR's willingness to offer credits, although it may well be true, as Willber points out that the USSR did open up a new era of forced economic growth in agriculturally over populated countries.[13] In India, while the adoption of overall objectives and strategy has been influenced more by domestic factors than by Soviet inspiration, the relative priorities of sectors and industries may have been influenced by the availability of East European credits which permitted the country to overcome the foreign exchange constraints prevailing at the time.

Soviet Aid and Industrial Development

The proportion of Soviet-bloc aid to India grew steadily from practically zero during the First Plan to under 6 per cent of total aid during the Second Plan and under 12 per cent during the Third Plan. The major portion of this aid came from the Soviet Union which supplied over 90 per cent of the total aid from this source over the entire period.

There was no significant external assistance in the First Plan, except in some isolated cases.[14] The plan was essentially to restore the economy form the effects of the devastation caused by the Second World War and the partition and to increase food production in which large deficit had developed after 1947 partition. The success of the First Plan encouraged a bolder and bigger Second Plan with its emphasis on the development of a 'heavy' industries base. The policy of non-alignment (which was considered "immoral" by American Foreign Secretary Dulles) together

12. Bhagwati, J. and Chakravarty, S .: *Contributions to Indian Econ. Analysis* p.12. Lalvani Publishing House, Bombay, 1971. American Econ . Review, Supplement, Part 2, Sept. 1969.
13. Wilber, C.K. : *The Soviet Model and Underdeveloped Countries,* University of North Carolina Press, Chapel Hill, 1969 (p.1).
14. It may be noted that the first instance of external assistance was a loan of $ 189.7 million from USA in 1951 to purchase 2 million tonss of wheat necessitated by the acute food shortage.

with the development of heavy industry in the public sector and the objective of establishing a "socialist pattern of society" were in consonance with the Soviet point of view. This, coupled with the shift in Soviet policy in favour of expanded technical assistance to underdeveloped areas can be said to be responsible for the beginning of Soviet aid in the Second and Third Indian Plans. while lending for industrial projects, the US and the World Bank tried to influence Indian policy in favour of the private sector, the USSR on the other hand was willing to help mostly projects in the public sector.

Indo-Soviet collaboration for development began with the signing of the first credit agreement on February 2, 1955 for the construction of Bhilai Steel Plant. This was the first major agreement of its kind signed by the Soviet Union with any non-communist country. It also marked the beginning of an end of long-standing barrier of isolation between these two countries.

Table 4.4

Soviet assistance authorised upto March 1975
(Rs. in cr. at post-devaluation rates)

	Loans	*Grants*
Upto the end of First Plan	102	-
During the Second Plan	503	1.8
During the Third Plan	158	4.4
During 1966-67	258	2.5
During 1967-68	-	0.8
During 1968-75	-	-
Total :	1021	9.5

Sources : Govt. of India, Ministry of Finance, External Assistance, 1974-75 (p.96).

During the two decades since then (1955-75), the Soviet Union has extended financial assistance to India to the extent of Rs. 1030.5 crores(loans Rs. 1021 crores and grants Rs. 9.5 crores) for a variety of projects in the public sector. Soviet assistance accounted for 8.8 per cent of the total foreign aid authorised to India upto the end of the Fourth Plan. Among all the aid-giving

countries, the Soviet Union's position was second only to USA whose share in the total external assistances was 56.5 per cent in 1972. Table 4.4 shows the amount of Soviet assistance authorised upto march, 1975.

Upto 1974, Soviet aided projects in India numbered 100 odd, of which 80 projects had already been completed or put into operation at least partially. A brief account of the project-wise Soviet credit authorised in favour in India upto the end of march 1974-75 is given in Table 4.5.

The Govt. of USSR had extended 8 credits upto 1974-75 for a total value of Rs. 1021.11 crores for the implementation of development projects of India's Five Year Plans in the Public sector. The notable projects are the Bhilai Steel Plant, the heavy machine building plant at Ranchi, the heavy electrical equipment plant at Ranipur, the mining machinery plant at Durgapur, the oil refineries at Bargarauli, oil exploration at Cambay and other areas, the drugs projects at Rishikesh, Hyderabad and Madras and the Steel plant at Bokaro. In addition, there are the coal mining project at Korba, the coal washery at Kathara, the precision instrument plants at Kota and Palghat, the Ophthalmic glass project at Durgapur and the pumps and compressors projects at Naini.

The entire assistance has been for the development of all these projects in the public sector. As the Soviet preferences has always been for loans, very little has been given by way of grants. The only grants given were for agricultural machinery valued at Rs. 124 lakhs for the Central Mechanised Farm set up at Suratgarh in August, 1956. A provision has also been made through an agreement, dated the 25th November, 1966 for the supply or agricultural machinery for setting up five Central State Farms at an estimated cost of Rs. 150 lakhs. The other grant for equipment worth about Rs. 57 lakhs had been received by the Indian Institute of Technology, Bombay under the Indo-Soviet Agreement signed in December, 1958. The "National Smallpox Eradication Programme" has been assisted by the Soviet Govt. by free supplies of thermostable potent freeze dried smallpox vaccine which is being utilised in the mass vaccination programme. 74000 lakhs doses of freeze dried smallpox vaccine have been received at an approximate cost of Rs. 617 lakhs. Emergency food aid in countries, the Soviet Union's position was second only to USA whose share in the total external assistances was 56.5 per cent in 1972. Table 4.4 shows the amount of Soviet assistance authorised upto march, 1975.

Upto 1974, Soviet aided projects in India numbered 100 odd, of which 80 projects had already been completed or put into operation at least partially. A brief account of the project-wise Soviet credit authorised in favour in India upto the end of march 1974-75 is given in Table 4.5.

The Govt. of USSR had extended 8 credits upto 1974-75 for a total value of Rs. 1021.11 crores for the implementation of development projects of India's Five Year Plans in the Public sector. The notable projects are the Bhilai Steel Plant, the heavy machine building plant at Ranchi, the heavy electrical equipment plant at Ranipur, the mining machinery plant at Durgapur, the oil refineries at Bargarauli, oil exploration at Cambay and other areas, the drugs projects at Rishikesh, Hyderabad and Madras and the Steel plant at Bokaro. In addition, there are the coal mining project at Korba, the coal washery at Kathara, the precision instrument plants at Kota and Palghat, the Ophthalmic glass project at Durgapur and the pumps and compressors projects at Naini.

The entire assistance has been for the development of all these projects in the public sector. As the Soviet preferences has always been for loans, very little has been given by way of grants. The only grants given were for agricultural machinery valued at Rs. 124 lakhs for the Central Mechanised Farm set up at Suratgarh in August, 1956. A provision has also been made through an agreement, dated the 25th November, 1966 for the supply or agricultural machinery for setting up five Central State Farms at an estimated cost of Rs. 150 lakhs. The other grant for equipment worth about Rs. 57 lakhs had been received by the Indian Institute of Technology, Bombay under the Indo-Soviet Agreement signed in December, 1958. The "National Smallpox Eradication Programme" has been assisted by the Soviet Govt. by free supplies of thermostable potent freeze dried smallpox vaccine which is being utilised in the mass vaccination programme. 74000 lakhs doses of freeze dried smallpox vaccine have been received at an approximate cost of Rs. 617 lakhs. Emergency food aid in the form of wheat, soyabean oil, milk powder, baby food etc. valued at Rs. 139.2 lakhs as on March 31, 1968 has also been provided.

It is interesting to note that the Soviet Union has assisted firms and industries in the private sector also, though on a much smaller scale. The first Soviet credit in the private sector was granted to the Hindustan Gas Company (Birlas) to whom equipment was sold in the autumn of 1954 on a deferred payment basis; Hindustan Files, Çalcutta, a subsidiary, received Russian technical aid; a private textile machinery plant was reported to be getting Russian help in 1962. Negotiations were begun for Russian aid in producing lorries in the private sector in 1961 but they provided abortive.[15] This was perhaps a tacit acceptance of the *status quo* implicit in the Mixed economy adopted by India.

Table 4.6 gives a purpose-wise distribution of Soviet aid upto march 31. 1965 and 1972.

Table 4.6

Purpose-wise distribution of Soviet aid

	1965 *(in percentages)*	*1972* *(in percentages)*
Steel	40.0*	53.0
Oil and Gas	19.1	16.0
Power	18.1	14.0
Coal Mining	6.5	5.0
Heavy Machine Building	7.2	9.0
Heavy Electrical Plant	4.9	--
Drug Project	3.1	2.0
Miscellaneous	1.1	1.0
Total :	100.0	100.0

* Excluding Bokaro project agreed to in January, 1965.

Source : External Assistance 1967-68, 1974-75, Ministry of Finance, Govt. of India, Deptt. of Econ. Affairs.

15. Kidron, M : *Foreign Investments in India*, 1965, Oxford University Press, London..

Steel Mill and Soviet Help

A significant development in Indo-Soviet economic relations was the conclusion of an agreement for the construction of a steel plant in India on 2 February 1955. Under this agreement the Soviet Union granted a credit for about 647 million rupees (Rs. 1019.6 mn. at post devaluation rate) for the construction of a steel plant at Bhilai, M.P. with an annual capacity of one million tons of steel, expandable to 2.5 million tons. When India become free her annual output of steel barely exceeded one million tons and even in 1955, about a million tons of steel was imported. The demand for steel was continuously increasing roughly at the rate of 12 per cent per year. The rising bills of the import of steel made it imperative for the Govt. of India to undertake construction of large steel plants in the public sector during the Second Plan period and approached for this purpose her traditional trade partners in the West. In response, the Govt. was given "sermons about creating a favourable climate for private foreign investment, about the advantage of importing steel from them rather than producing it here and the need to concentrate on infra structure".[16] When the West German firms Krupp and Demag were approached before the Bhilai transaction was concluded, they offered credits for building up a steel plant at an annual interest rate of 12 per cent and wanted even in share in the equity capital of the new enterprise.[17] It was in these circumstances that the Soviet Govt. was approached for technical and financial assistance for building a steel plant in the public sector. The USSR readily agreed to it and offered credits on terms then unknown to the Western world. It offered credits at 2.5 per cent interest to be repaid in 12 annual instalments with the export of Indian goods. In those days the Soviet Govt. was supplying complete industrial plants to China and Bulgaria and was conducting trade transition with Czechoslovakia in their national currency. But all these countries were within the Socialist bloc. The fact that India was offered similar terms only underlined the importance the USSR placed on strengthening its links with India.

16. Ten years of Soviet-Indian Econ. co-operation (Information Department of USSR of Embassy, New Delhi), p.30.
17. Ten years of Soviet-Indian Econ. co-operation (Information Department of the USSR Embassy, New Delhi), p.30.

The impact of Soviet offer of credit for Bhilai Steel Plant modified the Western terms for Rourkela and Durgapur Steel Plants in favour of India. For Rourkela Steel Plant the German firms granted a loan of DM 600 million in 1958 at an interest rate of 6.3 per cent for as short period as three years. This involved repayment liabilities of about Rs. 60 crores upto March 1963 i.e. even before the plant reached full production.[18] Though Bhilai Steel Plant started other than Rourkela Steel Plant, it reached its full production capacity before any other steel plant in the public sector. The Soviet Govt. sent its minister for engineering industries to personally direct the construction of the plant. The plant was designed to suit climatic conditions in India. In the words of Eral C. Smith, Chief metallurgist and Director of Research of the Republic Steel Corp. of the USA, Bhilai is "better designed for conditions production than anything that I have seen either in the USA or in Russia proper".[19] Since the beginning of the operations in 1959, the plant has produced 12 million tons of steel ingots and 10 million tons of rolled steel upto 1969. The plant has already exported to Japan, the USSR, Ceylon earning some Rs. 850 million in foreign exchange. Ingot steel was exported to Japan, rails to the Sudan, Ghana, Malaysia and assembled steel sections to Thailand and other countries. As early as 1966-67 the value of the exports of Bhilai Plant was estimated at Rs. 80 mn.[20] In 1969-70, the Bhilai Steel Plant exported steel worth Rs. 42 crores besides contributing about Rs. 150 crores to the state exchequer by way of excise duties and interest on state loans.

So far as the cost estimates of different Steel Plants like Rourkela with West German collaboration, Bhilai with Russian collaboration and Durgapur with British collaboration are concerned, Bhilai had the lowest cost of development among the three. Table 4.7 provides revised estimates of total cost for steel plants.

18. Roy, Ajit : *Planning in India - Achievement and Problems* (National Publishers, Calcutta, 1965), p.330.
19. Rao, V.K.R.V and Narayan, D : *Foreign aid and India's Econ. Development* (Asis Publishing House, 1963), p.45.
20. External Assistance, 1966-67, Govt. of India, Faridabad, 1968, p.95.

Table 4.7

Revised estimates of cost for steel plants. (Rs. in cr.)

	Item	*Rourkela*	*Bhilai*	*Durgapur*
1.	Coke ovens	17.50	10.78	18.88
2.	Blast furnaces	15.29	10.46	18.34
3.	Rolling mills	72.36	42.37	32.53
4.	Total including others	170.00	131.06	137.54

Source : Estimates Committee report 1958-59, 33rd Report, Feb. 1959 (P.13).

So far as the performance of Bhilai Steel Plant is concerned, the cost of production of ingot steel at Bhilai was the lowest, being Rs. 363 (1970-71) per ton. Table 4.8 shows the cost structure per ton ingot of steel for the year 1970-71.

Table 4.8

Plant	*cost per ton (Rs.)*
Bhilai open hearth	363
Rourkela open hearth	429
Rourkela LD	374
TISCO	413
IISCO	446
Durgapur	450

Source : Booklet issued by the Information Department of USSR Embassy in India, New Delhi.

Collaboration Agreement -- A Comparative Study

An underdeveloped country trying for economic development has to depend on other advanced countries for financial and technological help which are necessary for a breakthrough in the path of economic growth. Financial help may take the form of foreign aid; but technological help usually assumes the form of collaboration agreements between developed and underdeveloped countries. The objective of a collaboration agreement is to provide assistance in building the necessary infra structure for economic growth in underdeveloped countries. Indo-Soviet, Indo-German and Indo-British collaboration agreements of financial and technological collaboration for setting up steel mills in India can now be taken up for consideration.

The Soviet Union made the offer to build a steel plant in the middle of 1954. Final order for the plant at Bhilai was placed in April, 1956. For setting up a steel plant at Rourkela in Orissa, the Indian Govt. approached M/s. Krupp and M/s. Demag of West Germany in 1953. Consequently, a Memorandum of Association was signed with a combine of firms consisting of M/s. Fried Krupp Essen and M/s. Demag, Aktiengesellschaft, Dursburg. Negotiations were long-drawn because of the differences over the capacity of the plant and the collaborator's demand for holding 20 per cent of the shares of the company for a period of nine years. The final agreement was signed in July, 1955.

A technical mission with Sir Eric Coates as its head was invited by the Indian Govt. in 1955 to study economic and technical problems connected with the establishment of a steel plant. The mission submitted its report in August 1955. A consortium of 13 British firms known as the India Steel Works Construction Co. Ltd (ISCON) was formed which submitted a preliminary report and estimates in January 1956 and final estimates in May, 1956. The delay in making the final agreement was due to difference over the right of the collaborator to hold the shares of the company.[21]

Both the German and British collaborators raised many objections about policy, management and ideology which made the negotiations long drawn. But as soon as the Soviet Union came on the scene both the German and British collaborators softened their attitudes in favour of India.[22] The equity participation by the collaborators was ruled out in the final agreement. The delay in Soviet appearance on the scene was due to Indian doubts about Soviet technology and competence and what was

21. Committee on Public Undertakings, Reports 29, 30 and 11 are on Durgapur, Bhilai and Rourkela Steel Plants resctively.

22. Goldman, M. : *Soviet Foreign Aid*, Praeger, Washington, 1967 , p.86.

more important about Soviet intentions[23]

Table 4.9

The terms of credit for the aided steel projects : Bhilai, Rourkela and Durgapur

Projects	*Interest rates in percentages*	*Repayment period*	*Grace period*
Durgapur	Consolidated fund rate 5.50 to 6 per cent plus 0.25 per cent management fee	11 years	8 years
Durgapur expansion	Consolidated fund rate 5.50 per cent to 6 per cent plus 0.25 per cent management fee	25 years	7 years
Bhilai	2.50 per cent	12 years	1 year
Bhilai expansion	2.50 per cent	12 years	1 year
Rourkela	6.3 per cent	3 years	3 years
Rourkela services and maintenances	3 per cent	20 years	7 years
Rourkela expansion	5.75 per cent	20 years	5 years
Rourkela refinance	5.25 to 5.50 p.c.	12 to 16 years expect 1960-61 refinance for which only 4 yrs.	Variable

Source : Govt. of India, Ministry of Finance, External Assistance, 1964, pp. 36-40.

The terms of credit offered for Durgapur, Rourkela and Bhilai have been summarised in Table 4.9. The German-aided Rourkela provides the worst example in the bargain. It carried

23. Eldridge, P.: *The Politics of Foreign Aid in India*, Vikas Publication, Delhi, 1969, p. 138.

the highest rate of interest and the repayment period was only 3 years. In fact, it was nothing but purely a commercial transaction, the aid element lying only in the willingness to share the latest German know-how with the Indians. The commercial character was also prominent in the case of British aid to Durgapur. In the cases of both Durgapur land Rourkela, the Govts. of UK and Germany provided only a small percentage of the total aid. The bulk of the aid came from private companies of these countries. One of the important guiding principles of their aid was to derive adequate return for their investment. When they failed in their demand for equity participation, they insisted on building the plants on a turn-key basis and handing them over to India. By contrast, the Soviet collaboration was speedily executed. The terms and conditions of repayment contained concessional elements from the very beginning.

Estimates and Actual Cost of Construction of Rourkela, Durgapur and Bhilai Steel Plants

The original estimate for Bhilai Steel Plant for one million tons was Rs. 110 crores, followed by three revisions of estimates in 1957, 1961 and 1963. The final revised estimate of 1963 for Bhilai was 202.34 crores, the actual cost as on March 1970 being Rs. 199.86 crores. The foreign exchange content was originally estimated to be Rs. 64.7 crores. The final estimates settled down to Rs. 96 crores. In the original estimates foreign exchange constituted 58.8 per cent of the total expenditure, while in the final estimate the foreign exchange for the plant came down to 40.8 per cent of the total expenditure. In the 2.5 million tons expansion cost was Rs. 157.43 crores with foreign exchange content of Rs. 6.5 crores. The actual expenditure was Rs. 151.21 crores as on March 1970. The foreign exchange cost involved was about 32 per cent of total cost.

In case of Rourkela, the original cost estimated were Rs. 128 crores, followed by four revisions upto 1963 at the rate of Rs. 213.85 crores, Rs.221.35 crores, Rs, 223.20 crores and Rs. 230.69 crores. The foreign exchange cost estimated was Rs. 89 crores, but the actual foreign exchange expenditure was 122 crores. The percentage of foreign exchange for both works out to about 69.5 per cent and 52.9 per cent respectively. The expansion programme after a number of revisions finally cost Rs. 154.59 crores of which the foreign exchange content was Rs. 79.5 which works out to be 54.5 per cent of the total cost.

Table 4.10 provides project estimates and actual for Bhilai, Rourkela and Durgapur Steel Plants.

Table 4.10

Project estimates and actualls for Bhilai, Rourkela and Durgapur Steel Plants at the one million stage

(Rs. in crores)

Units	*Original estimates 1955*	*Revised estimates 1957*	*Revised estimates 1961*	*Revised estimates 1963*	*Actual estimates upto March 1970*
Bhilai	110.0	178.65	199.32	202.34	199.86
Durgapur	115.0	167.00	199.05	201.26	230.69
Rourkela	128.0	213.85	221.33	233.20	230.69

Project estimates and actualls for Bhilai, Rourkela and Durgapur Steel Plant's expansion.

(Rs. in crores)

Units	*Estimates drawn up by consultants*	*First estimates drawn up by HSL*	*Revised estimates drawn up by HSL*	*Estimates sanctioned by the Board*	*Estimates sanctioned by the Govt.*	*Actual upto March 1970*
Bhilai 2.5 mn	104.60 (1961)	157.30 (1962)	165.88 (1964)	164.35 (1965)	138.14 (1965)	151.20
Durgapur 1.6 mn	66.20 (1962)	64.61 (1963)	69.70 (1963)	60.59 (1965)	58.65 (1965)	64.43
Rourkela 1.8 mn	77.65 (1961)	113.17 (1962)	135.70 (1963)	124.48 (1965)	105.53 (1965)	154.59

Source : CPU-First Report, Hindustan Steel Ltd. Fifth Lok Sabha, 1971-72 (pp.97-98).

If we compare these figures about project estimates and actualls of Bhilai, Rourkela and Durgapur we find that the Soviet aided Bhilai offered better terms. In German-aided Rourkela, the share of foreign exchange to total cost worked out to the highest -52.9 per cent; whereas in Bhilai the figure was 40.8 per cent of total expenditure. The Germans at Rourkela wanted to bring everything, even "a carpenter" all the way from Germany. Moreover, only in Rourkela, the LD-process was employed for making steel in addition to the open hearth process. An examination of tables 4.11 and 4.12 shows that the capacity of Rourkela is only 1.8 million tons, the units are more complex and sophisticated than those of Bhilai. Besides the rolling mills which constitute a complex combination of many units, fertilizer and tube plants have been integrated into the project. By contrast, Bhilai represents a bigger unit; its process is simple and its final products consist mainly of pig iron, steel structural and rails. Accordingly, it is not very easy to compare the project cost unless we can get down to details about the structure of the plants.

Table 4.11

Various units of Bhilai Steel Plant, the products and capacity.

	Main equipment	*Product capacity (tons)*	*Yearly rated*
1.	6 coke oven batteries of 65 ovens each	coke (dry)	2,198,000
2.	3 blast furnances of 1033 cubic metre each and 2 furnances of 1719 cubic metre each	hot metal cold pig	2,361,000 3,30,000
3.	3 pig casting machines	pig iron	3,30,000
4.	3 sintering machines of 50 sq. metre hearth area each	fluxed sinter	1,520,000
5.	10 sationary basic open hearth furnaces-5 of 250 tones capacity each and 5 of 500 tons capacity	ingot steel	2,5000,000

(Contd.)

	Main equipment	Product capacity (tones)	Yearly rated
6.	1150 millimetre blooming mill with 13 groups of soaking pits	blooms (semis)	2,142,000
7.	1000/700/500 millimetre continuous billet mill with 12 stands	billet (semis)	1,263,000
8.	950/800 millimetre rail and structural	rails, structural	500,000 250,000
9.	350 millimetre rail and structural	rails, structural	500,000
10.	250 millimetre wire road mill	wire rods	400,000

Source : CPU-report 30, Bhilai Steel Plant of HSL, April, 1966.

Table 4.12

Various units Rourkela Steel Plant, Product and Capacity

	Units of the plant	*Product*	*Yearly rated capacity (tons)*
1.	4 coke oven batteries with 290 ovens	coke	1,880,00
2.	Byproduct plant treating coke oven gas of 105000	benzene, toluence, xylence etc.	-
	Blast Furnace		
3.	3 blast furnaces of 1000 tons per day and 1 blast furnace of 1500 tons per day	hot metal	1,600,000 (about)
4.	2 pig casting machine	pig iron	
	Steel Melting Shop		

(Contd.)

Units of the plant	Product	Yearly rated capacity (tons)
5. 4 basic stationery open hearth furnaces of 80 tons each	ingot steel	300,000
6. 3 LD converters of 40 tons each and 2 LD converters of 80 tons each	ingot steel	1,500,000
7. 2 sintering plants of 4000 tons fluxed sinter daily	fluxed sinter	1,200,000
3 mixers of 1100 tons each	-	-
5 vertical shaft lime kilns	-	-
2 vertical shaft dolomite	-	-
1 rotary calcium kilns	-	-
3 units of 100 tons/day	Oxygen	-
1 unit of 200 tons/day (plant)		
Rolling Mills		
Soaking pit : 11 batteries	-	-
Blooming and slabbing mill slabs	-	1,800,000
4 slab reheating furnaces	-	-
1 plate mill	plates	450,000
1 wide strip mill	plates	480,000
Cold rolling mill	rolled sheets	260,000
	hot tipped tin plates	50,000
	electrolytic tin plates	150,000
	galvanized sheets	160,000
1 continuous annealing line	-	-
48 hood type stack annealing furnaces	-	-

(Contd.)

Units of the plant	Product	Yearly rated capacity (tons)
2 continuous pickling line	pickled coils	768,000
1 electric sheet mill	electrical sheets	50,000
4 high single stand cold rolling mills one 5-stand tandom mill	plates	600,000

Source : CPU-report 11, Rourkela Steel Plant of HSL, May 1965.

Comparative Estimates of the Public Sector Steel Plants--Operational Costs

In respect of utilization of capacity in the three public sector steel plants, Bhilai showed a progressive improvement both in saleable steel and ingot steel. Capacity-utilization in ingot steel production improved from 45.2 per cent in 1964-65 to 77.23 per cent in 1970-71. It also improved in saleable steel production from 46.6 per cent in 1964-65 to 78.4 per cent in 1970-71. In case of Durgapur, capacity utilization in saleable and ingot steel deteriorated from 58.2 per cent and 62.88 per cent respectively in 1964-65 to 39.8 per cent respectively in 1970-71.[24] Though the performance of Rourkela is better than that of Durgapur, the capacity utilization has fluctuated between 51 per cent and 65 per cent. In Durgapur because of lack relative industrial peace there were slight prospects of improvement in capacity utilisation. Rourkela faced the prospects of very low capacity utilization because of the roof collapse and damages to the plant.

The actual production cost of steel in the various Indian units shows that Bhilai is the most economical unit even when compared with the two private sector plants. Table 4.13 provides the cost of production per ton of ingot steel produced in various steel plants in India.

24. Annual Report of HSL - various issues.

Table 4.13

Cost of production per tonne of ingot steel produced in various steel plants in India

(Rs. per ton)

Units		*1968-69*	*1969-70*
TISCO		320.00	320.00
IISCO		336.95	336.95
Bhilai		286.30	286.31
Rourkela :	Open hearth	316.75	316.75
	LD-process	323.02	323.62
Durgapur		335.19	355.19

Source : CPU-report 1, Hindusthan Steel Ltd, 5th Lok Sabha, 1971-72, p.34

Bhilai has also the lowest investment per ton among the public sector units. Table 4.14 shows the gross block investment per ton of steel ingot of various units.

Table 4.14

Gross block investment per ton of steel ingot produced by various steel plants in India

Units	Capacity (million tons)	Investment per ton of steel(rupees)
Bhilai	2.5	1,441
Rourkela	1.8	2,264
Durgapur	1.6	2,721
Bokaro	4.0	2,752
Tata Iron and Steel Co.	2.2	1,342
Indian Iron and Steel Co.	1.3	1,131

Source : CPU Report 1, Hindusthan Steel Ltd, 5th Lok Sabha, 1971-71, p.99

Financial Returns

Among the three public sector steel plants, Bhilai has shown the best financial returns. During 1959-1969, Rourkela provided profit only in three years, while Bhilai was able to make net profit in 6 years. Between 1966 and 1969 Indian engineering industries experienced a recession, in addition to breakdowns and labour troubles in Bhilai. Durgapur steel plant fared worse than the other two plants. Table 4.15 gives an idea of financial returns in these plants.

Table 4.15

Financial returns of the 3 public sector steel plants

Loss (-) Profit (+) (Rs. in lakhs)

Year	*Bhilai*	*Rourkela*	*Durgapur*
1959-60	+ 3.15	- 291.00	- 33.00
1960-61	+ 152.69	- 659.00	- 71.00
1961-62	- 388.57	- 1092.00	- 466.00
1962-63	- 448.93	- 1072.00	- 845.00
1963-64	+ 150.03	- 625.00	- 18.17
1964-65	+ 50.28	+ 350.20	+ 53.34
1965-66	+ 155.21	+ 503.64	- 231.31
1966-67	- 171.73	- 193.81	- 1316.41
1967-68	- 815.89	- 708.80	- 1737.95
1968-69	- 1119.41	- 305.50	-1749.08
1969-70	+ 305.00	+ 783.00	- 1550.00

Source : Annual Report of HSL, various.

Export

Bhilai is not only running on profit, but it has been exporting steel to 40 countries including USA, UK, France, Itlay, Japan, the UAR and other Far Eastern and Middle Eastern countries.[25] Upto 1969, Bhilai had supplied more than 6.2 million tons of pig iron and 13 million tons of steel products to the internal market.

25. F.M. Tahilraman (Public Relations Officer, Bhilai Steel Plant), "Bhilai, India's Biggest Steel Plant", Yojana, April 19, 1970, p.17.

In addition, export to other countries aggregated over Rs. 160 crores.

Bhilai's efforts in the field of export performance are brought out in Table 4.16.

Table 4.16

Bhilai's Export

Year	*Value of export of iron and steel (Rs, in crores)*		*Bhilai's share %*
	Bhilai	*All India*	
1966-67	5.64	20.00	28
1967-68	24.66	53.49	46
1968-69	31.97	69.60	46
1969-70	35.09	75.71	46
1970-71	46.07	66.71	69

Source : Annual Reports of HSL.

Bokaro Steel Plant

When we compare two or three steel plants, the costs differ according to the location, the production process, output and the raw materials used etc. Therefore in order to arrive at a meaningful comparison, it is necessary to ensure that the two or three projects under comparison should be similar in all essential respects. The best comparison is only possible where two or more bids are tendered for the same type of project. Bokaro Steel Plant provides such a case where the Govt. of USSR and American private steel firms offered their individual bids for the same kind of project. Table 4.17 provides the cost estimates of USSR and USA for the construction of Bokaro steel project.

The above table shows that the Russian bid was higher by about 25% than that of USA. There can be no question that the Soviet bid was inflated since the general experience with Soviet estimates has been that they leave out many items. On the other hand, it is difficult to judge the accuracy of American bid since it was never implemented. The constraining condition in the matter of acceptance of the American proposal was that the Bokaro steel plant would be under American management for a period of 10 years with a maximum number of 670 American technicians. But the consideration paramount to the growth of Indian steel industry was that such development should take place in the public sector. This constraint affected the strength of the Indian bargaining position in the outcome of Soviet-Indian negotiations on Bokaro.

Table 4.17

Total cost of construction of Bokaro Steel Plant

	Stage I	Stage II	Stage III	Cumulative
USA (m.$)	827.3	237.8	316.9	1,504.8
(m.Rs.)	3,939.6		1,506.2	7,147.8
USSR(m.Rs.)	4,860.0		6,940.0	10,273.32

Source : For the USSR : Dastur and Co. : Cost Reduction study on Bokaro Project (p.3, Table 4), Calcutta, May 1966.
For USA : Elliot, R. and Wagner, R. : Synopsis of a techno-economic survey of a proposed integrated steel plant at Bokaro (p.57, Washington D.C. 1963).

Note : The cumulative figures include capitalised interest, technical assistance before starting, personnel, recruiting costs, raw materials, stockpiles and miscellaneous items.

Soviet estimates, since they were not all comprehensive left out items such as design engineering, the cost of land, training commissioning, township, interest on investment etc. Within a year, the project-cost of Bokaro (stage I) increased form Rs. 5,400 million to Rs. 6,200 mn. This increase was due partly to devaluation of rupee in 1966 and partly to omission of a number of items.

By the time aid negotiations wear initiated for the establishment of Bokaro steel plant, India had already reached a stage of technological maturity with high local expertise in designing and construction. The prestigious Indian firm M.N. Dastur and Co. was actively associated with the early planning of the project and had the competence to assess critically the proposed Soviet designs. It was however muscled out by the Soviet negotiators from the final aid contract. The conclusion of Dastur and Co's report on the Soviet proposal was that the costs of Soviet project were too high "even after taking into account the increase in import duties and escalation of equipment and construction costs during the last two or three years". It is also known, from the report that "steel plants designed to produce flat products with facilities comparable to Bokaro are under construction or have been completed during the past few years in Britain, France, Italy the Japan at less than one-half the estimated cost of Bokaro".[26] Table 4.18 shows the estimates of total plant costs of different steel workers.

Table 4.18

Estimates of total plant costs of different steel works

Steelworks	*year of completion*	*Initial ingot steel capacity (mn tons per year)*	*Total plant cost (mn tons per year)*	*Plant cost per annual ingot tons Rs.*
Fukuyama (Japan)	1966	1.50	1,488	992
Spencer Works (U.K.)	1962	1.40	1,638	1,170
Taranto (Italy)	1964	2.50	2,153	860
Dunkirk (France)	1963	1.50	1,440	960
Bokaro				
(USSR proposal)	Stage I	1.70	4,860	2,860

Source : Dastur, M.N. and Co. : Cost Reduction Study on Bokaro Project, Calcutta, May 1966 (p.3).

It should be noted that although the plant listed in Table 4.18 were similar in terms of facilities and production programmes, there were important difference due to location and use of raw materials. A more accurate comparison would be in terms of difference in the costs of producing steel at Bokaro under Soviet and American initiative. Table 4.19 provides such a comparison.

26. Dastur, M.N. and Co : *Cost reduction study on Bokaro Project*, Calcutta, May 1966 (p.3).

Table 4.19

Comparison of Bokaro plant cost per annual ingot ton : the US and the USSR

	Step I	*Step II*	*Step III*
U.S. (Rs.)	2,479		1,447
($)	522	381	311
U.S.S.R. (Rs.)	2,860		1,735

Source : For the USSR : Dastur and Co. (p.3,Table 4).
For USA : Elliot and Wagner (p.57).

The foreign exchange cost in the American proposal was Rs.2,435 million which would be financed by a loan of 20 years at 5 3/4 per cent interest. But the foreign exchange component of the Soviet proposal was much smaller--190 mn. roubles which was revised later to 200 mn. roubles or Rs. 1,058 mn. at predevaluation exchange rate. The foreign exchange component was to be financed by Soviet credit to be repaid in 12 years at a 2½ per cent interest.

The basic difference between the Soviet and American approach to industrialization in less developed countries like India can be summarized as follows : the early American approach was opposed to the development of basic and heavy industry and the strengthening of the public sector. Although this attitude to a large extent has receded to the background in recent years and there is more purposeful collaboration in the development of light consumption industries, social overheads and some flows of aids to heavy industries, the basic dislike regarding this approach is still there. This can be understood from the outpourings of many Western economists who regard the creation of steel and capital goods plants in India as nothing but an example, of "conspicuous consumption" and dismiss such economic activities as an indication of economic inefficiency.[27]

M.I. Goldman observed correctly that "Bokaro could have provided a "flagship" project for the whole American aid effort.

27. Bhagwati, J. (1966) : *The Economics of underdeveloped countries,* World University Library, London, (p.166).

It could also have posed an effective counter to Soviet aid, not only in India but wherever the Russians made claim that Americans are unwilling to promote industrial projects".[28] But Americans failed to utililse this opportunity due to the predominance of the philosophy of private enterprise. Another source of dispute was regarding management and ownership. The Americans emphasized the 'turn-key' concept under which the American would build the plant, manage it for a period of 10 years and then hand it over to India in perfect working order. But the Soviet approach was more co-operative. As a donor country she respected and appreciated India's abilities and ideologies. Bokaro as it has been built up also represents virtually an example of turn-key project of the Soviets. But a distinguishing feature of Bokaro Steel Plant is that 63.5 per cent of its equipments, 92.5 per cent of its steel structures, 77 per cent of refractories and other materials have been supplied form indigenous sources like Heavy Electrical Equipment Plant at Hardwar and Precision Equipment Plant at Kota which were also set up with Soviet economic and technical assistance, while hardly 10 per cent of Equipment and structures were supplied from indigenous sources of Bhilai.

But all was well with the Bokaro Steel Plant. Dastur and Co. in their cost reduction study pointed out that although the Soviet design for the blast furnace and sinter plant were excellent, the proposed steel melting shops and rolling mills needed major modifications. Soviet project report provided for two separate steel melting shops for the four-million-stage plant. In the initial stage it was to have five 100-ton converters and two 250-ton converters in the next stage. Dastur Co's study argued in favour of installing large sized converters at the initial stage itself which would produce some advantages arising out of economies of scale. This argument was further supported by evidence indicating a world trend towards large sized converters for cost reduction purposes. Dr. Dastur in his evidence before the Committee on Public Undertaking (CPU) stated that the Russians have given India an antiquated design for LD Plant. 100-ton LD converters are not used for a big plant like Bokaro. According to him, 300 tonne LDs are absolutely standard and with one LD converter we can get 2 mn. ton of steel. So by putting four or five 100 ton

28. Goldman, M. (1967) : *Soviet Foreign Aid*, F.A. Praeger, Washington (p.92).

LD converters, capital cost and operating costs are raised. But these modifications for the steel melting shops were not accepted by the Soviet side. The 68th Report of the CPU reproduces the explanations given by the Soviet experts : "We can supply to India all the equipments which have been thoroughly checked up in operations in the Soviet Union. We can supply only equipments which can be commissioned straightway and which can be mastered on the basis of our experience at our own steel plants. We are producing 100-ton converters. Today we are not in a position to supply India other converters of higher capacities. The 250 ton converters are now being installed in some of the steel melting shops and we will be in a position to supply them to India after we have gained enough experience in their operations. for the second stage, we will be able to supply such converters."

Another equally damaging criticism centers round the proposed slabbing mill which was stated to be too large. The recent applications of the method of continuous casting were likely to render the proposed Soviet mill technologically by obsolete. The cost reduction study pointed out that the above technique had been well developed in the USSR and adopted at several plants. More specifically, it indicated that at the Novo Lipetsk plant, an LD converter shop and wide strip mill are now under completion together with a continuous casting plant in preference to a slabbing mill. The Soviet side rejected the alternative size of the slabbing mill as proposed by Dastur Co. on the ground that the saving expected would be marginal. According to Soviet experts the adoption of large-sized converters and the continuous casting method were of recent origin and the USSR had only just begun implementing these in its now steel plants. Therefore, it seems futile to insist that the Soviets should have done better than the best they could do by their own admissions. According to an OECD study, installation planned before 1964 for the Azovstal works was to consist of five converters, each of 250 ton capacity (to be increased to 300 tons). Again the converter sizes already planned for the new Novo Lipetsk Plants second stage of 3.8 mn. tons per annum was to have three converters of 250-ton capacity each. The study also pointed out that by 1960 the various economic and technical advantages of the continuous casting method were widely acknowledged by Soviet experts. From the above study it appears likely that if Bokaro were to be set up in the Soviet Union, it would have been designed with a provision for large-sized converters and without a slabbing mill.

To summarize the impact of Soviet assistance for the building up of the steel industry in India, one can point out that Bhilai Steel Plant (1955) and Bokaro (1964) are two significant milestones in the field of steel production in India. Steel production is the soul of industrialization. More than 50 per cent of India's total steel production now comes from the Soviet-aided steel projects. Moreover, Soviet entry into the field was an additional boon to India's steel productions. As Dr. V.K.R.V. Rao has pointed out "had there been no Bhilai, there would been no Rourkela or Durgapur".[29]

The late Nikita Khruschev was not wrong when he pointed out "you should write Rourkela and Durgapur Steel plants also to our account". If the Soviet Union did not exist, it is unlikely that imperialist powers would come to the aid of the underdeveloped countries[30] in their process of industrialization.

Oil Exploration

Oil plays a very vital role in the economic life of a country. Industrialization and modernisation would be stalled without the rapid growth in oil consumption. Oil is regarded as the most profitable commodity in international trade in recent times. But this commodity was being controlled by even major integrated oil companies of Western and American countries with the full support and co-operation of their Govts.

One should consider the problems of development of the oil industry in India against this background. Since 1957-58, the foreign exchange crisis became acute in Indian economy. The stagnation of India's exports had led to a widening gap between export earnings and import-requirements. Export earnings financed 83.4 per cent of India's total imports during the First Five Year Plan (1951-56). during the Second Five Year Plan the proportion of imports financed by current export earnings fell to 56.2 per cent.

29. Quoted by B. Natarajan in Soviet Review, Aug.17, 1970 (p.34).
30. Tansky, L: U.S. and USSR aid to developiing countries, New York, 1967 (p.5).

Import of capital goods constituted a major cause of foreign exchange crisis and consequently there was large scale withdrawal from foreign exchanges reserves accumulated during the 2nd World War. From 1951 to 1960 India's sterling balances were drawn down by Rs.7,360 million. Another reason for the aggravation of the foreign exchange problem was that the annual import bill oil had risen to a level of Rs. 100 crores per annum. So one of India's planning objectives was to achieve self-sufficiency in the matter of oil production. Standard Vacuum Oil Co. (Stanvac), California Taxas Oil Corporation (Caltex) of USA and Burmah shell of Great Britain enjoyed monopolist position so far as processing on crude oil in refineries and distribution were concerned. It was virtually impossible for a country like India to build her oil industry with the help of these 'oil majors'.

Regarding the question of co-operation between these oil companies and India Govt., important differences arose on the question of equity shares in refineries, the setting up of refineries and reduction in the price of crude. Being unable to get to the co-operation of these 'oil majors' the Indian Govt. determined to acquire the 'know-how' of oil production from whatever source was available and in the shortest possible time. The Soviet Union came forward with the objective of breaking private-sector monopolies in oil. After 5 months of study, the Soviet experts submitted their report in April 1956 and estimated that 40,000 square miles of prospective area of oil and natural gas were available in India and the reserves of oil would amount to 4 billion tons, while gas reserves would amount to 2 trillion cubic meters.[31] Following this, the Govt. took steps for the establishment of its own exploration agency, the Oil and Natural Gas Directorate and later ONGC. The Soviet Union offered all the initial help set up this agency by training a large number of fresh graduates in Geology in the various spheres of oil operations. The first success was achieved near Jawalamukhi in Punjab in the form of gas and later oil was struck in Cambay in Gujarat. The biggest success was the Ankleshwar oil deposits. The year 1961 is regarded as a "lucky year" for India since in that year oil deposits were discovered in Kalol and Rudrasagar in Navagam,

31. T. Nath : "India's Developing Oil Industry" Soviet Review, January 31, 1970 (p.49)

Lakhwa, Kadi, Sobasan and other places. More than 20 oil deposits had been discovered with Soviet collaboration. The Soviet Union has so far deputed more than 850 Soviet oil workers to India for rendering technical help, while 3800 Indian specialists got their training in the USSR. It is interesting to note that foreign oil companies were exploiting India throughout early 1950s, but they were not prepared to reduce their profit margins nor to explore for crude oil in India until the USSR emerged as a major oil exporter with the capacity to offer economic and technical assistance for establishing petroleum industry in the public sector. Thanks to the USSR's world wide campaign for breaking the stronghold of the major oil companies on the world market, India received benefit first in the form of lower prices of crude oil following Soviet entry and secondly through the establishment of the petroleum refining industry in the public sector.

In this connection it has been emphasized by Mr. Levy, one of the world's leading oil consultants and other western representatives of oil companies that developing countries should not undertake exploration of petroleum because it is highly risky with high costs and heavy overheads. According to Levy's estimate the average cost of exploration is to the tune of US $ 2,000 per cent barrel per day. "The capital costs of building up crude transportation, processing etc. which could add up to another US $ 150 million".[32] He also points out that investment in exploration is not associated with quick returns but matures very slowly. It appears that Mr. Levy puts too much emphasis only on the high risk-factor associated with this business. There must be equally compensating rewards, as otherwise nobody would be willing to participate in the business.

Tanzer in a book on politics and economics of oil has estimated that in 1966 earnings on petroleum investment accounted for 60 per cent of all US earnings in underdeveloped countries and the average rate of return on investment was 20 per cent with a maximum of 55 per cent.[33]

32. Levy, W.J.: *Search for oil in developing countries*, Report prepared at the request of IBRD, New York, 1960 n(Chap. 1).

33. Tanzer, M : *The Political Economy of International Oil and the Underdeveloped Countries*, Beacon Press, London, 1969, p.41-42.

Moreover, an oil-company handbook points out that the risk of failure in drilling can be reduced to a large extent at present due to advances made in geology and geophysics.[34] A report on the oil industry in the USSR says that the success ratio in the USSR has risen very rapidly, the success ratio of expiratory wells has been claimed to have gone up.by 50 per cent as a result of systematic planning and co-ordination of the geological, gravity-magnetic, seismic and structural drilling data.[35]

The Indian Refineries Ltd (Later ambulated with the Indian Oil Company Ltd to form, in 1964 the Indian Oil Corporation) established Rumanian collaboration and in Barauni and in Koyali with Soviet collaboration. The initial annual capacity of these 3 refineries was about 7 mn. tons, compared to the total approved annual capacity (in 1963) of 7.5 mn. tons for refineries of the oil companies.

Total investment in the petroleum industry amounted to about Rs. 4,000 million upto 1970. It was less than 2 per cent of total public sector outlays in the successive plans. Out of the above investment expenditure about Rs. 3,000 million was raised domestically and the rest which constituted the foreign exchange component of the programme was financed from external sources (mainly Soviet Russia). The important question here is : whether India could have obtained the same amount in external assistance from the private oil companies. From the behaviour of the private oil companies it is obvious that they were least interested in the matter as they had more than enough to offer in the market.

Another indirect benefit of Soviet entry was that the western private firms now made counter offers with more favourable terms for India. Refineries of Cochin, Madras and Haldia are examples to the point. Goldman has narrated the events as follows : "There was considerable evidence to indicate that the Indians had paid an exorbitant prices for Russian help. By the time the Indian had decided to build a third refinery at Koyali, the western firms realised the seriousness of the situation and began to make counter efforts. In addition, once the cartel had been

34. Royal Dutch Shell Ltd : The Petroleum Handbook London, 1959, p.71-72.
35. National Productivity Council of India : The Oil Industry in the USSR, Czechoslovakia and Rumania, NPC-Preport No.18, New Delhi, 1962, p.10.

broken, other western firms decided to enter the field. Consequently, Philip Petroleum Company of the USA, Amoco India (a subsidiary of Standard Oil of Indian) and the National Iranian Oil Company won the right to build the two joint-sector refineries for the Indian Govt. at Cochin and Madras. Their plan called for an initial capacity of 5.0 million tons per annum.

This provoked bids from ENI (The Italian State-owned oil corporation) and other western firms. Thus, for the first time, India was permitted the luxury of competitive offers.[36] As the Soviet Union is very sensitive about its image among the developing countries, it responded quickly by reducing the cost of the refinery at Koyali.

Table 4.20

(percentages)

Market share of private and Govt. Oil companies.

Year	*Indian Oil Corporation*	*Burmah shell, Esso. Caltex*	*Others*
1960	0.2	92.5	7.3
1965	21.0	73.4	5.6
1968	42.5	53.8	3.7
1970	51.5	44.8	3.7
1972	57.3	37.9	4.8

Source : "Market participation of Oil Companies", Indian Petroleum Handbook, 1973 (p.342).

With the pick up of indigenous curde production particularly from the ONGC's oil fields in Gujarat and the decline in the rate of growth of domestic consumption, the monopoly power of the foreign oil companies began to decline. While in 1960 the oil companies accounted for 100 per cent of the total installed feminine capacity, this figure had fallen to 92.12 per cent in 1963; in 1968 it was 64.4 per cent and in 1973, it was as low as 42.28 per cent. The situation was made more difficult by declining utilisation levels. Thus, utilised capacity as a percentage of installed capacity fell from 89.24 per cent in 1963 to 61.37 per cent in

36. Goldman, M .: *Soviet Foreign Aid*, Praeger, New York, 1967, pp.98-99.

1968 and to 55.99 per cent in 1973. Accordingly, the raked share of the Oil Corporation increased rapidly.[37] Table 4.20 shows the market share of private and Govt. oil companies during the period (1960-1972).

To sum up : If an investment is justified by its net result, investment in oil exploration which was about Rs. 400 crores upto 1970 was worthwhile form the Indian point of view. The investment in oil yielded better results than almost the same amount of investment in Rourkela and Durgapur Steel Plants which resulted in substantial cumulative losses.

Drugs :

Another important field in which Soviet contribution has been of great help is Drugs and pharmaceuticals. Upto 1953-54 about 95 per cent of total production in this sector was controlled by private foreign companies. In 1954 during the years of the First Plan, there were 1600 registered units out of which 28 units produced two-fifths of the total value of finished drugs. These 28 large houses were practically all foreign-owned. The patent rights in India favoured foreign firms till the new patents' bill was passed early in 1970. Foreign firms controlled nine-tenths of the patents granted in India and all the patents were in essential drugs upto 1958.[38] It is an irony of fate that the people of low income countries like India were forced to pay high price for drugs. Liberium, a tranquilizer was sold in India at Rs. 22,000 per kg, whereas it was sold in foreign countries at Rs. 303 per kg. Different brands of tetracycline whose cost was 48 cents per 16 capsules of 250 milligrams each were sold in India at 6.52 dollars per 16 capsules in 1959, An American Senate Committee made an important observation in this regard : "Prices in India for the broad spectrum antibiotics, aureomycin and achromycin are among the highest in the world. As a matter of fact, in drugs generally, India ranks among the highest priced nations of the world a case of an inverse relationship between per capita income and the level of drug prices".[39] The Pharmaceutical Inquiry Com-

37. All the figures are form "Indian Petroleum Handbook, 1973.
38. M. Kidron; *Foreign Investment in India*, Oxford Univ. Press, 1965 (p.211-12).
39. Cited in M. Kidron : *Foreign Investment in India*, Oxford Univ. Press, 1965 p.251.

mittee in 1954 and the Health Survey and Planning Committee in 1961 had found that patent rights were mostly responsible for exorbitant drug prices in India.

The Govt. of India was naturally looking for help to establish a dependable drug industry. No western country was willing to help without heavy royalty payments. The Soviet Union showed its willingness to assist India in the field of drugs, but the Govt. of India hesitated in accepting the offer because of the fact that Kane's Report recommended the adoption of Western technology for Indian Pharmaceutical Industry.[40]

After a year's hesitation, India accepted the Soviet offer and in April 1958, the Soviet Union made an offer of aid of Rs. 9.52 crores for establishing plants for the manufacture of synthetic drugs, antibiotics, surgical instruments, phyto-chemicals glandular products etc. in the public sector. This credit offer involved an interest payment at the rate of 2.5 per cent only per annum with no provision for royalty payment.

This Soviet offer was an important factor in the American Merck and Co's willingness to help another public owned company, Hindusthan Antibiotics Ltd. in Pimpri near Poona. But the agreement involved a fairly high royalty payment--2.5 per cent after tax on sales in India and 5 p.c. on sales abroad. Moreover there were provisions for the screening of scientist and classification of information about the plant applied to various parties according to Merck's satisfaction.[41]

Soviet aided IDPL projects could not make their expected impact on the drug market by bringing down the prices of drugs since they could not make any profit upto 1970. The performance of the plants improved after 1971 and gave rise to the hope that the expected impact would be realized. Although it is largely true that the poor performance of the Indian public sector undertakings has been due to inefficient operation, one should not for this reason discount the impact of Soviet aid in building up an independent drug industry in India.

40. CPU Report, Indian Drugs and Pharmaceuticals Ltd, 46th report, Lok Sabha, p.2.
41. M. Kidron : *Foreign Investment in India*, Oxford Univ. Press, 1965, p.164.

Heavy Engineering

One of the basic objectives of Indian planning was to secure rapid industrialisation with particular emphasis on heavy and basic industries. So far as the Soviet Union is concerned, the above objective was in keeping with her avowed ideology that basic heavy industry was essential for the economic independence of any country. The Govt. of India invited in the mid-50's two teams of experts to advise on the establishment of a plant for the manufacture of heavy machinery and equipment. One team was from the USSR and the other from the British Heavy Engineering Mission. The Soviet team's suggestion was for the establishment of an economically viable unit of 80,000 tons capacity to be expanded to 165,000 tons. The British team suggested, on the other hand, the establishment of a number of smaller units to be dispersed in different parts of the country. Although the Jehangir Gandhi Committee set up by the Govt. of India favoured the British proposal, the Govt. of India ultimately opted for the Russian proposal in 1957. The original plan was to have three units : a heavy machine building project, a foundry forge project and a coal mining machinery project. But in the final decision, the Coal Mining and Allied machinery project with Soviet help was decided to be set up at Durgapur and run as a separate corporation.

The Heavy Machine Building plant aided by USSR along with the Czechoslovakia-aided Foundry Forage Plant and Heavy Machine Tool Plant was constituted into another Corporation known as the Heavy Engineering Corporation Ltd.

The Heavy Machine Buildings plant at Ranchi, Bihar had designed annual production capacity of 80,000 tons of Heavy machinery and 25,000 tons of structural fabrication, to be achieved by 1975-76. It actually manufactured 23,850 tons of Heavy Machinery in 1968-69, 27,000 tons in 1970. There had been delays in the completion of the work, specially in the Foundry Forage Plant Section. So production was far below expectations. But the Ranchi plant supplied all structural and metallurgical equipment that was required for Bhilai's 6th blast furnace and over and above that it manufactured over 19,520 tonnes of structural and 7,056 tons of equipment towards its total share of 84,511 tons required for the first stage of construction of the Bokaro Steel

Plant.

Besides steel plant equipments, the Ranchi plant manufactures various sophisticated mechanical and metallurgical equipments required for the oil, mining, cement and other industries.

The Central Electrical and Mechanical Workshop at Korba, Madhya Pradesh had set up with Soviet assistance to meet the demand for major repairs and spare parts manufacturing facilities required for the operation of both open-cast and underground mining machinery and equipment in an around MP. The workshop consists of a large number of sections such as tool shop, main machine shop, auto-car shop and shops for heat treatment, forging, steel fabrication, repair. Apart from catering to the requirements of the NCDC (National Coal Development Corporation), the workshop would also be able to serve other sister industries in the MP region and Public enterprises like Bharat Aluminium Ltd, MP State Electricity Board etc.

Heavy Electricals

The Heavy Electricals equipment plant at Hardwar, Uttar Pradesh, built with Soviet economic and technical aid was expected to contribute towards the development of power engineering in India. The plant was to produce steam and hydraulic turbines of 2.7 million kw capacity comprising individual units with a capacity of 100,000-200,000 kw coupled with power generators. It was also to produce large DC and AC motors (upto 9,000 kw) for rolling mills.

The Mining and Allied Machinery Corporation, Durgapur, West Bengal is to become is to become a base for mechanising the Indian Coal industry. The Plant's manufacturing capacity of 45,000 tons of coal mining machinery and equipment per year will make it possible to mechanise mining of about 8 mn tons of coal a year.

Soviet Aid to other Sectors

The Precision Instrument Plant at Kota is another significant symbol of Indo-Soviet economic Co-operation. This is a crucial sector of the economy. The factory has started production in 1968. It produces automatic control instruments-"the nerves, eyes and ears" of large enterprises which are now coming up in the country. Core sector industries like power, fertilisers, steel, chemicals and oil refineries require complete sets of instruments of measuring and automatic control. Its annual turnover is about Rs. 4.5 crores and it also developed an export market.

Korba Aluminium Plant, Madhya Pradesh

The development of non-ferrous metals like copper, aluminium and zinc are of crucial importance of rapid industrialization of the country. Korba aluminium plant in the public sector, set up with Russian and Hungarian economic assistance is likely to go into full production in the near future. The country's aluminium need has been estimated at 2.5 lakh tons in 1978. With the price of aluminum rapidly rising in the world market, India should try to attain a stage of self-sufficiency in this regard by utilising its vast resources of bauxite. The Soviet Union has also offered to set up another plant with a capacity of one lakh tons in Madhya Pradesh, whose entire production the Soviet Union promised to buy over. This is an example of production collaboration programme which are dovetailed with trade between the two countries in their mutual interest.

Power Generation

Power is crucial both for industrial and agricultural development. At the time of Indian independence, the country's power generation capacity was about 2.3 million KWhs; in 1970-71 the figure went upto 17 mn. KWhs. The contribution of Soviet Union in this respect is very significant.

The Soviet Union has helped in setting up 16 power stations (11 thermal and 5 hydro-power stations). By the end of 1972, the total capacity of these power stations was almost 1.5th of the installed capacity of all the power stations in the country. Some of the important Soviet-aided projects in the field of power generation are as follows : Neyveli Lignite Power Station, Korba Power Plant, Singarauli Power Station, Bokaro Power Plant and Lower Silieru Power Stations.

Agriculture

Soviet aid to India mainly flowed into the industrial sector accounting for nearly 99 per cent of the total aid commitments.

Indian Agriculture received a nominal amount of Soviet aid. Perhaps one of the reasons is that in the Soviet model of development agriculture does not play any leading role. It has been "relatively unimportant sector" in the Soviet economy. There was hardly any incentive to improve productivity in this sector. On the other hand, in the West agricultural development consisted of increased production through price incentives and subsidies.

One should consider the role of Soviet aid to Indian agriculture against this background. The Green revolution that India enjoys at present is very much due to the help given by USA--both Govt. agencies and private organisations like the Ford and Rockefeller foundations--to develop improved hybrid varieties in wheat, rice, maize, cotton and some other important crops. USA also supplied a large quantum of foodgrains in the form of grants, rupee loans and long-term loans when India was facing acute food shortage.

Moreover, USA has given aid on easy terms to set up fertilizer plants in the country. Against this massive aid from USA towards agricultural development, the assistance from the USSR remains only a symbolic gesture of the country's willingness to help. The Soviet help to set up large scene agricultural farms in the public sector at Suratgarh, Rajasthan and Jetsar, Rajasthan, to build a tractor factory at Loni in UP in the private sector and the gift of a small amount of improved seeds did help in a small way to improve agricultural production. The total Indian investment in agriculture during the period from 1950 to 1972-73 is roughly over Rs. 5,000 crores; while USA's aid to this sector during this period would be between Rs. 1250 crores and Rs. 1300 crores, Soviet contribution would not be more than Rs. 50 crores. Contribution from UN agencies and other countries to Indian agricultural development during the same period would be between Rs. 750 crores and Rs. 1000 crores. The rest was contributed by national effort.

Coal

During 1962-68 the Soviet Union helped India in the development of several coal-mines in the country. The National Coal Development Corporation (NCDC) Ranchi, Bihar which is the largest single coal producing unit in India exceeded several projects with Soviet collaboration. These are : The Kathara Washery in the Bokaro-Kargil area in Bihar; the two underground mines of Banki and Surakachar and the Manikpur open-cast mine.

The Kathara Coal Washery, Bihar has an input capacity of 3 million tons of raw coal. It can wash coking coal varying in ash content from 13 to 39 per cent with help of modern cyclone method.

The Banki underground mine, Bihar, on reaching full capacity will produce about 50,000 tons of coal per month. And the manikpur open-cast mine, Madhya Pradesh is designed to produce over 83,000 tons of coal per month which will feed Soviet-built Korba thermal power plant of the MP Electricity Board.

Copper

Under the 15-year agreement with the USSR in 1973, the country will help India to develop its largest copper deposit in Malanjkhand (MP) which was discovered in 1968. While India's annual requirement is 63,000 tons, its production is only 10,000 tons and so India has to import copper worth Rs. 60 crores every year. When Malanjkhand benefication plant will go into full production it is expected to produce 30,000 tons of copper which will result in saving foreign exchange of about Rs. 30 to 35 crores. The recent discovery of high grade copper deposit in Mayurbhanj of Orissa holds further prospects of putting the country on the path of self-sufficiency, if it is properly explicated.

Soviet Military Aid

Military aid is not directly economic aid, yet it has some military assistance may be in the form of credits for projects which help to add to the total industrial production of the country and also to the development of employment potential of the country receiving that aid. This may be regarded as the direct economic effect of military aid. Moreover, the import of arms, ammunition and other defence materials has to be paid by the export of commodities or by convertible currency. If the import of arms is made through aid, the burden of repayment would depend on the nature of the aid. Hence, whatever be the nature of military aid, we have to recognise that some economic implications of that aid are always there.

In the disbursement of Soviet economic aid, India tops the list of developing countries; but her position is only 4th in the list of recipients of military aid. Until 1967, the proportion of known military aid to India was about 11 per cent of the total military aid to the less developed countries. This aid was about 44 per cent total economic aid given to India by the Soviet Union.

Soviet military aid to India assumed strategically significant proportions during 1963-64. As a background of this development, one may easily observe that immediately after the India-China war of 1962, the Govt. of India requested the US Govt. for $ 500 mn. of military assistance, to be spread over a period of 5 years, for the modernisation of India's armed forces. This amount was less than half of the military aid the USA had already given to Pakistan. But the American Govt. responded with only $ 70 mn. worth of military equipment and refused to grant any more, presumably for fear of offending Pakistan. In desperation, the Govt. of India then turned towards the Soviet Union which gave what was wanted and more. From that time onwards, the Soviet Union emerged as the biggest supplier of arms to India. In 1963 an agreement was signed to build an anti-aircraft missile complex, a training school costing 42 million dollars. In 1964, another agreement was signed which involved the supply 44 Mig 21s, over 50 surface to air missiles, some AN-12s and MI-4 helicopters, about 70 light tanks 6 submarines and various infantry weapons.

In the sphere of nuclear weapons construction the Indian venture has been assisted in an indirect way by the Soviet Union. The "atom for peace" agreement of 1961 envisaged co-operation in research and exchange of scientists.[42]

Of all the military aid which has been received so far by Indian from the Soviet Union, the agreement of 1962 to build the MIG-21 complex in India has a special significance for both India and the Soviet Union. This is because India till then was dependent for her aircraft requirements on UK and USA. This

42. P.J. Eldridge : *The Politics of Foreign aid in India*, p.164. Vikas Publications, Delhi, 1969.

dependence was used to the disadvantage of India when UK and USA a did not agree with Indian policies. The Soviet Union's emergence in this field was to break this monopoly element of the western powers. It was a definite help for India because India did not belong to any military group and she had to buy all her defence requirement on payment of foreign exchange. This was a great burden for the country. Soviet aid for supplying military hardwares to set up ordinance factories and to build supersonic fighter planes on rupee payment basis was real boon. The impact of this aid has been to enable India to avoid entering into military pacts. She has been able to plan her economy and defence on her own.

Conclusion

There is no denying the fact that the ideological desire of the Soviet Union to support the public sector has been in keeping with the aspirations of the Indian Govt. regarding the establishment of a sound and healthy heavy industrial base in the public sector. About 97 per cent of Soviet economic assistance is aimed at the construction of industrial enterprises in the public sector in the key branches of the economy. The United States on the other hand had followed a policy of catholic disbursement. Its preference for the private sector has been demonstrated improving such as Coolly Amendment Loans from P.L.480 counterpart funds which have to be made exclusively to the private sector. The difference between the Soviet and American economic assistance can be seem from the following table.

Table 4.21

Pattern of Soviet and American Economic Assistance (As on March 31, 1965) (in percentages)

Soviet Union		*USA*	
Steel	4.0	Steel & iron ore	1.8
Power	18.1	Power & irrigation	7.3
Oil and gas	19.1	Railways	3.8
Coal mining	6.5	Transport & communication	1.1

Soviet Union		*USA*	
Heavy machine building	7.2	Industrial development	25.0
Heavy electricals	4.9	Grants for technical assistance in health, agriculture, social and	
Drugs	3.1	Educational etc.	5.3
		1951 wheat loan, PL-480, 665 food and commodity	
Miscellaneous	1.1	assistance	55.7
	100.0		100.0

Source : P.J. Eldridge : The politics of Foreign Aid in India, London School of Econ . and Political Science, 1969, pp.11 and 18.

With the establishment of the Bokaro Steel Plant and the Mathura Oil Refinery with Soviet assistance, this pattern has been further oriented towards strengthening the capital goods base for industrial development. Table 4.22 shows the change in the pattern of Soviet and American economic assistance for India's industrial development in 1972-73.

Table 4.22

Pattern of Soviet and American economic assistance for industrial development as on March 31, 1972-73 (percentages)

USSR		USA	
Iron & steel	52.30	Steel & iron	1.00
Oil	16.20	Power & irrigation	7.00
Power	14.60	Railways	3.00
Coal mining	2.30	Transport & communication	2.00
Industry	12.00	Industrial development	26.00
U.SSR		USA	
Drug projects	1.50		
Others	1.10	Agriculture	61.00
	100.00		100.00

Source : External assistance, Ministry of Finance, Govt. of India, 1974-75; Fact sheet · U.S. Econ. Assistance to India, USIS, New Delhi.

In changing the industrial structure of the Indian economy, Soviet economic and technological assistance has played an important role. It is true that the USA has consistently been the major aid donor to India. Its share in total aid utilisation was 70 per cent in the First Plan, over 55 per cent in the Second Plan and 58 per cent in the Third Plan. In the later period the share declined though it remained dominant. But 50 per cent of this aid has flowed into supply of foodgrains or other consumer goods, whereas 97 per cent of the Soviet assistance has gone to build up the industrial base of India. If the rate of growth of capital goods output has increased to 10 or 11 per cent per annum in recent years, it is largely due to the Soviet-aided projects.

The emergence of heavy industries like steel, power, heavy engineering, heavy electricals and mining equipments, oil industries which are regarded as important pillars for accelerated industrial development has become largely possible on account of Soviet economic and technological assistance.

The Industrial Policy Resolution of 1956 made an attempt to define a number of industries where public sector projects were essential or desirable. Schedule 'A' of the Resolution listed 17 industries exclusively reserved for the public sector and schedule 'B' listed 7 industries which could be established both in the public and private sectors. Out of these industries, the Soviet assistance contributed in developing as many as 14 industries. The Soviet-aided projects in the crucial sectors accounted till the end of our Fourth Plan for 30 per cent of India's total steel production, 20 per cent of power generation, 35 per cent of oil production, 80 per cent of heavy machine building equipments and 60 per cent of heavy electrical equipments.[43] The 15-year agreement signed in 1973 is expected to increase further the contributions of Soviet-aided projects to the industrial output of the country in the crucial sectors.

The structure of industrial production has gradually shifted away from a preponderant role of consumer goods production to a growing role of capital goods and intermediates. The industrial

43. "Links of a Golden Chain", Soviet Desh, 1975.

production index with 1960 = 100 stands at 244.0 for capital goods industries, 140.2 for intermediate goods industries and 127.5 for consumer goods industries in 1965; the index changed to 243.5 for capital goods, 171.2 for intermediate goods and 168.2 for consumer goods industries in 1972 and the index numbers of industrial production in 1974 became 266.3 for capital goods industries, 177.7 for intermediate goods industries and 163.9 for consumer goods industries.[44] Soviet-aided projects played an important role in this transformation of Indian economy.

44. RBI Report on currency and finance, 1974-75, Statement 11, p.26.

CHAPTER 5

SUMMARY AND CONCLUSIONS

We have seen from our analysis in Chapter 1 that international trade has two important types of effects on the economic growth of the developing countries of the world. The analysis of the first type which runs in terms of positive effects of international exchange and capital flows upon the growth of developing countries is based on conventional static argument on the lines of the well-known comparative cost theory. The other main line of argument emphasising the beneficial impact of trade in the historical context in terms of international trade serving as an engine of economic growth.

The second important type of analysis puts emphasis on the detrimental effect of international trade in the less developed countries. This type of analysis emphasizes the "enclave character" of export development with its "backwash" effects on the rest of the economy, the destruction of indigenous industries by imported substitutes, the demonstration effects lowering saving propensities, thus hampering domestic capital formation and the tendency of secular deterioration in the commodity terms of trade.

In the light of these two contradictory approaches, it becomes difficult to draw a unique conclusion regarding the interconnections between foreign trade and economic growth. The safe conclusion that one may arrive at is that the historical impact of exports has varied from country to country and that there have been positive as well as negative effects from the development of exports. The 19th century British-economy provides a classic examples where exports of wool and textile sparked off economic development. The export of silk was the major propulsive factor in the early stages of Japanese economic growth. This is just one of the story. On the other side, it is equally widely accepted that the developing countries have not been as successful as developed countries in international trade. Besides experiencing a low supply-elasticity, the primary-producing countries are also faced with a declining demand for their products in the advanced industrial countries. As a logical consequence, the import-capacity of these countries which is generally measured by the trend in export-earnings becomes limited. It is now widely recognised that stresses and strains on the balance of payments of these developing countries that are created by this export-lag can be solved to some considerable extent by mutual trade expansion within the context of bilateral trade and payments agreements.

For India bilateral trade was important in the sense that it enabled her to import plant and equipment, industrial raw materials and components which were vital to Indian economic development in exchange for its stable products like tea, coffee and tobacco, crude materials such as iron-ore, leather-goods. The element of aid was demonstrated in terms of allowing India to pay for her imports in inconvertible rupee currency. In the growing export trade of India, the share of USSR is considerable. USA and UK who were once the largest purchases of Indian goods were relegated to the second and third position respectively in 1970. Table 5.1 shows India's exports to some important countries between 1960-61 and 1974-75.

Table 5.1

India's exports to some important countries (Rs. in crores)

Countries	*1960-61*	*1965-66*	*1970-71*	*1974-75*
All countries	642.32	805.64	1535.71	3304.0
USSR	28.81	92.09	209.85	418.2
USA	102.15	168.04	235.30	375.8
UK	172.48	145.71	170.44	307.0
Japan	35.27	57.12	230.48	295.2

Source : DGCI and S : Monthly Statistics of Foreign Trade of India.

From the Soviet point of view also bilateral trade with emphasis on bilateral balancing was convertible foreign exchange in its trade dealings with the Less Developed Countries. Moreover, there was an element of certainty about the commodities and quantities to be exchanged in such an approach to trade. In centrally planned economies like that of Soviet Russia, there is much advantage in knowing in advance what will be available from foreign import-sources and what must be provided for despatch abroad. It is true that the USSR and other East European Countries has faced and still now face the problem of shortage of free foreign exchange. Bilateralism was decidedly of help in the import of much needed tropical goods (consumers' goods) in exchange for Soviet industrial products. Thus bilateral trade mechanism was helpful to both trade partners--India and the USSR. The UN World Economic Survey of 1958 was quite explicit regarding the significant increase in the exports of primary commodities by the Less Developed Countries as a result of their entry into bilateral trade and payments agreements with the Soviet Bloc countries.

As a whole, Soviet Bloc aid to developing countries like India has been useful in more ways than one. The Soviet Bloc extended financial assistance to the extent of Rs. 1011.8 crores (loans Rs. 10002.4 crores and grants Rs. 9.4 crores) upto 1973-74.* In quantitative terms, Soviet Bloc aid was not much compared to the aid from the consortium countries, but the quantum was not the correct indicator of the impact of Soviet Bloc aid to India. The Soviet Bloc introduced a new style of aid-giving which was guided by three important principles specially suited to the desires and needs of developing countries like India: (a) to give loans rather than grants, (b) to charge low rates of interest and (c) to accept repayment in kind. By putting less emphasis on grants these countries wanted to show some respect for the developing countries; the Third World countries were treated as equal partners in international trade and commerce. The Soviet Bloc was also pioneer among developed countries in extending loans on soft terms. Right from the beginning, Soviet credits carried a nominal rate of interest of 2.5 per cent per annum. Soviet loans were repayable over a period of 12 years (except in the case of credit for drug projects). Repayments, however, were to begin one year after the completion of deliveries of equipment for setting up the respective projects.

* (a) Economic Survey, Govt. of India.

(b) Conversion in rupees at pre-devaluation rate of exchange ($ 1 = Rs. 4.76) upto the end of the Third Plan and at post-devaluation rate of exchange ($ 1 = Rs. 7.50) for the subsequent years.

So far as utilization of Soviet Bloc credit is concerned, we find that upto 1973-74 these countries had authorised Rs. 1002.4 crores and India utilized Rs. 711.1 crores. This shows that more than 70 per cent of the total credits had been utilized by India. We find a considerable degree of improvement in utilisation in view of the fact that upto the end of the Third Plan about half of the total aid disbursed remained unutilized. The widespread drought in the mid 1960s and the industrial recession that followed it were responsible for the slackening of the pace of utilization. The nature of the projects for which Soviet aid was provided for was also an important factor in show utilization of aid. Soviet aid mostly concentrated in the fields of steel making, heavy machine building, oil refining, power equipment and mining machinery--all of which required detailed planning and designing, elaborate processes for tying up delivery schedules and a host of other arrangements. In other words, a long period of gestation was inherent in such projects.

But not everything is satisfactory in respect of Soviet aid. the Indo-Soviet credit agreements contain a gold parity clause in which the gold content of the rupee is indicated as 0.186621 gm. of fine gold per rupee. The amount of credit was indicated in rupees in the agreement on Bhilai plant and in other agreements the amounts were expressed in roubles. In the agreements where the amounts were expressed in roubles the gold content of the rouble was indicated. Thus the liability was guaranteed in terms of gold. There was an unconditional gold clause in the Bhilai agreement which provided for proportionate revaluation of the balance in the credit repayment account in case of a change in the gold parity of the rupee. A compromise was understood to have been arrived at, while negotiating for the Third Plan credits, which stipulated that the question of revaluation of accounts would not arise when the change occurred as a result of the revision of the official price of gold. When the rouble was revaluated in 1961, the amounts of credits in rupees had also been revalued in accordance with the new gold content of the rupee. Thus India's liability increased substantially. It would be desirable to remove the gold clause entirely from the agreements or least to soften the increase in the burden of repayment. This insertion of a "gold clause" displayed the strictly commercial nature of the

Soviet Bloc's transactions with India.

Some attractive features of Soviet aid seen in the earlier period seem to have disappeared in recent years. Bhilai was a "prestige issue" since it was the first project undertaken by the USSR. All efforts were made to make it an outstanding success in competition with Durgapur and Rourkela projects. But Bokaro Steel Plant shows a somewhat attitude taken by the Govt. of USSR owing to a shift in the policy.

Despite some such disadvantages, many developing countries including India have to lean more towards Soviet Bloc than to USA or UK Soviet aid which is generally project tied, places more emphasis on the development of key industries in the public sector such as steel, coal mining, oil exploration, heavy electricals and machinery, power generation etc. Thus the Soviet Union ushered in a new era in economic co-operation between a developed country and a developing country by providing financial and technical assistance in building up a self-reliant economy. Moreover, Soviet-aided projects in India do not involve any equity participation by the USSR Besides, Soviet co-operation in building any project generally provides for training of requisite Indian personnel to take charge of the operation of the project at the earliest possible time. Another important point is that both payments of interest and loan repayments are made in rupees and not in rouble or any hard currency. These rupees are utilised by the Soviet Union for the purchase of goods and services in India according to the according to the bilateral trade agreements. Lastly, the Soviet Union's entry into aid-giving business had changed the aid-climate in favour of soft-term loans to developing countries.

The most important questions center round the net cost and net benefit of Indo-Soviet trade. In Chapter 3, we discussed this questions in detail. Out finding has been that from 1950's Soviet trade expanded by about 50 per cent every five years. In the most recent period (1971-74), there has been a further acceleration. In the 1970's the USSR has become one of India's major trade partners. It is obvious that bilateral trade and payments agreements have brought about this important development.

Regarding the point whether rupee trade meant any diversion

of India's trade from traditional Western markets, we found that there was some amount of diversion for India's export-commodities like tea, coffee, spices and jute goods from the western markets to East European markets. A careful scrutiny of India's exports of tea to USSR and East Europe reveals that beginning with the 1960's India has been exporting mainly high-grade variety of tea to these countries under bilateral trade agreements. It is believed that almost the whole amount of Darjeeling tea is being exported to USSR. In respect of common-quality tea, USSR and Eastern Europe provided an outlet for Indian tea under the bilateral trade agreements at a time when the world demand for such common-quality tea from India was stagnant. Hence, with respect to common-quality tea, the question of diversion does not arise. Moreover, one should note some likely beneficial aspects regarding the emergence of USSR and East European markets for Indian tea. Larger off-take of tea by these countries was a helpful factor in the matter of price stabilisation for India's tea. The other factor to be taken into account is that in the absence of the markets of USSR and Eastern Europe, if India were to try and maintain its share in the traditional Western markets, there would have been a further fall in tea-prices, thus hampering India's foreign exchange earnings form tea exports.

Regarding exports of jute manufactures, our finding has been that India's capacity of producing good quality jute being limited, exports of Hessian cloth, which needs good quality raw jute in their manufacture, was diversionary; but exports of sacking bags may be regarded as largely additional in nature. The fact that the stocks of jute manufactures over the year-ends were on the increase is sufficient to prove that U.S.S.R. and East Europe had little to do in the matter of any loss of markets in convertible currency.

The emergence of USSR and East Europe as an important market for coffee made a difference to India's exports of coffee to the rest of the world. In terms of value, the trade diversion amounted to Rs. 4 mn. annually.

Regarding cashew kernel, we have found that a vast potential market for cashew kernels exists in the convertible currency markets. So if India could have exported larger amount of the commodity, it would, in all probability, find markets in the western countries. All available evidence shows that the East European Countries (including USSR) were re-exporting considerable amount of cashew nuts to the western markets. If this was so, India could easily sell the amount that it was selling under bilateral trade agreements to Eastern Europe. so this export of cahsew nuts to USSR and Eastern Europe cannot be regarded as a net gain to India.

Regarding the exports of pepper to Eastern Europe, out analysis has shown that India's exports of pepper to the rest of the world suffered as a result of increase in pepper-exports to Eastern Europe. India's pepper production remained stagnant during the period 1961-73. So large scale purchases made by USSR and East Europe ultimately led to an artificial price-rise in the domestic market making exporters unwillingly to export to other countries.

India produces a special type of raw wool which is used for making carpets, besides other things. This wool was generally in high demand in western markets. But besides being required for increased defence supplies within India, firm commitments of exports to USSR and other Socialist Countries were responsible for decline in exports of this commodity to the rest of the world.

Regarding hides and skins, it is believed that Indian hides and skins have got a special market among the shoe and hand-bag manufactures. The reason is that Indian hides and skins are smaller and free of fat. USSR and other East European countries diverted the exports of hides and skins from the western markets by paying a higher price.

The last item in our present analysis is tobacco unmanufactured. Since USA itself is a major producer and exporter of tobacco, there is perhaps no scope for increased exports of tobacco to USA. So far as India's exports to tobacco to the UK market is concerned, there was severe competition by Rhodesia. If these factors are taken into account, exports of tobacco to USSR and Europe could very well be regarded as an welcome addition.

The commodities, so far discussed constituted the bulk of

India's exports to USSR and Eastern Europe upto India's fourth Five Year Plan. We wish to stress the point that trade with USSR and Eastern Europe did not imply any large scale diversion of India's exports from the western markets. Such diversion as may have occurred is to be regarded as the unavoidable cost of finding new markets in the Soviet Bloc. But in case some of the commodities imported form India by USSR and Eastern Europe are found to be reexported by these countries, there will surely arise an additional cost in the sense that India is thereby deprived of free foreign exchange earnings.

Of course, the basic reason for reexports of Indian or other Third World products by the Soviet Bloc countries is that the whole of Soviet Bloc is very much in need of free foreign exchange since they suffer from adverse balance of payment problems with convertible currency areas.

The question of reexports cannot be really answered without full knowledge about domestic production and consumption in the countries of East Europe over and above figures relating to trade. Some difficulties may arise also in estimating the actual amount of re-exports. This is because (1) there will be no mention of the country in the foreign trade statistics of Western Europe unless that country is a big exporter of the commodity concerned. (2) Many commodities are often exported through third countries. So in order to solve these problems we need a comprehensive survey regarding trade, production and consumption of all Western and Eastern Europe.

Soviet trade statistics also do not provide any evidence regarding re-exports. The reason is : Official trade statistics of the USSR and other East European Countries do not distinguish between exports and re-exports. Moreover, goods purchased from one country and resold to another by a foreign-based but Soviet-owned commercial enterprise are included in Soviet exports as well as imports. This makes it impossible to verify the question of Soviet re-exports.

In spite of such statistical difficulties, a general impression regarding re-exports may be formed in the following manner. When USSR imports tea from India not for meeting increasing domestic consumer demand, but to enable the country to increase her exports of tea, this must be considered to be a case of re-export. In 1971 and 1972, USSR exported 1367 and 81 tons of tea respectively to the UK at prices of 536 and 546 rouble per ton. But it paid higher prices to India and Sri Lanka. The USSR also sold substantial amounts to the Third World Countries like Morocco and Afghanistan in 1972 and 1973 but at a lower price. Soviet Union's own production of Georgian tea plus the imports from India enable her to engage in tea re-exports. Similarly, larger off-take of cashew kernel and oilcakes by USSR may also lead us to the same conclusion regarding re-exports. In the Algiers meeting of the "Group of 77" and in Lima Conference many developing countries including India have registered their protests against such re-exports and the Socialist countries have agreed in general terms to limit such re-exports.

During 1969's and early 1970's India seems to have obtained slightly higher prices for her exports to the USSR and other East European countries for some commodities, but it was difficult to judge whether these prices were significantly higher than what were obtained elsewhere because of quality differences. The commodities which fetched high prices in Indo-Soviet/East European trade were tea, coffee as well as hides and skins. In case of commodities like cashew kernel, jute fabrics, tobacco unmanufactured, coir and coir manufactures, India appears to have received low prices for her exports to Soviet Bloc countries. One of our findings has been that unit value fluctuations of India's exports to the USSR were confined within very narrow limits. On the other hand, India' unit value index number of exports to the rest of the world declined continuously over the period 1960-61 to 1964-65. The fall in index number of India's exports to the rest of the world was as wide as 21 points, whereas it was only 2 points in case of India's trade with the USSR.

So far as prices of current imports, specially imports of Industrial raw materials are concerned, they were not generally higher prices from the Soviet Bloc and the rest of the world were comparable. So for merchandise trade alone, India's net barter terms of trade was in no way inferior to what it obtained from the rest of the world. But India's current imports from Soviet Union and other East European countries constituted only 25-30 per cent of India's total imports from these socialist economics.

Machinery and equipments alone constituted more than 50 per cent of India's total imports from the countries. Prices of Soviet machinery and equipments supplied to India being generally higher than world market prices, the logical conclusion is that India's net barter terms of trade with the Soviet Bloc, taking into account all imports and exports has tended to be inferior to that with the rest of the world.

Although in general, the Soviet Union offered decent prices for its imports from India and other Third World countries, its ultimate gain was higher due to relative overpricing of its machinery, turn-key projects etc. which constituted and still constitute the lion's share in Soviet exports.

The USSR enjoyed substantial gain from her trade with India and other Third World countries, because with the exception of a few years and commodities the secular trend of worsening terms of trade for Third World primary goods has continued from 1950's to this day. The USSR and Eastern Europe like all other countries have taken full advantages of this situation. But this does not mean that India and other Third World countries do not reap any benefit form their trade relations with the socialist countries. What is important is that there has been unequal distribution of gains form trade between India (and other Third World countries) on the one hand and the Soviet Bloc on the other.

Regarding the question whether India was successful in getting high-priority goods at competitive prices from the Socialist countries, we have found that India had no absolutely free choice with respect to its purchase from the USSR and other East European countries. India's imports from these countries were always regulated by import licences and it would be fair to assume that Govt. of India should grant a licence only when the good is necessary. If this is so, the question of buying low-priority goods does not arise.

The question of quality of imports must remain open since the most important imports from these Socialist countries are machinery and equipments, quality-comparisons are meaningful only when the imported-goods are identical or at least similar in important respects to goods from other sources. The general feeling has been that East European products are not good enough to compete with Western products. Long standing familiarity of Indian businessmen with the western machinery and equipment as well as techniques and technology make them dependent on imports from western countries. Price advantage, if any of East European products has little impact on the demand for such commodities.

On the whole, India has till now managed to secure mainly high-priority goods from the Soviet Union. While in money terms the US economic assistance to India is the highest, only 50 per cent of the American aid has flowed into supply of foodgrains or other consumer goods, whereas 97 per cent of the Soviet assistance has gone to build up the industrial base of Indian economy. In addition to economic assistance, India received and is still receiving military aid, the repayment of which is to be made by the exports of Indian goods.

It is sometimes argued that rupee trade reduced the flexibility of India's trade policy with the USSR and Eastern Europe. But this does not accord with the facts. The objective of a rational trade policy is to extend the opportunities of trade between countries. Under different Indo-Soviet trade agreements, one cannot fail to notice the gradual change in the export-import commodity combination between the two countries. During the early trade agreements, machinery and equipment particularly turn-key machinery played a very dominant role in India's import list from the Soviet Union. There was some obvious reason for this. India's planning strategy was to lay particular emphasis on the development of heavy industries for the rapid industrialisation of the country and this necessitated capital goods import from its trade partners. But equal emphasis on turn-key projects was on the decline in India's import list form the Soviet Bloc countries; at the same time, industrial raw materials and spare parts were regarded as the most important items of India's imports from these countries. Similarly, Soviet imports from India were weighted gradually in favour of non-traditional items like hosiery goods, cotton textiles, engineering goods and products of Soviet-assisted projects which helped India to sustain her production programme. This shows that on the whole the Agreements have given rise to a flexible pattern of trade between the two countries.

Soviet economic and technical assistance have been available on a wide front creating additional productive capacities in the crucial sectors of Indian economy, influencing Indo-Soviet trade in its volume and composition over the years. Nearly 100 projects in the crucial sectors of Indian economy received Soviet economic assistance and technical know-how. These projects include : metallurgical projects, hydro-power production, power stations at industrial projects, hydro-power stations, oil industry, off-shore seismic survey, oil refining, mining, pharmaceuticals, agriculture and miscellaneous industries. Besides, Soviet technical assistance is available to as many as 15 institutions all over the country.

While the industrial sector of Indian economy accounted for about 99 per cent of total Soviet aid to India, agricultural sector of the country received only a nominal amount of Soviet aid. Soviet military aid to India has also some economic implication for Indian economy. Such aid also provides for increasing the total industrial production of the country. In 1963, an agreement was signed between the two countries to build an anti-aircraft missile complex, a training school costing 42 million dollars. Soviet aid for supplying military hardwares to set up ordinance factories and to build supersonic fighter planes on rupee payment was a real to India.

What, then, are the future prospects of Indo-Soviet aid and trade? India has gained in many ways by promoting trade with the Soviet Union and other East European countries. But uptil now India has not taken full advantage of the opportunities available in the countries of this region. In fact, India's share in their import trade, far from increasing, has been declining. India's share in Soviet Russia's imports fell from 2.31 per cent in 1970 to 1.88 per cent in 1974. In case of other countries like Hungary, Bulgaria, Romania, Czechoslovakia, there has been a similar trend. Although India's exports of non-traditional goods to these countries have increased, it has not been of a substantial nature.

Certain factors emanating from the structural changes of Indo-Soviet trade should be kept in view while framing India's trade policy with the USSR. First, for further expansion of Indo-

Soviet trade, there arises the need for overall directional planning of India's trade. As is the experience, there is a lot of adhocism in the trade policy which is so much dependent upon the terms of trade agreement.

Secondly, while offering its own term, India should also take into account the pricing policies of these countries. As in the Soviet Bloc countries, prices are influenced by the objective of securing investible surplus, prices of imports from these countries do not reflect their comparative cost position. Hence, while brgaining for price terms, adequate consideration should be given to the reciprocal comparative cost positions.

Thirdly, as a result of changing technology in use in these countries and because of sophistication in their industrial structure, their requrements for new inputs are increasing and for this they are bound to have to look upto the countries of the Third World. In this context, it should be noted that India should give adequate thought to the possible draft on her irreplaceable natural resources, particularly minerals consequent on the accelerated rate of their exploitation.

As a result of structural changes in both the trading camps, the strict complementarily in trade is on the wane. As a consequence, the problem of accumulation of surpluses would lead to perversion of trade practices such as switch trade, exchanging of non-essential goods and artificial manipulations of prices and exchange rate. In with disfavour and we should seriously think whether the time is not ripe for switchover to some extent towards multilateral convertibility. At the present moment any set back to India's exports arising form the change to the new system could be looked after by the accumulation of the large foreign exchange reserves. However, that the country now enjoys the volume of trade with the USSR being quite sizeable and economic relations with the USSR being of basic importance, a switchover to free currency trading arrangement with the USSR should be postponed for the time being, while experiments in such trade with other East European countries provides some guide-lines for taking suitable decision regarding the future pattern of Indo-USSR trade. It may be noted that India terminated her rupee trade with Yugoslavia in the mid-1970's. We should make a careful study of the impact of this new policy before we take any new steps in the direction of modifying the nature of Indo-Soviet trade.

CHAPTER 6

A REVIEW OF THE CURRENT PERIOD: 1975-1990

The main purpose of the postscript is to extend out previous cost benefit analysis of Indo-Soviet Trade to the current period (1975-90). A careful scrutiny of Indo-Soviet trade during the current period can only substantiate and strengthen our basic observations in this regard. In this period, Indian economic had to pass through her 5th & 6th Five-Year Plans. On the other hand over the same period, Indo-Soviet trade had completed its fifth and sixth bilateral trade agreements--The Fifth Trade Agreement (1976 - 80) and the Sixth Trade Agreement (1981 - 85). During the 6th agreement period, rupee trade crude crisis came to the forefront. Indo-Soviet trade protocol for 1984 was signed in New Delhi on December 9, 1983, coinciding with the visit of the Deputy Prime Minister Ivan Arkhipov. The main object of the trade protocol was to find out pragmatic solutions for rupee trade crisis. Another significant milestone in Indo-Soviet economic relation was Mikhail Gorbachev - Rajiv Gandhi-10 point joint declaration, popularly known as New Delhi Declaration '86' primarily intended for larger economic and technical co-operation between the two countries.

A careful scrutiny of the growth of Indo-Soviet trade shows that he value of Indo-Soviet trade which was Rs. 726.47 cr. in 1975-76 increased to Rs.3457.97 Cr. in 1984-85 - a growth of about 5 times within a decade. Value of India's exports to USSR increased from Rs. 416.69 Cr. in 1975-76 to Rs.1654.59 Cr. in 1984-85. During the same time India's imports from Soviet Union rose from Rs. 309.78 Cr. to Rs.1803.38 Cr. Delhi Declaration of 1986 proposes an expansion of trade target between India and USSR by two and half times by 1992. Few could have visualised during the time of Indian Independence that trade between the two countries with different economic and political systems would grow so rapidly and at such a phenomenal pace. Total Indo-Soviet trade in 1950-51 was barely 0.22 cr. While in 1984-85, it crossed Rs.3400 cr. This spectacular growth in trade in a span of a little more than three decades in example of fruitful trade and economic co-operation between the two countries with different social systems. Bilateral trade, aided by the self-balancing "rupee payments" mechanism grew rapidly between India and USSR in the 1960's, 1970's and early 1980's and has perhaps now reached a qualitative, though not a quantitative plateau. Added to this was the appreciable amount of economic assistance extended to India by USSR that gave further stimulus to growth in trade between India and the Soviet Union. Between 1977-78 and 1985-86 the amount of authorisation of external assistance by USSR towards India has increased from Rs. 208.3 cr. to Rs. 1143.4 cr. During the same period, utilisation of external assistance also rose from Rs. 54.6 cr. to Rs. 130 cr. In 1984-85, India's exports to East European countries recorded a strong increase of 23.3 p.c., with those to the USSR alone growing by 26.p.c. on the other hand Indian exports to OECD countries rose by 22.5 p.c and to the OPEC and developing countries (non-OPEC) showed a small increase of 6.3 p.c and 1.1 p.c. respectively in 1984-85. USSR alone constituted a share of 14.3 p.c. of total Indian exports in 1984-85 a close second to USA, with a percentage share of 15.3.

On December 2, 1983 India and Soviet Union celebrated the 30th anniversary of the first long-term trade agreement between the two countries. 1953, India and Soviet Union have had six trade agreement between them. These agreements were set out to achieve several objectives, viz. (1) to establish direct contact with USSR and other centrally planned East European countries, (2) to obtain capital goods and raw materials without straining India's convertible foreign exchange reserve, (3) to stabilise prices of India's traditional exports, (4) to create markets for India's traditional export markets, (5) to create markets for India's non-traditional products and (6) to maintain a balance between export and import values--a bilateral balancing of trade.

In this postscript, we intend to study primarily the extent to which the fifth (1976-80) and sixth (1981-85) trade agreements have been successful in achieving these objectives. An objective study is all the more important since Indo-Soviet relations is perhaps the unique subject on which there is a consensus, among almost all sections of political opinion in India--the opposition as much as the Government, the right as much as the left. At the same time, many doubts have also been raised regarding the overall benefits of Indo-Soviet trade to India. The doubts raised mainly relate to (a) whether there is a real trade diversion from the convertible currency areas and thus losing valuable free foreign exchange, (b) whether India is trading at a loss in terms of prices and (c) whether the imports from USSR are of comparable quality.

In order to assess the costs and benefits of Indo-Soviet trade during the 5th and 6th trade agreement periods, we again propose to consider the following important points as we did previously ; (1) whether India could have established links with USSR to get an increasing share of its trade without the rupee payments agreements ; (2) whether rupee trade led to any diversion of Indian trade from the traditional markets; (3) how far India, under rupee trade agreement was able to get prices for her exports and imports comparable to world market prices; and (4) how far the rupee trade mechanism restricted the flexibility of commercial policy of trading countries.

Regarding point (1) our main conclusion still stands in the current period that it would have been difficult for India to establish and maintain increasing trade links with USSR without rupee trade agreement. In absolute terms India's exports to USSR which stood at Rs. 418 Cr. in 1974-75 crossed Rs. 3400 Cr. in 1984-85. This remarkable expansion would perhaps have been impossible without rupee trade agreements.

Prior to 1958, all the trade agreements had a clause stating that payment relating to commercial and non-commercial transaction between India and USSR were to be effected in Indian rupee or pound sterling. Any balance in the rupee account which is maintained in the authorised banks of either country, was to be converted into sterling on demand at the usual banks' selling rate for sterling. Since 1959, when it was decided that all payments between the two countries were to be settled in Indian rupees, "true bilateralism" was thus introduced between India and USSR.

Under this rupee trade system, India was in a position to have a more balanced international trade with USSR. The self-liquidating nature of the agreement has added to the possibility of further expansion and growth of trade between India and USSR. Bilateral trade with bilateral balancing is helpful not only from Indian but also from Soviet point of view. In centrally planned economies like that of USSR, it is always of much advantage in knowing in advance what will be available from foreign sources and what must be provided for despatch abroad. Thus bilateralism provides and easy way of disposing the accumulated surpluses in each economy. There is no denying the fact that shortage of free foreign exchange is one of the important problems that the USSR is still now facing in international transactions. In this context bilateralism was undoubtedly of help in the import of much need tropical goods (consumers' goods) in exchange for Soviet industrial products. Implicit in the trade agreement were the principles of reciprocity and mutuality. Thus bilateral trade mechanism was helpful to both trade partners--India and the USSR. But one must take care of the defects of bilateralism compared to multilatoral exchange; bilateralism besides being primitive, narrows down the choice of imports and markets too and the quality of goods is unlikely to be of the best standard. India with a weaker bargaining position should believe cautiously in her future dealings in trade with USSR.

Regarding the question of diversion of India's trade from her traditional markets like that of Western Europe and America, our conclusion still holds in the current period. There is some amount of trade diversion towards the Soviet Bloc countries. In Tea exports, such diversion is possible because India committed herself to export good quality tea to the USSR under the terms of trade agreements. This quality of tea could have been sold easily in the convertible currency markets of Western Europe and so India was losing its convertible currency earnings from high grade variety of tea. But this observation is not applicable for common quality tea. Not only India but also countries like Sri Lanka, Bangladesh and China are now the sources of supply of tea to Soviet Union. The share of India has slightly declined in the recent years. A comparison of unit value of tea imported into USSR with international market price shows that the Soviet Union was able to procure tea at a lower price than the prevailing international prices. It is a fact that intensive an extensive measures soviet Union is able to increase its tea production by more than two-fold during 1975-85. Over 90 p.c. of this tea was produced in Georgia and the rest in Azerbaijan and Russian Federal Republic. Soviet production of tea in 1983 was more than 120,000 tons. Imports plus increased her exports of tea during early 1980's to socialist countries such as Mongolia, Hungary, GDR Mongolia regularly imported about one-third of total Soviet exports. Unit value of exports was generally lower than unit value of imports. This might have been mainly due to the export of low quality tea produced domestically by the USSR In 1982, the unit value of export of tea was 710 roubles per ton against 1,555 roubles per ton for imports. However, unit values of export to GDR and Czechoslovakia were higher than unit value of imports. In 1080 per capita consumption of tea in USSR at 0.56 kg. was low compared to 3.3 kg in UK, 2.1 Kg in Iraq and 1.52 Kg in Sri Lanka. Since tea is a common beverage of the Soviets and there is a rising preference for Indian tea to Georgian tea, it is expected that demand for Indian tea will rise in future with the rising income of the Soviet citizens. Soviet market for this quality of tea was helpful in stablizing the prices of tea in the inter-national/domestic markets.

Soviet Union in 1980's imported raw tobacco from a large number of among them being Bulgaria, Yugoslavia, Greece, Democratic Republic of Korea and India. On the other hand Soviet union is a regular exporter of raw tobacco, exporting to the tune of 1,000 - 2,000 tons per year during early 1980's.

In case of cotton textile fabrics, Soviet Union imports from as many as seven countries--Hungary, GDR, Poland, Czechoslovakia, India, Pakistan and Egypt. At the same time, Soviet Union is an exporter of cotton fabrics and expecting in a few years to be a net exporter of the same. In spite of some year-to-year fluctuations, the over all picture in respect of tea, coffee, black pepper, jute bags and packaging materials and cotton textiles, there is a general increasing trend of Soviet imports import market in respect of Coffee, black pepper, raw tobacco and cotton textiles during the current period. If we follow a wider interpretation of re-exports, it can be pointed out that when the USSR's import of a commodity from India is not meant for increasing domestic consumer demand, but enables USSR to increase her exports of the same, this may be regarded as a case of re-export of Indian goods.

Regarding the important question of comparative price advantage, our previous conclusion remains the same. India's net barter terms of trade with USSR are perhaps inferior to those with the rest of the world, if we take all export and imports together.

Regarding the last point centering round the question of flexibility of commercial policy of trading countries, our observations that Indo-Soviet bilateral trade agreement have provided for the diversification of import - export trade of the Indian economy to quire a significant extent. Indian imports over the years moved more in favour of industrial raw materials, spares and components of Soviet assisted projects. Imports of conventional types of plant and machinery on a turn-key basis have been on the decline. In the commodity composition of India's export, agricultural products are gradually yielding place to engineering products.

After careful consideration of all these factors, our broad judgement has been that Indo-Soviet trade, on the whole has benefited India during the current period too. But it would be difficult to say whether the extent of benefit is the same as it was during the period (1953-74) One cannot be fully sure whether a solid foundation for the future development of this trade has been laid or not. There are still the same two important sources of uncertainly regarding the future development of this trade : (1) India is not an indispensable supplier of any commodity to the Soviet Union and therefore India's bargaining power is still relatively weak. This position has to be changed (2) If Sino-Soviet relations improve further, India may not be so much needed because at one stage i.e. after Sino-Soviet rift) Indian supplies had replace those from China.

The industrial sector of Indian economy accounted for about 95 per cent of total Soviet aid to India. Soviet military aid to India is having now important economic implications for Indian economy. Such aid for supplying military hardware to set up ordinance factories and to counteract the supply of sophisticated US arms (including possibly AWACS) to Pakistan on a rupee payment basis in the current period is a real boon to India.

We observed earlier that due to structural changes in both

the countries, the strict complementarity in trade is on the decline. As a consequence, the problem of surplus accumulation may pose a serious threat to the future growth of trade. Rupee trade crisis arose mainly out of the heavy adverse balance of trade against Russia over the past few years, particularly in 1932 when it reached Rs. 668 cr. This is due to the fact that India finds it can import mainly items like oil and petroleum goods and has little need for Russian equipment and machines. Indo-Soviet protocol for 1984 had its focus on economic co-operation, but this is really meant for finding ways by which imports of capital equipment and machinery could be increased so that balance of trade can be restored. In 1982, India exported Rs. 1921 cr. worth of goods to Russia and its imports amounted Rs. 1253 cr. Although this meant a record trade turnover of Rs. 3174 cr. and made Russia India's single largest trading partner, it also meant that the Soviet Union was forced to accept heavy "technical credits" of Rs. 668 cr. The planned balance in 1983 is somewhat less but the slow down by Russia in making purchases from India suggests that Moscow fears it will again be large. Faced with declining imports of Soviet machinery by India's public sector undertakings, the Soviet Union has pragmatically shown a keen interest in industrial collaboration with India's private sector--a proposal which was ideologically unacceptable a decade back. The recent visits of FICCI team and an ASSOCHEM Delegation to Moscow have created hopes in the minds of the Soviet policy makers about active participation of India's private sector in increasing Soviet engineering exports to India. As a step in that direction, the Soviet Government have decided to permit large and established Indian firms to open their offices in Moscow.

Prospects of Indo-Soviet trade in 1980's appear to be bright provided India can fill up its increasing quota regarding the import of engineering goods from Soviet Union.This depends to a large extent to India's private sector which now holds the key to the growth of Indo-Soviet trade.

The economic and technical co-operation agreement signed during Gorbachev's visit to India in 1986 bears the imprint provides for a fresh soviet credit of 1.2 billion roubles to pay for import of Soviet equipment and services for 4 projects listed in the agreement. More significantly, Soviet Union is to extend an additional credit of 300 mn roubles specifically to meet the rupees costs of one of the 4 projects--the 2400 MW Tehri hydro electric projects. This is a reflection of Indian Govt's inability to raise resource to finance development projects in such high priority area as power generation. It is also interesting to note what is explicitly stated in the co-operation agreement that each of the four project is to be undertaken by Soviet Union on a turn-key basis, though all the projects--Tehri power project, reconstruction and modernisation of Bokaro Steel plant, setting up four underground mines in Jharia and off-share oil exploration in West Bengal--are in areas in which considerable development of Indian technological and engineering skills is supposed to have taken place. Clearly given its inability to raise resources to finance even the domestic component of the cost of the projects, the Govt. of India is in no position to take stand against turn-key projects which India does not really need now. This again shows India's weak bargaining power in trade negotiations with USSR.

In spite of all these short comings, we find an increasing trend rate of growth of growth of Indo-Soviet trade over the years. This cannot but be regarded as one of the significant achievements in India's trade policy. Since India now maintains her exchange rate under a "System of managed floating", the rupee has been devalued between 1980 and 1986, to the extend of 38 p.c. against dollar, 54 p.c. against yen, 26 p.c. against Deutsche mark an only 11 p.c. against the pound. But the devaluation of the rupee has not really helped much to improve the country's export performance. The World Bank has drawn attention to the fact that Indian export growth in the last decade has been less than 2 p.c. in real terms and has lagged behind overall world trade growth. The World Bank and the IMF have been frequently urging the country to devalue her currency. In this context the growth of Indo-Soviet trade is a matter of pride and real boon to Indian economy.

The situation has not changed even in the most recent time period. This is clearly evident from the observation of the two co-chairmen of the Indo-Soviet Joint Commission of 1990 that "the existing system of trade between the two countries has been and continues to be beneficial and should therefore, be continued." In other words, Indo-Soviet trade relation in 1990 is an affirmation of *status quo.* This may appear incongruous in the sense that when revolutionary changes are taking place in the Soviet domestic and foreign economic relations under "perestroika" and major changes are taking place in India's internal and external economy, the framework of Indo-Soviet Trade relations should remain unaffected. In fact, the memorandum of understanding signed by the leaders of both the countries observed that "major, structural changes in the economy and foreign trade of both the Soviet Union and India currently underway would require adjustments in the Indo-Soviet economic relations". In spite of all these, the countries are willing to have the existing trade relations in the framework of rupee trade and bilateral balancing of trade etc., this reveals the truth that both countries are somewhat compelled to maintain the continuity of the existing trade relations between them. In other words, the existing pattern of trade between the two countries followed over a period of three decades is till now a policy of convenience and compulsions on both sides.

If we consider the rationale for following the existing trade strategy from the Indian side, we find that it is extremely difficult for Indian economy to do away with the rupee trade and bilateral balancing mechanism. The Soviet Union now standard as one of the largest trade partners of India. Its trade turnover with the USSR constitute around 15 p.c. of total trade. This fact itself constitutes an essential precondition for maintaining the existing trade in order that India's foreign trade is not adversely affected at this juncture. This is all the more important when India has been under acute economic strains with huge budget deficit, high rate of inflation and unemployment etc.

A careful scrutiny of India's imports from the Soviet Union reveals that India is still dependent on the Soviet Union for critical import items such as oil, fertilisers, non-ferrous metals, newsprint etc. Thanks to rupee trade, there is no outgo of converting foreign exchange under conditions of acute balance of payments difficulties. It would not be wise for India to lose the secured supply of these critical inputs to Indian economy in the immediate future. India's dependence on Soviet Union has been magnified all the more after the Iraqi invasion of Kuwait. Internal spot market price of oil has jumped from $ 14 per barrel to about $ 20 per barrel as a result of t the above invasion.

If we consider the need for Soviet market for India's exports, we find that Indian has substantial stake in retaining Soviet marked for the export of non-traditional items. India has really been successful in diversifying its trade structure with the U.S.S.R. India now exports a wide range of manufactured goods and machineries to Soviet Union. In value terms, this constitutes more than one third of total exports to the Soviet Union. Trade statistics reveal that several branches of industry such as knit wear industry in Ludhiana are able to flourish primarily due to the Soviet market.

So far as the Soviet Union is concerned, it also favours continuation of the existing system of trade and economic relations with India. Again, it is a matter of convenience and compulsions from the Soviet side. As far the domestic economy of the Soviet Union is concerned, it is facing a serious economic crisis--budget deficit (R 60 bn official and R 120 - 150 bn unofficial estimate), Low economic growth (2 - 3 p.c. as compared to the first half of 1989) inflation of 8-10 p.c. shortage of wide range of consumer goods and so on. Perestroika has not so far improved the economic condition. The Soviet Union has also suffered a trade deficit in 1089 and it is persisting in 1990. There was a decline in trade with its CMEA trade partners of east Europe. Under the circumstances, the Soviet Union is rather compelled to retain its trade level with India which has increased significantly during 1988-89.

India has supplied a wide variety of consumer goods such as tea, coffee, knitted and ready-made garments, soaps, detergent etc. India is also exporting some hi-heal products like xerographic machines, computers, electronic items etc., to Soviet Union. Some of these items are imported by India and re-exported to the USSR that suit Soviet interest. Thus it is advantageous for the USSR to retain this arrangement of Indo-Soviet trade.

It is often argued that the rupee-rouble exchange rate is not favourable for India. In fact there are two or three different exchange rates for different categories of transactions, for example R 1 = Rs. 29 for tourists, Rs. 20 for commercial transactions and Rs. 16 for Govt. transactions. These are official rates of exchange which are radically different from the market rate of exchange. R 1 = Rs 4 or 5. The Soviet Policy makers are keen to retain these artificially high official exchange rates. This surely goes against India's economic interest. From the Indian side, efforts are made to arrive at an acceptable exchange rate though mutual discussions. But the fact remains so long as both the currencies are not freely convertible, it is difficult to find a satisfactory solution. Negotiations are not likely to yield better result from Indian point of view, since the country is on the lower side of the bargaining scale. India is heavily dependent upon the Soviet supply of defence machinery and equipment. Although details are not available, in some years it amounts to 12 - 15 p.c. of total imports from the Soviet Union. India is constrained to import Soviet defence equipment and spare parts. It is a matter of compulsion of Indian side no doubt. But we must not forget that this suits Soviet interest which has surplus of defence equipment as a result of detente with the West.

Moreover, India cannot ignore the improvement in Soviet political relation with China and South Korea. In fact, Soviet trade with China increased six fold between 1980 and 1988. It can supply a similar basket of agricultural and industrial products to USSR as India does. It is quite likely that India's ability to export to Soviet Union may be affected without the mechanism of rupee trade. Besides china, the potentialities of a newly industrialised country like Korea must not be underestimated. It can export a wide range of industrial goods and hi-tech products to USSR

Improved Soviet political and economic relations with the advanced capitalist countries have added another dimension to Indo-Soviet Trade. Soviet policy makers are keen to modernise their economy with the liberal Western credit from governmental and non-governmental sources. Import of consumer goods from the West is the at present at the lower scale of the Soviet priority list. So it is unlikely that India's exports to USSR would be affected. But it would wise for India not to rely heavily on this source. Some Soviet experts feel that if rupees trade is discontinues, the USSR will be able to meet more easily her export requirements for manufactures consumer goods from the developed countries.

Thus it is evident that although there are some constraints

for both India and USSR to retain the existing framework of trade, the degree of compulsion is more on India than the USSR. For her own interest, India must try to be more competitive in the Soviet market. She must no longer take Soviet market for granted. Perhaps days of political intervention and goodwill of Soviet leadership are over. This is quite likely as the regimented Soviet economy passes towards the market economy.

BIBLIOGRAPHY

Allen, Robert L. : Soviet Economic Warfare, Public Affairs Press, Washington D.C., 1960.

Agarwala, A.N. and Singh, S.P. (eds). : The Economics of Underdeveloped, Oxford University Press, New York, 1963.

Arnold, H.P. : Aid for Developing Countries, Bodley Head, London, 1962.

Arya, P.N. : A Study of India's Bilateral Trade and Payments Arrangements, U.S. Aid Mission, New Delhi, 1958.

Ahuja, K. : India's Trade with Eastern Europe, Indian Econ. Journal, January, 1962.

Arnold, H.J.P : Aid for Development, Paperback Editions National Academy, Delhi, 1968.

Asher, Robert. : Grants, loans and local currencies : Their role in Foreign Aid, the Brooklings Institution, Washington, 1961.

Berliner, Joseph. : Soviet Economic Aid : The New Aid and Trade Policy in Underdeveloped Countries, Council on Foreign Relations, New York, 1958.

Bhagwati, J. and Chakravarty, S. : Contributions to Indian Economic Analysis : Survey", American Economic Review Supplement, part 2, Sept. 1969.

Bhagwati. J. and Desai, P. : "India : Planning for Industrialisation". Oxford University Press. London, 1970.

Bhagwati, J. : International Trade, Penguin Modern Economics, England, 1969.

Benham, F. : Economic Aid to Underdeveloped Countries, Oxford University Press, London, 1964.

Baykov, A. : Soviet Foreign Trade, Princeton University Press, Princeton, 1946.

Baner, P.T. : United States Aid and Indian Economies Development, Washington D.C., 1959.

Billerbeck, K : Soviet Block Foreign Aid to Underdeveloped Countries, An analysis and a prognosis (trans. J. Bolkamper), Hamburg Archives of World of Economy, Hamburg, 1960.

Bergson. A. and Kuznets, Simon (eds). : Economic Trends in the Soviet Union, Harvard University Press, Mass. 1963.

Behari, Bepin. : The Facts of Foreign Aid, Vora and Co., Bombay, 1968.

Balassa, B. : Trade Prospects for developing countries, Richard P. Irwin, Illinois, 1964.

Brown, W. and Opie, R. : American Foreign Assistance, Brookings, Washington D.C., 19953.

Carter, J.R. : The Net Cost of Soviet Foreign Aid, Praegar, New York, 1971.

Chenery, H. and Clark, P. : Inter-industry Economics, Wiley. New York, 1962.

Cohen, B. : "The Stagnation of Indian Exports", Quarterly Journal of Economics, March 1964.

Chandrasekhar, S. : American Aid and India's Economic Development, F. Praeger Publishers, New York, 1965.

Dastur, M.N. and Co. : Cost Reduction Study on Bokaro Project, Calcutta, May 1966.

Dagli, V. : Indo-Soviet Economic Relations : A Survey, Vora and Co., Bombay 1971.

Datar, A. : India's Economic Relations with the USSR and Eastern Europe 1953-69, Cambridge University Press, 1972.

Dave, S. : India's Trade Relations with the East European Countries 1952/3 to 1959/60, Indian Econ. Journal, July 1961.

Dasgutpa, A.K. (ed). : Trade Theory and Commercial Practice in Relation to Under Developed Countries, Asia Publishing House, Bombay, 1965.

Deshpande, S.N. : The Fourth Five-Year Plan, Reserve Bank of India Bulletin, July., 1970.

Domar, E. : Essays in the Theory of Econ. Growth, Oxford University Press, New York, 1957.

Eldridge, P. : The Politics of Foreign Aid in India, Vikas Publications, Delhi, 1969.

Elliot, R. and Wagner, R. : Synopsis of Techno-economic Survey of a Proposed Integrated Steel Plant at Bokaro, Washington D.C., 1963.

Friedman, W. and Kalmanoff, G. International Financial Aid, Columbia University Press, New York, 1966.

Fryer, D. : World Economic Development, McGraw Hill Book Co., Tokyo, 1965.

Goldman, M. : Soviet Foreign Aid, Praeger, New York, 1967.

Goldman, M. : The Soviet Economy : Myth and Reality, Prentice hall, Englewoodcliffs, N.J., 1968.

Goldwin, R. : Why Foreign Aid ? Rand McNally Chicago, 1963.

Hazari, R.K. : Foreign Collaboration : Report and Proceedings of the Seminar by the Center of Advanced Studies, University of Bombay, 1967.

Hawkins, E. : The Principles of Development Aid, Penguin Modern Economics, England, 1970.

Hirschman, A. : The Strategy of Economic Development, Yale University Press, New Haven, 1958.

Harrod, R. : An Essay in Dynamic Theory, Econ. Journal, March, 1939.

Hejmandi, J : Volume of Indo-USSR Trade Rises, Journal of Industry and Trade. May, 1966.

Hoblik, K. : The U.S., The Soviet Union and the Third World Hamburg, 1968.

Indian Institute of Foreign Trade, India's Trade with East Europe, Ministry of Commerce, Govt. of India, New Delhi, 1966, 1973.

Johnson, H. : "International trade and Economic Growth", George Allen and Unwin, London, 1958.

Jackson, R. : The Case for an International Development Author ity, Syracuse University Press, N.Y., 1959.

Johnson, William. : The Steel Industry of India, Oxford University press, Bombay, 1967.

Kidron, M. : Foreign Investments in India, Oxford University Press, London, 1965.

Kidron, M. : Pakistan's Trade with Eastern Bloc Countries, Praegar Publishers, New York, 1972.

Kiser, M. : Comecon : Integration Problems of the Planned Economies, Oxford University Press, London, 1967.

Knorr, K, : Ruble Diplomacy, Center of International Studies, Princeton, 1956.

Kulkarni, M. : Indo-Soviet Political Relations, Vora and Co., Bombay, Princeton, 1956.

Kurien, K. : Impact of Foreign Capital on Indian Economy, People's Publishing House, New Delhi.1966.

Kodachenko, A. : Developing Countries : Economic Co-operation, Novosti Press, Moscow, 1971.

Kovner, M. : The Meaning of Co-existence, Public Affairs Press, Washington D.C., 19961.

Little, I.M.D. and Clifford, J.M. : International Aid. Allen and Unwin, London, 1965.

Lakdawala, D. : International Aspects of Indian Economic Development, Oxford University Press, London, 1931.

Levy, W. : The Search for Oil in Developing Countries, Report prepared at the request of IBRD, New York, 1960.

Lubell, H. : Soviet Oil Offensive and Interblock Economic Competition, Rand Corporation, Santa Monica, California, 1961.

Mahalanobis, P. : The Approach of Operational Research to Planning in India, IST Statistical Series No.18, Calcutta, 1963.

Mahalanobis, P. : Talks on Planning, IST Statistical, Series No. 14, Calcutta, 1961.

Malenbaum, W.M. : Prospects for Indian Development, Macmillan and Co., New York, 1962.

Meier, G. : International Economics of Development : Theory and Policy, Harper and Row Publishers, New York, 1968.

Mikesell, R. and Allen, R. : Economic Policies Towards Less Developed Countries, Joint Economic Committee, U.S. Congress, Washington D.C., 1961.

Mikesell, R. and Behrman, J :Financing Free World Trade with Sino-Soviet Bloc, Princeton, New Jersey, 1958.

Muller, K. : The Soviet Bloc and the Developing Countries, Thacker and Co., Bombay, 1970.

Myrdal, G. : Asian Drama : I, II and III, Penguin Books, New York, 1968.

Macbean, A. : Export Instability and Economic Development, George Allen and Unwin Ltd, London, 1966.

NCAER, Export Strategy for India, New Delhi, 1964.

NCAER, Export Prospects of Vegetable Oil and Oil Seeds, New Delhi, 1965.

Nurkse, R. : Pattern of Trade and Development, Blackwell, Oxford, 1962.

Nove, A. and Donnelly, D. : Trade with Communist Countries, I.E.A., London, 1960.

Nesterov, M. : The Soviet Union's Foreign Trade, Foreign Language Publishing House, Moscow.

Nove, A. : The Soviet Economy, George Allen and Unwin, London, 1968.

Ohlin, G. : Foreign aid Policies Reconsidered, OECD, Paris, 1966.

O.E.C.D., Flow of Resources of Developing Countries, 19576-63, Paris, 1964.

Patel, S. : Export Prospects and Economic Growth : India, Econ. Journal, September, 1959.

Patolichev. N. : USSR Foreign Trade : Past, Present and Future, Novosti Press, Moscow.

Pant, P. and Mehra, K : Prospects of Exports in the 4th Plan, Foreign Trade Review, Jan - March, 1969.

Pincus, J. : Costs and Benefits of Aid : An Emperical Analysis, UNCTAD, Geneva, 1967.

Prebisch, R. : Towards a New Trade Policy for Development, Report by the Secretary General of UNCTAD, UN, New York, 1964.

Pisar, S. : Co-existence and Commerce, McGraw Hill Book Co., New York, 1970.

Rao, V.K.R.V. : Foreign Aid and India's Economic Development, Asia Publishing House, Bombay

Roy, H. : Tea Price Stabilisation; The Indian Case, World Press, Calcutta, 1965.

Rudra, A. : "Trade between Developing and Socialist Countries", Foreign Trade Review, January-March, 1962.

Robinson, R. (ed). : International Co-operation in Aid, Cambridge University Press, London. 1971.

Samuelson, P. : International Economic Relations : Proceedings of the Third Congress of the International Economic Association, Macmillan St. Martin's Press, New York, 1969.

Schwartz, Harry : The Soviet Economy since Stalin, j.P. Lippincott Co., New York, 1965.

Srivastava, S.K. : Trade of India, S. Chand and Co., Delhi, 1956.

Streeten, P. and Lipton M. : The Crisis of Indian Planning : Economic Planning in the 1960's Oxford University Press, London, 1968.

Singh, M. : India's Export Trends and Prospects for Self-sustained Growth, Clarendon Press, Oxford, 1964.

Singh, R.K. : Prosperity through Exports, Engineering Export Promotion Council, Calcutta, 1965.

Spulber, No. : Soviet Strategy for Economic Growth, Indian University Press, 1964.

Stanislans, M. Sebastian : Soviet Economic Aid to India, N.V. Publications, New Delhi. 1973.

Tanzer, M. : The Political Economy of International Oil and the Underdeveloped Countries, Beacon Press, London, 1969.

United Nations : Economic Bulletin for Europe, Geneva (various issues).

Vassilev, U. : Policy in the Soviet Bloc on Aid to Developing Countries, OECD, Paris, 1969.

Varghese . D.K. : India's Foreign Trade, Allied Publishers, Bombay, 1964.

Vertikar, V.S. : Commercial Policy and Economic Development in India, F.A. Praeager, New York, 1969.

Wilber, C.K. : The Soviet Model and Underdeveloped Countries, University. of North Carolina Press, Chapel Hill, 1969.

Indian Govt. Publication

Department of Commercial Intelligence and Statistics : Monthly Statistics : of Foreign Trade of India.

Ministry of Finance : Utilisation of External Assistance (4th LokSabha), 11th Report.

Ministry of Finance : Economic Survey (annual) various issues.

Reserve Bank of India : Report on Currency and Finance (annual).

Reserve Bank of India : Monthly Bulletin.

Planning Commission :

The First Five-year Plan, New Delhi, 1952.

The Second Five-year Plan, New Delhi, 1956.

The Third Five-year Plan, New Delhi, 1961.

The Fourth Five-year Plan, New Delhi, 1969.

Other Publications :

U.N. Year Book of International Trade Statistics, New York (various issues).

Vneshniaia Torgovlia SSSR, Moscow (various issues).

INDEX